ENTANGLED SENSEMAKING AT SEA

Sustainable commercial fishing, species conservation, and bycatch are contentious topics. Great emphasis has been placed on the sustainable sourcing of particular species that we buy at the store and order in restaurants, but how can we trust that the fish on our plates, from a system-wide perspective, have been appropriately sourced? Even in what are commonly considered to be the best-managed fisheries in the world (i.e., Alaskan fisheries), thousands of tons of fish are wasted each year in the interest of providing certain species in certain ways to certain people, at certain prices. Are the management practices and regulations that we think are helping actually having the desired outcomes in terms of the effective use of natural resources?

This book presents a framework that can enhance our understanding, research, and regulation of frontline organizing processes in commercial fisheries, which may be generalized to other resource extraction industries. It enables readers to better grasp and respond to the need to develop practices and regulations that involve effective use of all natural resources, rather than just a chosen few. The book is especially important to researchers and practitioners active in the fishing industry, and natural resource managers and regulators interested in understanding and improving their management systems. It is also highly relevant to organization and management researchers interested in coupled human and natural systems, ecological sensemaking, the role of quantum mechanics in organizational phenomena, sociomateriality, and sustainability.

The book uses the real-world case of an Alaskan fishing fleet to explore how the commercial fishing industry (which includes businesses, management agencies, regulatory bodies, and markets, among others) entangles itself with natural phenomena in order to extract resources from them. After gaining a better understanding of these processes can we see how they can be improved, especially through changes to regulatory management systems, in order to foster not only more sustainable, but also less wasteful (these two goals are not necessarily interdependent in today's regulatory management systems), natural resource extraction and use. Such an understanding requires exploring how regulations, natural phenomena, human sensemaking processes, and market forces entangle at sea to materialize the fish that make their way to our plates - as well as those that, importantly, do not.

Jason Good holds a master's and PhD in Natural Resources and Environment from the University of Michigan, USA. Prior to his graduate work he was a fisheries scientist, working primarily in Alaskan waters. His research focuses on business sustainability, circular economy, and coupled organizational and natural systems.

ENTANGLED SENSEMAKING AT SEA

Bycatch Management that Makes Good Social and Ecological Sense

Jason Good

Routledge
Taylor & Francis Group

LONDON AND NEW YORK

First published 2021
by Routledge
2 Park Square, Milton Park, Abingdon, Oxon OX14 4RN

and by Routledge
52 Vanderbilt Avenue, New York, NY 10017

Routledge is an imprint of the Taylor & Francis Group, an informa business

© 2021 Jason Good

British Library Cataloguing-in-Publication Data
A catalogue record for this book is available from the British Library

Library of Congress Cataloging-in-Publication Data
A catalog record has been requested for this book

ISBN: 978-1-78353-811-9 (hbk)
ISBN: 978-1-78353-745-7 (pbk)
ISBN: 978-1-003-05066-7 (ebk)

Typeset in Bembo
by Taylor & Francis Books

MIX
Paper from
responsible sources
FSC
www.fsc.org
FSC® C013985

Printed in the United Kingdom
by Henry Ling Limited

CONTENTS

FIGURES

PREFACE

What this book is about

Daft and Weick (1984) begin their article "Toward a Model of Organizations as Interpretation Systems,"[1] which is a seminal part of the 'interpretive turn' in organization and management studies, as well as a precursor to the sensemaking domain of research that this book is situated in, with the following analogy:

> Consider the game of 20 questions. Normally in this game one person leaves the room, the remaining people select a word that the person is to guess when he/she returns, and the only clue given about the word is whether it signifies an animal, vegetable, or mineral. The person trying to guess the word asks up to 20 questions that can be answered yes or no in an effort to guess what the word is. Each question is designed to provide new information about the correct word. Together, the questions and answers are the process by which an interpretation is built up by the person who is 'it.'
>
> Organizations play 20 questions. Organizations have limited time and questions, and they strive for the answer. The answer is discovering what consumers want that other organizations do not provide. The answer is finding that there is a market for pet rocks, roller skates, encounter groups, erasable ball-point pens, or zero population growth. Many organizations presume that there is a correct answer to the puzzle of 20 questions. They query the environment with samples, market surveys, and test markets. They may establish specialized scanning departments that use trend analysis, media content analysis, and econometric modeling to obtain answers about the external environment.
>
> *(Daft & Weick, 1984, p. 284)*

Few academic papers have given us such a creative introduction. The reproduction of Daft and Weick's analogy here serves to highlight how organizations, and the people in them, make sense of their place in the world; a somewhat different version of the analogy, however, can also help us understand such sensemaking, although from a very different, yet complementary, perspective.

Let's examine Daft and Weick's analogy in more detail before we move to the second version of the game. First, note that in this version the organization (or person) assumes that there is some *thing* to be interpreted that is separate from it. Thus, the thing (e.g., animal, vegetable, market demand) exists as a distinct, fully formed object prior to the organization examining its environment (or the player questioning the other participants). Also note that the organization's goal is to gain as accurate an interpretation of the distinct, fully formed object as it can. This accuracy is mediated by such things as 'trend' and 'media content' analyses, and 'econometric models.' Taking the organization, the external thing, and the analyses and models together, there is what Karen Barad, whose work this book draws heavily from, calls a 'tripartite arrangement' (Barad 2003, 2007): there are people or organizations who are doing the interpreting, there are separate, external, fully formed objects, whose boundaries, properties, and meanings are pre-existing, that are the subjects of interpretation, and there are representations of those objects, either in the form of answers to questions (for the game) or in the form of samples, market surveys, or test markets (for organizations). These representations in turn facilitate the interpretive process by mediating the relationship between the people or organizations and the objects of their interpretation, such as 'pet rocks, roller skates, encounter groups, erasable ball-point pens, or zero population growth.' The nature of the tripartite arrangement, in which representations bridge the gap between organizations or people and objects, naturally raises concerns for the accuracy of those mediating representations; such concerns in turn engender efforts aimed at improving the representations used in analyses and models, which occupy enormous amounts of scientific, governmental, and private-sector resources. This separation- and mediation-based tripartite arrangement is largely our current approach to studying, managing, and regulating how organizations engage with the phenomena they are embedded in, including how various organizations in various industries extract resources from natural systems.

Now take the following non-tripartite, non-separation, non-mediation-based version of the same game, as crafted by renowned theoretical physicist John Wheeler as a way to describe quantum mechanics (as told by political scientist Alexander Wendt). This version of 20 questions also starts with a group of participants and a player who leaves the room:

> while the first player is out of the room the group decides *not* to choose a word. Instead, they agree that as the first player goes around the room asking questions, the members of the group will still answer yes or no, but are required in each case to have some word in mind that is consistent with all the other answers that have already been given. [Quoting Wheeler:] "… the

information about the word was brought into being step by step through the questions we raised … if we had chosen to ask different questions we would have ended up with a different word … with a different story."

(Wendt, 2015, pp. 67–68)

In the first version of the game, the object is a stand-alone entity that exists independent of the questions, while in the second version, the object is given boundaries, properties, and meanings through the act of questioning and answering; in the first version, only the right questions can unveil the pre-determined right answer, while in the second version, different questions would have determined a different answer. Thus, in the second version there may be a desired answer, but there cannot be a *right* answer. Further, in the second game it is only when an answer is produced that the 'right' questions can be known. Thus, the first version is all about subjects crafting an accurate interpretation of a separately constituted object, while the second is all about crafting the constitutions and separations that lead to a separate object, and therefore to separate subjects. Prior to the start of the questioning process, potential answers are superpositioned (the boundaries between possible answers are indeterminate, existing as a field of possibilities), and only through the process of coherent asking and answering is some *thing* differentiated into unambiguous form, which only becomes 'the' answer after the somewhat arbitrary cut-off point of the 20th question. Thus, the first version is about organizations operating under the assumption that there is an inherent separation between themselves and their environments, which they mediate through interpretive practices, which produce representations of inherently individual and pre-existing things lying in wait in that environment. The second, however, involves the creative mutual constitution and differentiation (i.e., entanglement) of organizations, environments, interpretive practices, and objects.

The first and second versions of the game can provide mutually exclusive versions of the same reality, in which both would be required to understand that reality. Thus, together the versions exhibit 'complementarity,' which is a central aspect of viewing the world through the lens of quantum mechanics (which is one of the primary perspectives used in this book). To be complementary is to be 'mutually exclusive but jointly necessary,' such that 'a complete description of the system requires both; each by itself is only a partial representation' (Wendt 2015, p. 48). Daft and Weick's version starts with a determined answer and depicts how organizational beliefs in the existence of pre-determined things, as well as in inherent boundaries between organizations and environments, shape which activities organizations undertake. Wheeler's version, on the other hand, starts with an *in*determinate answer, and depicts how activities not only create the boundaries, properties, and meanings that constitute things, but also help make 'the organization' and 'the environment' what they are (in this case a questioning and answering apparatus) and are not. Thus, the first version of the game involves a *pre*-existing determined object that is discerned through *inter*-active practices; in those practices, entities relate with one another, but doing so changes neither the entities nor the nature of what emerges through their relations; the second involves a *post*-existing determined object that is created through *intra*-active practices, in which the activity of relating not only differentiates and constitutes what materializes through them, but also makes the entities what they are (and are not). The more we focus on determinacy and *inter*-actions, in which existing individual things *act on* other individual things, the tougher it is to examine *in*determinacy and *intra*-actions, in which individual things *emerge though* inseparable activities. Like the apparatuses at the center of famous debates between Niels Bohr and Albert Einstein about the nature of light (and reality), in which light can either be elucidated as a wave or particle, but never both within the same apparatus, Daft and Weick's and Wheeler's analogues of interpretive practices are mutually exclusive (though the framework that Daft and Weick go on to create in their paper, especially its 'enacting' component, would likely lead to a 'game' that would look very much like Wheeler's), yet they complement one another in terms of what they can help us understand about organizational phenomena.

This book aims to help transform our understanding of, research into, and ultimately regulation and management of how organizations interpret and engage with natural phenomena; it is a transformation from solely crafting and deploying analyses and models, in both academic research and regulation and management systems, that depend on separation-based tripartite arrangements between organizations and nature to also including those that account for the entangled nature of organizational and natural phenomena, in which they mutually constitute what each is and is not, can be and cannot. Thus, in the current approach to research, regulation, and management, the starting point is largely separate human and natural phenomena, from which academics, regulators, and managers attempt to understand, manage, and regulate how, when, where, and to what extent organizational and natural phenomena come together, act on, and impact one another. This approach has the tripartite arrangement at its core, and its nearly invariable goal is to, in some way, shape, or form, coerce frontline managers—those who directly engage with natural phenomena on a day-to-day basis (e.g., fishing captains, loggers, fracking operators, oil explorers, miners)—to spend great amounts of effort crafting more accurate representations of the effects that their actions will have on separate natural phenomena. The problem is that when the assumption is that representational accuracy, primarily in terms of the future effects that organizational activity will have on natural phenomena, is attainable, regulatory and management systems choose to (or paradoxically *have* to) give great leeway to frontline practices for their *in*accuracies. Thus, in management systems where a tripartite arrangement is taken for granted, and in turn accuracy is not only presumed to be possible, but becomes the goal of the system (but in reality is not actually attainable), *in*accuracy follows as a necessary, pervasive, and prominent property of those systems. This phenomenon is a sort of 'accuracy trap,' in which the large-scale wastage of natural resources, such as fisheries bycatch, agricultural 'uglies,' and even whole swathes of rainforests, or how the pervasive pollution of natural phenomena, such as groundwater infused with fracking compounds, greenhouse gas emissions from oil sand operations, and runoff from mining, become normalized parts of management systems (even as they are vilified). Such effects are necessary accompaniments of the assumption that what we deal with are separate human and natural systems, which in turn directs us to marshal all our resources toward attaining accurate understandings of our interactions with, and effects on, separate and distinct phenomena.

But accuracy *can't* be the name of the game any longer. That game is (or should be) over, for we have lost. And by 'we,' I mean everyone, nearly everything. Our shift into the Anthropocene Epoch, the growing intensity of climate change, the increasing frequency and strength of storms, fires, and other natural disasters, the expanding loss of human and non-human habitat, among various other overt and emerging socio-environmental problems, all attest to the fact that whatever the game is, it has been going extremely poorly for us. Regardless of our pretentions to grandeur in terms of our ability to accurately know and manage what is happening and what will occur, nature, and our entanglement with it, keeps reminding us that it is not deterministic; "Determinism is the view that there is no inherent randomness in nature, that what happens in the present and future is completely fixed by the laws governing the motion of matter in the past" (Wendt, 2015, p. 62). Like Wheeler's version of the game of 20 questions, natural phenomena keep telling, or rather shouting to, us that we cannot know for sure what will materialize, both in the short and long term, through our entangled relations with it until those relations have already occurred.

Thus, rather than determinism, indeterminism is the name of the game, and it defines the rules. Yet as quantum mechanics teach us, "The existence of indeterminacy," from the level of the electron to the level of human society to the level of nature, "does not mean that there are no facts, no histories, no bleeding – on the contrary, indeterminacies are constitutive of the very materiality of being" (Barad, 2014, p. 177). There is a lot to learn about how indeterminacies shape our organizing practices (and vice versa), especially as they are entangled with natural phenomena, and in turn there is a lot to learn about how to manage and regulate those entangled practices, for such efforts are always constitutive of that which they attempt to shape and control.

This book is about understanding what indeterminism looks like and what its 'rules of the game' are in terms of organizing processes at the *intra*section of industry and natural phenomena. The particular organizing processes it looks at are sensemaking in general, and ecological sensemaking in particular, as these are the processes that, in terms of organization and management studies, most concern how frontline managers understand and organize with natural phenomena. More particularly, this book examines what indeterminacy looks like and what its 'rules of the game' are in ecological sensemaking through a qualitative study of an industrial context where organizational and natural phenomena are overtly entangled—commercial trawl fishing in the Gulf of Alaska. The goal of its examination is to move our understanding of how human organizing processes are entangled with natural phenomena, including what effects materialize through those entanglements, forward in a way that does not adhere to age-old, dualistic (and disproven) versions of reality.

The book's focus on indeterminacy, and in turn the mutually differentiated and constituted, or entangled, nature of human and natural phenomena came not from the outside, not merely from what is on the cutting edge of organization and management studies, but rather from the qualitative study the book is based on. Thus, the framework and theory that the book uses were not imposed *on* the data, but rather emerged through many years, embedded in which have been multiple iterations of attempting to tell a data-based story of how frontline managers make sense of natural phenomena, of what that sensemaking means for what materializes through it (e.g., catch and bycatch), and of what it all means for regulating and managing those, and other, natural resource extractive processes and industries. This effort has been shaped by the often difficult but always present principle— which is both contained in the data and emerged from around five years of working on the decks of fishing boats (and nearly 700 days at sea)—that a story of organizing practices in a natural resource extraction context that takes a dualistic perspective, meaning that it starts out assuming the separation of those practices and nature, not only ignores a critically important and ever-present relationality (namely the inescapable entanglement of human and natural phenomena), but also skips over what is perhaps the most important part of those practices, their regula- tion, and their management—the story of their mutually enacted constitutions and differentiations. As Barad argues, "the point is that the very practices of differ- entiating the 'human' from the 'nonhuman,' the 'animate' from the 'inanimate,' and the 'cultural' from the 'natural' produce crucial materializing effects that are unaccounted for by starting an analysis after these boundaries are in place" (Barad, 2011, p. 124). We cannot take responsibility for how we constitute and thus shape natural phenomena if we do not also, or perhaps first, enact our responsibility for understanding and accounting for how we differentiate ourselves from the natural phenomena that we in turn 'impact.'

Whenever the focus is on indeterminacy, quantum mechanics will, until fully embraced, continually attempt to elbow its way into the conversation. This is because quantum mechanics has indeterminacy at its core (Barad, 2007; Wendt, 2015). Therefore, to tell the story of the entanglement of human organizational and natural phenomena at the front line of a natural resource extraction industry, without ignoring the inherent indeterminacy of the boundaries and properties those phenomena, this book fuses ecological sensemaking with quantum mechan- ics, primarily in the form of Karen Barad's 'agential realism' (e.g., Barad 1998, 2003, 2007, 2014). Agential realism brings to light the mutual constitution of quantum mechanics and social phenomena, and provides a way of understanding reality in general, and the entanglement of natural and human organizing phe- nomena in particular, that is both consistent with, and takes key lessons from, quantum physics. Yet ecological sensemaking and agential realism are not simply juxtaposed in the ensuing chapters, this book relies on the process philosophy of Alfred North Whitehead to help accomplish their fusion. But because, as Wendt (2015, p. 7) states in his own book that involves the interplay of quantum mechanics and social theory, the "start-up costs for thinking in quantum terms are high," this book starts with some basic principles and premises of agential realism in the Introduction, and gradually elaborates how they change our understanding of ecological sensemaking from one chapter to the next (getting help from White-head's process philosophy along the way).

The work contained in this book, however, did not start with the intention of involving agential realism (or quantum mechanics). While this book effectively started in 2013 as I started in earnest to write my doctoral dissertation, the infusion of agential realism has only developed over the past two years (and thus my own understanding of and thinking about the subject is in its relatively early stages, and its embryonic nature surely shows throughout the book, resulting in explanation and arguments that are not as quite sharp as I would like, as well as undoubtedly too much of my own sensemaking on the topic). Thus, this book draws on only what it needs from the realm of quantum thinking and agential realism in order to make sense of the data and to tell its story of the entanglement of organizational and natural phenomena at the frontline of a fishing industry. Further, only after completing the chapters to follow did I come across the work of Alexander Wendt (as well as Hahn & Knight, in press; Lord, Dinh, & Hoffman, 2015), who looks at the interplay of quantum thinking and international relations, which in turn introduced me to whole literatures on quantum decision theory and quantum brain theory, among other interdisciplinary explorations of quantum mechanics and social theory. Yet in the little I have admittedly delved into these literatures, I not only found the 'start-up costs' to be quite high, but I also did not find them necessary to tell the story I wanted to tell in this book. That is because this book tells an empirical story, and as such it develops both theoretical understandings and practical implications from data; it is not a treatise on the interplay of quantum mechanics and social science, nor on the embedding of agential realism in organization and management theory. For the reader who wants to know more about quantum mechanics and the social sciences, I refer the reader to Wendt's excellent book (Wendt, 2015), as well as to the other works it points to. To the reader who wants to know more about what quantum mechanics says about the entangled nature of humans and nature, or who is inspired to know more about agential realism, I refer the reader to Karen Barad's work, which, to me at least, is unparalleled in dealing with this entanglement that is the core and the periphery, and all that is in between, of our existence. For the reader who specifically wants to know more about agential realism and organization and management theory, see such excellent works as Orlikowski (2007), Orlikowski and Scott (2008, 2014), and Hultin and Mähring (2017). In fact, even though I cite the paper in the ensuing chapters, I did not fully realize until after completing them that Hultin and Mähring (2017) makes similar arguments that I do regarding the role that agential realism should play in our understanding of and investigations into sensemaking. Though our work concerns very different contexts, produces very different (though not incompatible) findings, and my work specifically concerns ecological sensemaking, there is generative overlap.

Words of gratitude

As previously stated, this book started with my dissertation. My first words of gratitude go to the people who guided me through that process: Andy Hoffman, Jim Diana, Wayne Baker, and Karl Weick. Each of these men have been an inspiration to me both personally and professionally. Karl Weick, a 'god' of organizational theory (which would make him cringe), and especially sensemaking, was almost always the most humble and curious person in the room. He never presumed to know 'the' story, and always wanted to know more about my story. Wayne Baker was always a generous and insightful motivator. Jim Diana, a natural science, 'fish guy,' often displayed more perspicacity within qualitative sociological research (like mine) than many qualitative sociological researchers I have known. As for Andy Hoffman, he has been a champion of this project all along. Without him, this book would not exist. Through the years Andy has been an unwavering supporter, even in times when I felt that, due to one or another set-back, such support was not warranted. Andy's work, approach to life, and generosity, are an inspiration. Of the other people who have also more professionally guided me along the way, I have to give special thanks to Bryan Husted, whose openness to different ways of working and seeing, and whose pleasant and generous way of working is such a pleasure to be involved with, has allowed me to not only complete this work, but to also complete other projects.

I also want to thank several friends whose support has made this possible. Garima Sharma is the friend and colleague one always wants, yet rarely encounters. I have been lucky to have her on my side; yet I can't mention her without mentioning Pranay and Arnav, who are two of the best guys around. I also want to thank Sara Rueda Raya, whose friendship throughout the past year has enabled me to survive, and Andrea Thorpe, a co-author and friend, one who has had the perhaps unfortunate experience of trying to make sense of what is in my brain, and whose talent with directness and lucidity I both admire and have benefitted from. I further want to thank Julie Bonney and Katy McGauley, who generously offered me immense help in getting the qualitative, empirical research that this book is based on both off the ground and completed in far off Kodiak Alaska. Both are tireless and inspiring practitioners. I know this outcome of the study took much longer than they thought it would, and I am sure is much more theoretical than they had anticipated, but I know they support me nonetheless.

Finally I want to thank family members who have been unwavering supporters for, well, my lifetime. I can always depend on them, and the freedom and security that it gives me has allowed me to complete various tasks, such as this book. Now that this is done, let's spend more time together.

Note

1 And which currently sits at over 7,700 citations, according to Google Scholar (https://scholar.google.nl/scholar?hl=en&as_sdt=0%2C33&q=Toward+a+model+of+organiza tions+as+interpretation+systems&btnG=).

1

INTRODUCTION

What does metaphysical individualism have to do with sustainability? What does it have to do with the business of resource extraction (e.g., commercial fishing, logging, mining)? What does it have to do with natural resource management? The answer to these questions should be, 'as little as possible.' The unfortunate answer, however, is something along the lines of 'a lot.' Though your actual response might have been, 'What the heck is metaphysical individualism?' 'Meta' literally means 'beyond' or 'on a different level,' as in a meta-analysis, which is a study that examines other studies on a topic in order to learn something new (i.e., an analysis of analyses); 'meta' also has more colloquial uses, such as when a comment is deemed 'meta' because it says something relatively more abstract about more concrete things. For instance, a 'meta-joke' is a joke about jokes; a 'meta-movie' is a movie about movies (e.g., *Adaptation, Get Shorty, The Player*). In terms of the other part of the word 'metaphysics,' 'physics' refers to the entities whose commonalities or connections are the subject of the 'meta' part of the phrase. Such things include objects, people, organizations, and so on; they include whatever can be considered to be a 'this' or a 'that.' 'Metaphysics' as a domain of philosophy concerns fundamental connections or commonalities among individual things, which necessarily go beyond any one thing.

Don't worry, this book is not actually about metaphysics. Instead, it offers an alternative to the metaphysical individualism that molds how scholars and regulators treat the entanglement of human and natural phenomena in resource extraction contexts. Thus, to understand what this book is about, we first need to clarify what it is both arguing against, and offering an alternative to: the metaphysical individualism-based approach that experts and decision-makers commonly take to studying, regulating, and managing the business of natural resource extraction in general, and the business of commercial fishing in particular.

Such a an approach grounded in metaphysical individualism goes something like this:

> OK, here is a reality we are concerned with; it is constituted by these individual things; these things inter-act; their inter-actions may or may not be obvious, measurable, or even perceivable; nonetheless, what are they? What are their effects? Who is to blame for them? And, how can we control them?

At the heart of metaphysical individualism is the assumption that the world is composed of inherently separate things, each having its own roster of non-relational characteristics (Barad, 2007, citing Teller, 1989). By 'non-relational characteristics,' I mean boundaries, properties, and meanings that are not only inherent to what makes a 'thing' a 'thing,' but their existence is not dependent on the actual or potential activities of other things. Thus, the properties of a thing are self-contained to that thing, and the nature of the thing is not necessarily derived from the its relations with other things. This means that the boundaries and properties of the thing exist *prior to* any sort of relation; the individual thing's relations with other things are therefore meta- (occurring after the) physical (thing). From a metaphysical individualism-based perspective, for instance, we need look no further than the zebra to understand its stripes (and can ignore the environmental conditions that the zebra thrives in, for they are ultimately separable); to understand an isolated tribe that lives on an otherwise uninhabited island we just need to study the tribe itself (and not the outside world that exists beyond the tribe's boundaries, without which its boundaries would make little sense); an individual's criminal behavior is simply a decision made by that individual, for which the individual is solely responsible (and the institutional and cultural arrangements that he or she grew up in, was embedded in at the time of the behavior, and without which the bad decision would make little sense).

From the perspective of metaphysical individualism, things may come together, impact, and change one another, but those things exist as separate stand-alone entities prior to those relations, and therefore prior to future relations. Such a perspective paves the way for scholarly and regulatory efforts that focus on preventing certain unwanted interactions among separate things from occurring, and, if they do happen to occur, seeking out an individual who is responsible for the occurrence. That individual is then punished and/or isolated as a way to prevent those unwanted interactions among the inherently separate individuals from re-occurring. Thus, the interaction that might re-occur *after* the existence of the individuals, or *in addition to* their individuality, is blocked. Such an approach, grounded in metaphysical individualism, has deep roots and a pervasive presence in Western society, not only shaping the ways in which academic theory and research are performed in prominent academic departments like economics and political science, but also how we structure our legal and regulatory systems, and enact the management processes that flow from them.

Readers steeped in philosophy will likely object to my unsophisticated description of metaphysics. Yet philosophical sophistication is not the point; my point is that scholars and practitioners tend to approach humans and nature as if they are individual entities, and then attempt to study, manage, and regulate their connections as if they occur *in addition to* the entities' individualities; thus, their approach is grounded in metaphysical individualism, much to the detriment of our understanding, management, and regulation of humans and nature.

Let's look at an example of metaphysical individualism and its metaphysical methodology at work. For many decades corporations have produced annual financial reports; in the past decade or so more and more corporations have begun producing 'sustainability reports.' Just as financial reports detail a firm's financial goals, its strategies for reaching those goals, and the progress it has made in implementing those strategies and reaching those goals, sustainability reports detail a firm's ethical and sustainability-oriented goals, its strategies for reaching those goals, and its progress toward implementing those strategies and reaching those goals. Often these reports speak to social governance principles, guidelines, and benchmarks, such as the family of ISO 14000 standards and the UN Sustainable Development Goals. Research indicates, however, these reports are highly metaphysical in terms of how they communicate firms' relationships with natural phenomena (Csabai, Good, & Parham, 2020). For instance, in their 2018 sustainability report, energy giant BP had this to say about how they manage their relationship with biodiversity:

> Every year we review the location of our operations in and close to the most sensitive areas. This can change from year to year as governments update protected area designations. We evaluate new projects to determine whether planned activities could affect protected areas. If our screening process shows that a proposed project could enter or affect an international protected area, we conduct a detailed risk assessment to better understand any potential impacts. Executive approval is required before any physical activities can take place.
>
> *(BP, 2018, p. 52)*

What is missing from this passage, and from all passages in BP's report, is an assessment of how (non-human) natural phenomena and BP's activities, as well as the activities of firms along BP's supply chain, have constituted one another through time, and in turn how that mutual constitution shapes BP's actual and potential relations with protected areas, as well as their understanding of them. Thus, in this passage BP discusses how they manage the potential *impacts* that their planned activities could have *on* protected areas, but they fail to account for the role that BP, and the firms that constitute its supply chain, have played in the natural and socio-political constitution of those protected areas (by 'constitution,' I mean the boundaries, properties, and meanings that define what things are and are not, can be and cannot). Were past actions by BP, as well as by other firms along its supply chain, part of the materialization of the protected areas that they want to manage their interactions with? Has BP and/or the other firms acted, intentionally or unintentionally, knowingly or unknowingly, directly or indirectly to shape the constitution of those protected areas? Are the natural phenomena that are in the protected areas *already* partly constituted by the activities of BP and the firms in its supply chain? If we take activity to be the fundamental stuff of reality, as many eminent scholars from multi-varied backgrounds urge us to do (e.g., Barad, 2007;

Bergson, 2007; Butler, 1990; Haraway, 1991; Latour, 2005; Weick, 1979; Whitehead, 1978), and then we assume that BP's activities have had a hand, in some way, in the materialization of the protected areas they are concerned with impacting, then boundaries between BP and those areas are not as distinct, and BP and the protected areas are not as separate, as BP's language indicates.

If nature were not constituted the way it is, BP and other firms along their supply chain would not be constituted the way they are. Likewise, if BP and other firms along its supply chain were not constituted the way they are, nature would not be constituted the way it is (to a increasingly alarming degree). There is a strategic reason BP is operating within or near protected areas, for BP's business activities are, at their core, inseparable from the activities of the natural phenomena that constitute those areas.

For one thing to 'impact,' 'act on,' or 'affect' some other thing requires that other thing to first exist apart from the one thing, and to then come into contact with it. If we assume that BP's actions have in some way had a hand in the constitution of the protected areas, and that the natural phenomena in the protected areas have played a role in BP's actions, how are we to understand BP's attempts to manage its actual and potential *impacts on* those areas? BP would, in part, be managing its interactions with itself. Thus, assuming that BP and the firm along its supply chain have helped constitute the protected areas in some way, and that the natural phenomena in and around those protected areas help constitute BP in some way, does the idea of 'impact' still make sense? Does it capture what is really going on, and thus what needs to be managed?

Issues with BP's metaphysical individualism based-approach emerge when we appreciate the fact that BP, and the firms that constitute its supply chain, are almost certainly *already* entangled with the protected areas that BP is concerned with impacting. But issues related to a metaphysical individualism-based approach do not stop there. In attempting to understand its potential impacts on some*thing* else, in this case on the protected areas, BP has to first understand the protected areas in their individuality, as they exist prior to its actions; then BP has to prospectively study its actions that would cross the divide between itself and the protected areas; and finally BP has to predict or 'measure' how those actions could change the protected areas. We can set aside all the problems with building models based on future probabilities (and there are many), for this approach has something more fundamentally problematic about it: it relies on the inherent separation of the measuring process from that which is being measured, which is yet another iteration of metaphysical individualism. Such separation has long been empirically rejected by quantum physics (Barad, 2007; Bohr, 1958, 1963; Mermin, 1998), and, because the lessons of quantum physics are not isolated to the 'micro' world (Barad, 2007, Mermin, 1998), such lessons need to be integrated into our research into, and management of, 'macro' phenomena. The issue is that, in attempting to predict, or 'measure,' its impacts on some other thing (i.e., on the protected areas), is BP actually able to maintain a clear division between itself, its measuring activities, and that other thing? Or is the dividing line between BP and the protected areas, between subject and object, humans and nature, *always* inherently indeterminate (as quantum mechanics teaches us)? And if the dividing line is always indeterminate, requiring determinacy to be imposed by the measuring process, what is BP really evaluating and assessing? Thus, not only do questions arise as to whether BP and the protected areas are separate *prior to* any sort of evaluation and risk assessment, questions also arise as to whether BP can keep its evaluation and assessment practices separate from that which it is attempting to evaluate and assess.

At the heart of these issues is the fact that any identification of a business's *impacts on* natural phenomena is inherently self-referential. Proposals of potential, and accountings of actual, impacts between businesses and natural phenomena materialize from:

1. the manner in which (non-human) natural phenomena, such as breeding behaviors, migratory patterns, and morphological characteristics, make themselves intelligible to scientists and managers;
2. the ways in which scientists study and managers understand their own activities, the firms' activities, and the activities of natural phenomena; and
3. how scientists and managers define 'impact.'

In other words, an identified impact is inherently constituted (i.e., given boundaries, properties, and meanings) by both human and non-human activities; this in turn means that such impacts cannot be understood outside of an understanding of how they are articulated by entangled human and natural phenomena. Adherence to *a priori* assumptions of a separate 'nature,' and separate business practices, involving a supposed inherent boundary between human and natural phenomena, overlooks key organizational practices through which such boundaries are created and wedged into place, and then paradoxically treated as if they were there all along (see Whitehead, 1919, 1967b for rich examinations of this pervasive phenomenon, what he calls, 'The Fallacy of Misplaced Concreteness'). Such boundary-making practices are not only part of what makes organizations what they are and are not, they are largely unexamined by organization and management scholars (Good & Thorpe, 2019). An assumption of separation creates individuality where there is none, which in turn blocks appreciations and accountings of entangled constitutions, while also impairing clear understandings of how bad (or good) outcomes are articulated, and who is responsible for them. Thus, in practice, as well as in the current organization and management literature, the separateness of firms, such as BP and protected areas is taken for granted. The reality, however, is that humans, organizations, and nature constitute one another, including the organizing practices through they differentiate themselves *from* one another (Barad, 2007; Good & Thorpe, 2019).

Much like classical physics, metaphysical individualism is based on the idea of the stand-alone individual entity; but just as quantum physics, which empirically rejects the idea of the non-relational entity, has supplanted classical physics, we need to revise our metaphysical approach to studying, regulating, and managing how businesses relate with the natural world. This book, based on an ethnographic research project conducted in a fishing fleet that operates in the Gulf of Alaska, contributes to such a revision.

An alternative to a metaphysical individualism-based approach is an 'entanglement' perspective. To be entangled, according to Barad (2007, ix), "is not simply to be intertwined with another, as in the joining of separate entities, but to lack an independent, self-contained existence." Entangled entities (e.g., atoms, activities, objects, persons, organizations, systems) lack individually determinable or isolatable boundaries, instead gaining such qualities through their differentiating and constituting relations. 'Entanglement,' as it is understood here, is not merely an epistemological issue; thus, it is not only about how one comes to know something. Rather, entanglement is the ontological (i.e., inherent, physical, real) inseparability of 'objects' and 'agencies or instruments of observation' (or measurement, interaction, engagement, etc.). Thus, entanglement is the impossibility of drawing any sharp, unambiguous distinction between the behavior of what is being interacted with (the 'object') and the conditions or context of that interaction (the 'agencies of observation') (Barad, 2007). Put differently, there is an inherent indeterminacy regarding the boundaries that separate 'objects' and 'agencies or instruments of observation.' Entanglement is both the mutually constitu*ted* nature of what we consider to be individualities ('objects'), as well as the mutually constitu*ting* nature of our acts of consideration (or any act of engagement, from observations to measurements to experiments). Because of this inherent indeterminacy, determinacy must be continually enacted, i.e., performed, such that separation that is necessary for unambiguous meaning is imputed (or 'cut') where it does not ontologically exist. As we will see later in the book, such meaning is found in the differential-yet-entangled responses to differential articulations of entanglements. Importantly, entanglement is not just a human, or even merely a quantum, affair; it occurs 'all the way down,' from the world of very large stuff to the world of very small stuff, and all the way back, from the present far back into the past (Barad, 2007; Butler, 1990; Slife, 2004).

Thus, from an entanglement perspective the isolation of phenomena into a separate thing renders the boundaries, properties and meanings of the isolat*ed* thing at least partly constituted by the isolat*ing* activity; likewise, the isolat*ing* activity is inseparable from the phenomena being isolat*ed* as a thing, for the phenomena being isolat*ed* gives boundaries, properties, and even meaning (to greater and lesser degrees of course) to the isolat*ing* activity (note that this is the case for all activity, human and non-human). Taken together, the appearance or notion of an isolat*ed* thing is a materialization that is performed by entangled (i.e., mutually constitutive) isolat*ing* and isolat*ed* activities, as well as the entangled phenomena that those activities are part and parcel of. Actions can never be isolated in and of themselves because they are always, whether intended or not, performing the boundaries, and contributing to the properties and meanings, through which actions (and things) take shape. We never encounter individual actions, or *inter*-actions, only *intra*-actions (Barad, 2007). Thus, the absolute isolation of an action, or a thing, cannot actually occur, for it is inseparable from the isolating activities. Crucially then, not only can actions and things never be isolated as stand-alone entities, but neither can their boundaries. Boundaries are always mutually constituted by differentiating activities, and therefore 'belong' to whatever entities are both bounded and are doing the bounding. Put differently, boundaries are ambiguous when viewed through the lens of individual entities; they always are performed by, and belong to, more than one individual. Differentiation does not imply separation, and entanglement does not imply sameness. As Barad states, "Entanglements are not unities. They do not erase differences; on the contrary, entanglings entail differentiatings, differentiatings entail entanglings" (Barad, 2014, p. 176). This is entanglement in a nutshell.

From an entanglement perspective the boundaries that isolate BP and the protected areas they are wary of impacting are ambiguous. By this I mean that they are mutually constituted by the entangled activities of multiple actors, including BP's actions and the actions involved in non-human natural phenomena, and therefore cannot be isolated to one or the other. Thus, if BP had a hand in the constitution of the protected areas, then BP and those areas, 'are not simply intertwined with another, as in the joining of separate entities, but lack an independent, self-contained existence.' Which is to say, they are entangled. Failing to account for current and past relations among BP and the protected areas overlooks critical information on the contemporary organization of BP's relationship with protected areas. In short, to start from a such highly organized place, i.e., that of separation, is to ignore most of the story. As Barad argues in terms of the inherently entangled nature of human and natural phenomena:

> To exclude the human from the realm of nature and sequester him or her in the realm of culture is not only to install the nature-culture divide in the foundations of the theory but to forgo the possibility of understanding how this boundary gets drawn.
>
> *(Barad, 2007, p. 339)*

For BP to fully assess how they 'impact' something that is not separate from them, they would first have to analyze how the boundaries between that something and themselves are articulated, and then they would have to re-define 'impact' to better align with the realities of entanglement rather than the fictions of separation.

Thus, a key aspect of entanglement is that the boundaries that create and separate individuals are inherently ambiguous. And we see such ambiguities play out all the time: Anybody who has thought beyond a superficial level about Cartesian dualisms (e.g., human–nature, inside–outside, subject–object, word–world, organization–environment, ontology–epistemology), which take the world to be constituted by separate and opposing objects, each with their own roster of non-relational boundaries, properties, and meanings (Farjoun, 2010), has frustratingly run up against the inherent ambiguity of the very elements, i.e., separate boundaries, that define them. Fellow teachers will identify the frustration that students experience when we task them with dividing up an entangled world into un-entangled, discrete categories, such as 'the organization' and 'the environment,' or the political, natural, technological, sociocultural, and economic dimensions of 'the environment.' Anybody who has wrestled with the question, or even the science, of who is responsible for climate change—humans or nature—will find themselves frustrated by the inherent ambiguity at the heart of the question. The question of whether or not climate change is caused by humans is, from an entanglement perspective, a nonsensical question, a distraction, perhaps even a red herring, for it is grounded in metaphysical individualism. A metaphysical approach to climate change becomes highly problematic when our determinations of what should be done about it, and who should do it, rest upon its Potemkin foundation.

Concerns with inherent, deleterious, and widespread changes to natural phenomena, and therefore to human phenomena, always materialize from the inherently entangled nature of human and natural phenomena. Yet people dealing with those concerns also all too often tend to approach them from a non-entangled, metaphysical individualism-based perspective. For example, scientists from various disciplines (but starting with geologists) are arguing that we have entered a new epoch, which they call the 'Anthropocene.' The Anthropocene, according to leading scholars on the topic,

> implies that the human imprint on the global environment is now so large that the Earth has entered a new geological epoch; it is leaving the Holocene, the environment within which human societies themselves have developed. Humanity itself has become a global geophysical force, equal to some of the 'great forces of Nature' in terms of Earth System functioning.
>
> *(Steffen et al., 2011, p. 741)*

Thus, our new geological time period is defined by the inherent role that humans play in the ongoing materialization of nature, which has important implications for our understanding of humans and their relationship with nature; as organizational scholars Andrew Hoffman and Devereaux Jennings state, "The Anthropocene Era represents an emergent awareness of a fundamental change in the intellectual, cultural, and psychological conceptions of who we are as humans and how we relate to the world around us" (Hoffman & Jennings, 2015, p. 9).

But if this is the case, if the change is indeed 'fundamental,' then why are scholars framing this 'new' relationship between humans and nature as if it involves separate things? For example, Lewis and Maslin, writing in a top scientific journal, state that, in this new epoch, "Human activity profoundly *affects the environment*, from Earth's major biochemical cycles to the evolution of life" (2015, p. 172, citing Palumbi, 2001; emphasis added). Similarly, Dirzo et al. (2014), elaborating the 'defaunation' (i.e., loss of animal populations and species) that will accompany our journey further into the Anthropocene, state, "Human *impacts on* animal biodiversity, particularly, are an under-recognized form of global environmental change" (emphasis added). Likewise, in an edited volume on the Anthropocene, Crutzen, one of the early proponents of the new geological designation, writes, "Human activities are exerting increasing *impacts on the environment* on all scales, in many ways *outcompeting* natural processes" (Crutzen, 2006, p. 13, emphasis added).

Each of these discussions, and many others, assumes a separation of humans and the very nature that scholars argue that humans are now a constitutive part of (though social scientists, such as Hoffman and Jennings, whose work more often straddle human and natural differentiations, often have a better appreciation of the entangled nature of human and natural phenomena in the Anthropocene). Thus, in appreciating how humans 'impact,' 'affect,' and 'outcompete' 'the environment' and 'biodiversity,' we are required to first cast human and non-human phenomena (i.e., the environment and biodiversity) as separate things, and to then appreciate that one (humans) impacts the other (the environment, biodiversity) to such an extent that one (humans) is now fundamentally part of the other (the environment, biodiversity). While the deleterious effects described in the quoted material above are undoubtedly occurring, framing the problem as an issue of humans 'impacting,' 'affecting,' and 'competing with' something that otherwise exists apart from them, but which they are a constitutive part of, creates a paradoxical way of approaching the problem. The approach has metaphysical individualism at its core, even as it seemingly attempts to fight against it. As Alfred North Whitehead long ago stated in his analysis of the same troubled approach that requires one to first bifurcate inseparable phenomena into separate human and natural realities, and to then to take such bifurcation to be foundational to those realities, "This is surely a muddle" (Whitehead, 1919, p. 21).

The muddled approach lies in framing the issue as one of impacts, opposition, and competition, and therefore adhering to the idea of the separation of humans and nature—yet simultaneously attempting to make the case that the two are inherently inseparable. If the whole point of the concept of the Anthropocene is to recognize and account for humanity's inherent role in how (non-human) nature materializes through time, does it make sense to frame the issue as a problem of human activity impacting, affecting, or competing with nature? Are we to assume that, while humans now play a fundamental, i.e., constitutive, role in how nature unfolds, that humanity and nature are also separate? Is it perhaps the case that humans are entangled with how nature materializes, but (even more paradoxically) nature is not entangled with how humans materialize? Each of these options smack of human exceptionalism, whereby man has both distance from and elevation above nature, and is then burdened with all the paternal responsibilities that such deistic endowment demands. The arbitrariness of the separation of humans and nature becomes more apparent the more it becomes apparent that it does not exist. How can we expect to understand, and then regulate and manage, our short and long-term, direct and indirect, near and distant relations with the natural world, if we erroneously characterize them from the start?

In the Anthropocene, as well as in the time of climate change, reality has 'fundamentally changed,' but our approach to understanding it has not. The perspective of reality in general, and particularly of the relations among human and non-human phenomena, explored in this book, i.e., entanglement, should deeply inform the theory and frameworks used to understand, and the structure used to discuss, study, manage, and regulate such issues as climate change and the Anthropocene. If we can get a grip on the entanglement of humans and nature, including how they mutually constitute, while at the same time differentiate themselves from, one another, then we can begin to better understand how humans are constituted by nature (and in turn how humans constitute nature), and why our duty to act is much more profound than assumptions of the separation of humans and nature lead us to believe. If we continue to clumsily plod into this new epoch, and approach such dire issues as climate change with the outdated and empirically disproven idea that humans and nature are separable, we will continue to dangerously overlook critically important relations among humans and nature, and our concordant responsibilities to do something about them.

Analytical approach

This book is focused on answering the following questions:

- How do frontline managers in a commercial fishing industry make sense of, and in turn organize with, natural phenomena?
- What does that sensemaking mean in terms of material outcomes of fishing, and in turn how such resource extraction practices should be regulated and managed?

To answer these questions, this book argues that we need to take an entanglement-based approach to understanding and managing relations among humans and nature, particularly the relations that can involve unwanted outcomes. It takes on the task of understanding natural resource extraction practices from a place of realistic entanglement rather than an assumption of fantastical separation, with the ultimate goal of similarly shifting natural resource management and regulation from dealing in fantasies to working with realities. The book makes its case through the analysis of the front-line practices of a particular natural resource extraction industry—commercial trawl fishing in the Gulf of Alaska, and asks how a particular unwanted outcome—fisheries bycatch—continually materializes, who bears responsibility for it, and what can be done about it. This analysis is conducted through the combined perspectives of Karen Barad's agential realism (e.g., Barad 1998, 2003, 2007, 2011, 2014) and Karl Weick's organizational sensemaking (e.g., Weick 1979, 1995, 2009), and, to a lesser extent, Alfred North Whitehead's process philosophy (e.g., Whitehead 1967a, 1968, 1978). In the following I briefly discuss how Barad's agential realism and Weick's sensemaking can help us answer the questions outlined above. Each perspective, including Whitehead's process philosophy, is more explored in more detail in the ensuing chapters.

Barad's agential realism

Karen Barad, scholar of theoretical physics, feminist theory, and new materialism, has elaborated a perspective of reality in general, and of the mutual constitution of humans and nature in particular, that takes on the seemingly intractable problem of attempting to know an entangled world through disentangled perspectives and methods. While other scholars have also taken on this problem in somewhat similar ways (e.g., Michel Callon, Ian Hacking, Donna Haraway, Bruno Latour, John Law, Andrew Pickering), Barad's treatment, grounded in quantum mechanics, not only encompasses both humans and nature, but is also the one that most clearly, directly, and equitably, at least to my reading, gives nature its due in terms of accounting for its role in the ongoing materialization of the human (and natural) condition. Callon, Latour, and Law's actor–network theory would seemingly be a natural choice for an examination of the entanglement of human and natural phenomena in natural resource extraction industries; in fact, Callon's influential 1986 article, "Some elements of a sociology of translation: domestication of the scallops and the fishermen of St Brieuc Bay," focused on biologists as they studied scallop populations that were part of a fishery in France. Yet actor-network theory, constituted by a complex vocabulary, and weighted down by opaque internal disagreements, lacks clarity and accessibility (at least in terms of the limited capabilities of this author). Further, actor-network theory does not bring with it the expansive cross-disciplinary legitimacy that agential realism does, which bridges quantum mechanics, primarily drawing on the work of Nobel laureate Niels Bohr, with various social theories, drawing on such scholars as Michel Foucault, Judith Butler, and Donna Haraway.

Some may understandably question how applicable an approach that is grounded in quantum mechanics is to human-scale phenomena. First, let's put to rest the notion that there is some sort of dualism between quantum and non-quantum, micro and macro words. There are not, as Barad clearly puts it, "two separate domains of nature, one macroscopic and one microscopic" (Barad, 2007, p. 338; for experimental papers demonstrating the same argument, see Fein et al., 2019; Gerlich et al., 2011; Ma et al., 2012, among various others). No such dividing line exists, and claims of its existence commit the fallacy of misplaced concreteness (Whitehead, 1967b), in which they stitch the dualisms we use to infuse our modes of thinking and communication with determinacy into the indeterminate empirical thing that we think and communicate about; then they interpret those dualisms as having existed in the empirical thing all along (prior to thought and communication about them). Instead, quantum mechanics "is the most successful and accurate theory in the history of physics, accounting for phenomena over a range of twenty-five orders of magnitude, from the smallest particles of matter to large-scale objects" (Barad, 2007, p 110). Arguments for distinct macro and micro worlds become even less tenable once we appreciate that the findings of the experiment at the heart of quantum mechanics—the double-slit experiment (see Barad, 2007, among a multitude of other texts, for an explanation of this famous experiment)—hold for both quantum-sized material, such as atoms and electrons, and human-sized material, such as sand particles, bullets, and basketballs. The double-slit experiment, according to Nobel laureate Richard Feynman, is "a phenomenon which is impossible, absolutely impossible, to explain in any classical way ... [it] has in it the heart of quantum mechanics. In reality, it contains the only mystery" (Feynman, Leighton, & Sands, 1964, as quoted in Barad, 2007, 2014). What we find, thanks in large part to Barad's work (e.g., Barad 1998, 2003, 2007, 2010, 2014), and others that apply and extend it (e.g., Fitzgerald & Callard, 2015; Hahn & Knight, in press; Shotter, 2014), is that the solution to the mystery of the double-slit experiment holds important lessons for our understanding of the human, and the inseparable natural, condition.

The question of the suitability of applying agential realism, due to it being grounded in quantum mechanics, to human-scale phenomena has in fact already been settled. As Hollin, Forsyth, Giraud, and Potts (2017) note, "Agential realism is deployed across a range of scales, in an array of different spaces, and it has jumped these scales rather smoothly" (p. 10). Most notably for our purposes, agential realism is the heart of the burgeoning domain of management theory and research known as 'sociomateriality' (e.g., Berthod & Müller-Seitz, 2018; Leonardi, 2011; Nicolini, 2011; Orlikowski & Scott, 2015; Stigliani & Ravasi, 2012). Introduced by Wanda Orlikowski, 'sociomateriality' was born out of the ontological and epistemological problems associated with treating human and non-human phenomena (in this case primarily technology and other artifacts) as if they are inherently separate (Orlikowski, 2007; Orlikowski & Scott, 2008). The underlying assumption of sociomaterial scholarship is that (human) social processes and their material artifacts "start out and forever remain in relationship" (Slife, 2004, p. 159, as cited in Orlikowski & Scott, 2008, p. 455). Thus, the social and the material are inherently inseparable, and you cannot understand social processes without understanding their materiality, and you cannot understand their materiality without understanding social processes (Orlikowski, 2007). The social and the material are, in other words, "ontologically fused" (Orlikowski & Scott, 2008, p. 456). Like Orlikowski and colleagues, this book also draws heavily on Barad's work (e.g., Barad 1998, 2003, 2007, 2014), but expands the sociomateriality literature's convention of only examining materiality in the form of artifacts (e.g., de Vaujany & Vaast, 2014; Scott & Orlikowski, 2012) to include natural materiality which, unlike artifacts, "can exist outside of society" (Bansal & Knox-Hayes, 2013).

But at least one more reason remains, a more empirical and experiential one, for choosing agential realism as one of the two primary interpretive lenses used in this book. Agential realism is the analytical approach that, after five years of searching for a satisfying way to understand the data at the heart of this book, not only finally makes it all make sense, but also rings true to someone who has spent several years working on fishing vessels in the cold Alaskan waters, who later did his doctoral research both on those fishing vessels and in a local community that is dependent on natural resource extraction for its livelihood, and who has spent many hours observing nature through the lens of a camera. In Barad's agential realism, humans and nature are inseparable, yet a key concern is the entangled activities through which humans and nature both constitute and differentiate themselves from one another, and the effects of those practices on one another. Within this perspective, the agency of both humans and nature is given equal treatment; each one's level of responsibility for deleterious outcomes is given equal weight, even as their unequal accountability for responding to those outcomes becomes explicit. Agential realism argues that humans and nature are entangled (i.e., mutually constitutive), and that this entanglement increases (rather than reduces) *our* responsibility for shaping how our relations with nature unfold. Both humans and nature have agency in what each is and is not, can be and cannot be, yet only one can hold themselves accountable to the extent the world needs.

In other words, agential realism is 'posthumanistic.' 'Posthumanism,' as it is used here, means that agential realism is not, to the extent possible, "calibrated to the human" (Barad, 2007, p. 136). Although we cannot escape the humanistic confines of our perceptions, thoughts, languages,[1] social structures, and processes, we can be mindful of how we perceive, think, talk, write, socialize, structure, and organize ourselves in relation with phenomena that are not entirely human (and all phenomena are not entirely human). While there are several versions of 'posthumanism' out there, Barad's posthumanism is

> about taking issue with human exceptionalism while being accountable for the role we play in the differential constitution and differential positioning of the human among other creatures (both living and nonliving). Posthumanism does not attribute the source of all change to culture, denying nature any sense of agency or historicity … Posthumanism does not assume that man is the measure of all things.
>
> *(Barad, 2007, p. 136)*

Posthumanism recognizes the interpretive, social, and physical differentiation of humans and what humans call (i.e., differentiate as) 'nature,' but not their separability. The lack of separability at the heart of posthumanism is demanded by findings of experiments in quantum mechanics: As Barad recounts, "According to Bohr, the experimental evidence forced on us a recognition of quantum non separability" (2007, p. 340). If quantum mechanics makes it clear that there is non-separability at the quantum level, and if there is no ontological division of quantum and non-quantum realities, and if quantum mechanics shapes phenomena at all levels (Barad, 2007; Mermin, 1998; Wendt, 2015), then we must at least wrestle with, and attempt to account for, the non-separability of our social and organizational realities. Taking 'non-separability' seriously means that posthumanism assumes a 'relational ontology,' which psychologist Brent Slife describes in the following:

> Relationships are not just the interactions of what was originally nonrelational; relationships are relational 'all the way down.' Things are not first self-contained entities and then interactive. Each thing, including each person, is first and always a nexus of relations.
>
> *(Slife, 2004, p. 159)*

Whether we look at our reality from the bottom-up (quantum mechanics) or the top-down (psychology, sociomateriality, etc.), we end up in the same place: The entangled nature of our reality in general, and of our relationship with nature in particular.

As a result, a posthumanistic perspective of entanglement sees the differentiating of humans and nature as something that should be questioned and interrogated, not taken for granted. While humans and nature are regularly treated as different from one another, due in no small part to their differentiating biological, conceptual, physical, social, and organizational processes, humans and nature are not biologically, conceptually, physically, socially, or organizationally separable. Differentiating processes are never separable from whatever it is that they are differentiating. Differentiation is a mode of entanglement; it cannot, by definition, be a characteristic of separate entities. And due to the cataclysmic state of our relations with nature, the differentiation of humans and nature cannot be assumed to not matter, and therefore be taken for granted, for it is perhaps what matters most.

As noted above, agential realism draws heavily from Nobel laureate Niels Bohr's work on quantum physics. In fact, according to Hollin et al. (2017, p. 16), "Barad's concept of agential realism largely reframes the work of Niels Bohr for a new audience." In doing so, Barad pays special attention to what she calls Bohr's 'central lesson of quantum mechanics.' This is the lesson that "we are part of the nature that we seek to understand" (Barad, 2007, p. 247). Implicit in this lesson is its logical extension, that the nature we are part of and seek to understand is also part of us and our processes of understanding, as well as what materializes through them, whether it be physical or conceptual, human or non-human (by 'what materializes,' I mean what comes to matter, that which emerges into being; a 'difference which makes a difference'). Another version of the lesson 'we are part of the nature that we seek to understand' is Bohr's finding from his analysis of the famous double-slit experiment and its 'wave-particle duality paradox,' that "concepts are meaningful, that is, semantically determinate, not in the abstract but by virtue of their embodiment in the physical arrangement of an apparatus" (Barad, 2007, p. 117). The wave-particle duality paradox captures a long period in history in which the world of physics, involving such renown figures as Isaac Newton, Albert Einstein, Max Planck, Werner Heisenberg, Erwin Schrödinger, and Niels Bohr, attempted to determine the nature of light (which, it turned out, also involved determining the nature of determining, and the nature of nature). From the late 1600s to the beginning of the 1800s, scientists understood light to be a particle. After much debate, in the mid-1800s they determined it was a wave. Both during this time and later, some thought it was both.

Niels Bohr's 'central lesson' was his resolution of the wave-particle duality paradox. But it was not only that, Bohr believed it to be a re-working of Western epistemology (Barad, 2007). Bohr resolved the paradox by showing that the unambiguous determination of light to be a wave or a particle is beholden to the physical apparatus through which such determinations are made; light itself is ambiguous in terms of the concepts of 'wave' and 'particle.' In fact, there is no 'light itself,' for whatever our knowledge of light is, that knowledge is inseparable from the relations that constitute the apparatus through which the knowledge of 'light' emerges, through which light is known. 'Apparatus' takes on special meaning in this context: it is an arrangement of entangled activities that articulates specific boundaries into inherently ambiguous phenomena, materializing certain properties, and allowing clear, unambiguous meanings to be derived (Barad, 2007; Foucault, 1978; Haraway, 1991). Apparatuses are posthumanistic discursive practices, or "specific material configurings of the world through which determinations of boundaries, properties, and meanings are differentially enacted" (Barad, 2007, p. 335). Specific apparatuses perform specific arrangements of 'material discursive practices,' through which specific meanings are enacted, whether humans are involved or not. 'Material-discursive practices' are the boundary-, property-, and meaning-making contemporary and historical, human and natural activities that constrain and enable what is said and done, and in turn what "counts as meaningful statements" (Barad, 2007, p. 63).

Foucault, who famously also studied apparatuses (or 'dispositifs'), understood them to be specific socio-historical relations that produce the very subject matter that they attempt to control (such as legal systems that articulate their criminals). Barad, on the other hand, drawing on Bohr, Butler, and Foucault), finds apparatuses to be *physical* socio-*natural*-historical arrangements that articulate particular matters and meanings into experience, to the exclusions of other particular matters and meanings. Apparatuses are contemporary and historical, human and natural articulations of physical phenomena through which certain boundaries, properties, and meanings materialize from a field of possibilities, and other (mutually exclusive) boundaries, properties, and meanings do not. To work with apparatuses, from an agential realist perspective, is to insist on the material articulation of meaning (Barad, 2007). Everyday practices, such as measuring, observing, thinking, communicating, extracting, organizing, and sensemaking, are apparatuses—they all involve the physical articulation of both what matters and what is excluded from mattering. In fact, sensemaking, as a meaning-making apparatus operating at the frontline of commercial fishing practices, is the central concern of this book.

Critically, the subject-matter of an apparatus is always a constitutive part and parcel of the apparatus through which it is known. In fact, the subject matter is only differentiated as 'a subject,' or as 'a thing,' with its 'own' boundaries, properties, and meanings, through the apparatus. As Orlikowski and Scott (2014, p. 873) describe, "apparatuses are 'not passive observing instruments' that simply mirror nature; rather, they are 'productive of (and part of) phenomena,' simultaneously producing and organizing the phenomena they observe" (citing Barad, 1998, p. 98). Thus, that which is being measured is always a constitutive part and parcel of the act of measuring; that which is being observed is always a constitutive part and parcel of the act of observing; that which is communicated is always constitutive part and parcel of the act of communicating, and so on. A ruler is only a ruler through its acts of measuring; a lion is not 'a lion' outside of its manifestation in the apparatus that is human observation (it is certainly something, but the lion is not known to itself, to other lions, or to the impala, through their own processes of knowing, as we know it—as our concept 'lion'); the phrase 'let's go measure that lion with this ruler' will not have the same meaning each time it is communicated, for each utterance will involve a different arrangement of boundary-, property-, and meaning-making activities; each different arrangement is an apparatus through which certain meanings materialize, and others do not. While the activities and constitute an apparatus are only known through that apparatuses, the constituents of the apparatus are *real*, and their particular boundary-, property-, and meaning-making activities have *agency* in what materializes, and what does not; this is 'agential realism' in a nutshell. Apparatuses enact what matters and what is excluded from mattering, and these pervasive performative processes occur regardless of whether humans are present or not.

What holds true at the human level holds true at the quantum level (and vice versa) (if properly interpreted). Light is part of the apparatus through which it materializes, and the determination of light as a particle or as a wave is grounded in the specific configuration of the measuring apparatus. Which is why, according to Bohr, a specific apparatus is needed to elucidate light as a particle, and a *different* specific apparatus is needed to elucidate light as a wave; in fact, the two apparatuses are mutually exclusive—the apparatus that elucidates light as a wave cannot elucidate light as a particle, and the apparatus that elucidates light a particle cannot elucidate light as a wave (see Barad, 2007, for a thorough explanation of this phenomenon). Yet the apparatuses are complementary in that they each tell us something different about the phenomenon of light. Also notice that the apparatuses are posthumanistic—they are constituted by both human and (non-human) natural phenomena, as is what materializes through them (e.g., light as having the properties and meaning of being a particle, or as having the properties and meaning of being a wave).

Agential realism is a robust rendering of quantum mechanics that inherently expands it beyond the tiny world of electrons, photons, and atoms. It means that we are part of the nature we seek to understand, that the boundaries and properties that define 'we' and 'nature' are inherently entangled prior to and throughout knowledge processes, and that it is not just 'we humans' perform such processes (in which 'knowledge' is posthumanistically understood as the differential-yet-entangled response to the world articulating itself differently). Further, agential realism holds that what emerges through knowledge processes does not exist as a determinate entity, with clear-cut boundaries and individual properties and meanings, prior to those processes; it is the particular arrangement of human and non-human materialities, which intra-actively enact differences which make a difference, that perform what emerges as locally and contingently determinate (in which the problem of indeterminacy is resolved through entangled intra-actions; entanglement itself never ends). Material relations define, i.e., have agency in, the boundaries, properties, and meanings of what emerges. More broadly, an apparatus is an entangled array of differences which make a difference in the boundaries, properties, and meanings that constitute whatever it is that emerges through it, whether that 'it' is a mere idea, a sense of what is happening, or a physical object. If realism is "a belief in the correspondence between theoretical terms and physical reality" (Barad, 2007, p. 318), agential realism is the articulation of terms, or things that come to matter, by apparatuses (posthumanistically understood).

The central lesson of agential realism for this book, which will be made clear in the ensuing chapters, is that unambiguous meaning is derived from its mutually exclusive physical articulation by apparatuses, which are constituted by both human and natural phenomena. Thus, unambiguous meaning is a property of the apparatus through which meaning is materialized; it is not inherent in that which is observed, measured, or communicated, or in whatever does the observing, measuring, or communicating. Rather, unambiguous meaning is a product of the entanglement through which a separation, or 'exteriority,' is enacted, creating a semantically-determinate boundary (i.e., a boundary in meaning) between what is observed and what is doing the observing. As Bohr found, and Barad elaborates, theories, ideas, thoughts, arguments, etc., are *actual physical phenomena*, and the extent that they are meaningful, i.e., unambiguous, is the extent to which they are exclusively articulated by physical arrangements of entangled activities, resulting in differentiated boundaries, properties, and meanings, such that all other theories, ideas, thoughts, arguments, etc., save the one being articulated (and its synonyms and analogs), are omitted. Such omissions are 'constitutive exclusions,' resulting in 'exteriority within' phenomena (Barad, 2007). This is 'the materiality of meaning-making,' and it is grounded in Bohr's quantum mechanics, as elaborated through Barad's agential realism.

Weick's sensemaking

This book makes the case that sensemaking is an apparatus for making unambiguous meaning at the frontline of commercial fishing, through which certain organized entanglements, and their material outcomes, emerge (and certain others do not). According to the current literature, sensemaking is an organizing process through which a sense of what is happening now and what will happen in the future is both determined and in turn enacted into ensuing experience, which shapes both how organization forms and what it looks like (Gephart, 1993; Weick, 1979, 1995; Weick et al., 2005). According to the current literature, sensemaking is triggered when actors unexpectedly perceive cues that run counter to, or perhaps are foreign to, their expectations (Bean & Eisenberg, 2006; Jett & George, 2003; Patriotta & Gruber, 2015; Rerup, 2009; Weick, 1995, 2010; Weick & Sutcliffe, 2007). The sensemaking that follows such perception is characterized by seven properties: it is *social* (in which 'social' is the actual or imagined presence of others), informed and driven by *identities* (i.e., who an individual or organization is and wants to be), *retrospective* in orientation,[2] focused on and by *extracted cues*,[3] *ongoing* (we are always, at some level and to a certain extent, both making sense of experience and shaping the experience we make sense of), beholden to *plausibility* rather than accuracy,[4] and both shaped by and dependent upon *enactments*.[5] The following outline of a sensemaking process depicts the relationships among these properties: "Once people begin to act (enactment), they generate tangible outcomes (cues) in some context (social), and this helps them discover (retrospect) what is occurring (ongoing), what needs to be explained (plausibility), and what should be done next (identity enhancement)" (Weick, 1995, p. 55), which in turn shapes people's context and what cues they generate.

In this book I investigate the day-to-day sensemaking at the frontline of a resource extraction industry. More specifically, I investigate the day-to-day sensemaking that vessel captains in a commercial trawl fishery in the Gulf of Alaska engage in as they organize their entangled relations with natural phenomena, with the goal of reliably shaping what materializes through them (e.g., target catch), and what does not (e.g., bycatch). A fishing captain's primary duty is determining where to fish next (Gatewood, 1984; Gezelius, 2007; Orth, 1987), whether it is the next set, the next trip, the next season, or the next year. What is "perhaps the fundamental problem of ordering and organizing" is a salient issue in the practice of commercial fishing: "the problem about what will come next" (Cooper & Law, 1995, p. 242). Determining what comes next in the face of ambiguity and equivocality is a primary function of sensemaking (Weick, 1995), which encompasses the activities through which actors answer the questions, "what's the story here?" and "now what should I do?" (Weick et al., 2005, p. 410). To answer these questions is to create a "workable level of certainty" (Weick 1969, p. 40); workable levels of certainty "suggest plausible acts of managing, coordinating, and distributing" (Weick et al., 2005, p. 411). Acts of managing, coordinating, and distributing are key organizing processes that constitute the organization (Chia, 2003; Czarniawska, 2004; Law, 1994). Thus, the relationship between sensemaking and organizing is one in which "People organize to make sense of equivocal inputs and then enact this sense back into the world to make it more orderly" (Weick et al., 2005, p. 410). In other words, the relationship is recursive in that people organize to engage in processes collectively known as sensemaking, yet it is through such sensemaking processes that they are able to organize. It is safe to assume that what holds true for the trapper in the arctic wild (Whiteman & Cooper, 2011) and the firefighter in the Montana wilderness (Weick, 1993) holds true also for the commercial fishing captain: they engage in sensemaking as they work to answer the questions, 'what's our story here?' and 'what do we do next?,' and in doing so organizes their entanglement with natural phenomena.

Current commercial fisheries scholarship assumes that fishing practices can be analyzed through rational decision-making theory, assumptions, and frameworks (e.g., Acheson, 2006; Branch et al., 2006; Grafton et al., 2006; Hilborn, Orensanz, & Parma, 2005; Plummer & Fitzgibbon, 2004). This scholarship has largely overlooked how fishing captains make sense of novel, confusing, or otherwise indeterminate experience involving natural phenomena in order to make key decisions about how to organize with such phenomena and thus extract resources from them. Fisheries management scholar Daniel Holland speaks to this void in the following:

> When modeling fishing decisions, there should be more explicit consideration given to how fishermen incorporate information into complex decisions, and how they actually make decisions ... If our goal is to understand and predict fishing behavior and design more effective fishery management tools, it is critical to understand how fishermen actually make decisions, not how economic theory suggests they should make them.

> (Holland, 2008, p. 342)

Svein Jentoft, another fisheries management scholar, suggests some of what is needed to fill this void:

> We should not only be looking for causal factors external to the individual actors involved, but also to the motivations that guide their behaviour and the interpretations and meanings they attribute to the particular circumstances that they find themselves in and the choices they make.
>
> *(Jentoft, 2006, p. 678)*

This book examines sensemaking, through an agential realist lens, in order to understand (1) the interplay of motivations, behaviors, interpretations, meanings, attributions, and circumstances through which captains and natural phenomena together form particular organized entanglements at the frontline of commercial fishing, and (2) what those entanglements mean for forging desirable and sustainable outcomes.

If it is through sensemaking that organization emerges, it is through ecological sensemaking that organization involving both human and natural phenomena emerges. As defined by Whiteman and Cooper (2011) in their research into the land management practices of indigenous peoples of the Canadian Arctic, specifically the Cree tallymen, ecological sensemaking is "the way actors notice, bracket, make, and select connections and act on spatial and temporal cues arising from topography and ecological processes" (p. 905). Whiteman and Cooper's work draws heavily on what was perhaps the first ecological sensemaking study (conducted before 'ecological sensemaking' was coined), Weick's 1993 analysis of the disastrous efforts made by 'smokejumpers' to fight a woodland forest fire in Montana in 1949, which Normal Maclean (author of *A River Runs Through It*) examined in his book *Young Men and Fire*. Whiteman and Cooper, examining both their own research and Weick's, argue that to understand how people make sense when embedded in natural phenomena, we have to account for the depth and breadth of their experience in such phenomena. Ecological sensemaking occurs over large swaths of time and space, and the extent of one's embeddedness influences which ecological cues actors notice and incorporate into their sensemaking, how they interconnect those cues, what sense they make of the distant past and the passing present, and what sense they retain for the ensuing future.

Whiteman and Cooper's work on ecological sensemaking makes the case that how ecological sensemaking unfolds is inseparable from the *ecological materiality* it is embedded in. 'Ecological materiality,' according to Whiteman and Cooper (2011, p. 892), is "the interaction of dynamic biological and biophysical processes and organic and inorganic matter over space and time." Together Weick (1993) and Whiteman and Cooper (2011) elaborate how ecological materiality that is bracketed and imported into, as well as excluded from, ecological sensemaking influences how effective (safe, reliable, even lifesaving) that sensemaking is.

While the relatively small ecological sensemaking literature (more recent additions include Bond, 2015; Linnenluecke, Griffiths, & Winn, 2012; Tisch & Galbreath,

2018) helps us understand that ecological materiality is critical for effective functioning, there is an important part of the story that is missing. Though we may read between the lines to see that both non-human phenomena and humans constitute 'the natural environment,' and therefore what is not 'the natural environment,' the literature (e.g., Weick, 1993; Whiteman & Cooper, 2011) fails to capture, from a post-humanistic perspective, how non-human phenomena is a constitutive part of sensemaking, how those phenomena have agency in terms of what sensemaking looks like, and what sort of materiality (i.e., that which has the property of mattering) is articulated through that sensemaking. In the current literature ecological sensemaking is understood as a sort of internal process of mapping external phenomena, in which what is considered to be important about the external environment, based on past experience, is internally depicted, either in one mind or across multiple minds; in this view ecological materiality is an external subject of internal objects, which humans individually and socially assemble into representational configurations, i.e., sense, of that external matter. The boundaries, properties, and meanings of ecological materiality, as they occur in ecological sensemaking, are performed by humans, for humans.

The key problem with this current version of ecological sensemaking is that it adheres to the much and long-criticized (e.g., Butler, 1990; Callon 1986; Haraway, 1991; Pickering, 1995; Latour, 2005; Levins & Lewontin, 1985; Whitehead, 1919), as well as scientifically debunked (e.g.,Bohr, 1958; Mermin, 1998; Schrödinger, 1935/1983), dualistic view of humans and nature. In taking a dualistic view, in which ecological materiality is something external that is made sense of inside human social processes, the current version of ecological sensemaking robs nature of its agency in terms of how sense is made and what materializes through ecological sensemaking, both in terms of meaning and matter. While ecological materiality, in the current literature, may 'act on' and 'impact' humans sensemakers, it takes a passive role in terms of how it is articulated and what sense is made 'of' it. Barad makes a similar point in the following:

> Nature is neither a passive surface awaiting the mark of culture nor the end product of cultural performances. The belief that nature is mute and immutable and that all prospects for significance and change resides in culture merely reinscribes the nature-culture dualism … To presume a given distinction between humans and nonhumans is to cement and recirculate the nature-culture dualism into the foundations of [theory], foreclosing a genealogy of how nature and culture, human and nonhuman, are formed.
>
> *(Barad, 2007, p. 183)*

Our sense of nature, of its materiality (i.e., what comes to matter), is not a mere output of human phenomena. Natural phenomena do not merely await human activity for their boundaries, properties, and meanings; instead, nature is, as Barad argues, an active boundary-, property-, and meaning-making agent in its processes of materialization, whether humans are involved or not. The idea that humans exists apart from nature, and that the two come together at times to 'interact with,' 'act-on,' 'affect,' and 'impact' one another, is inherently intertwined with the belief that nature, in terms of how it materializes in 'human' phenomena, is merely a blank slate onto which humans etch its import and meaning.

The assumption of the separation of humans and nature shapes a vast array of scientific findings, leaving us with incomplete understandings of a vast array of phenomena, from atoms to technologies to genders to organizations to nature (Barad, 2007; Butler, 1990; Good & Thorpe, 2019; Haraway, 1991; Rouse, 2002). And we can see its influence hampering our understanding of ecological sensemaking. For example, although Whiteman and Cooper (2011) state that the purpose of their study was to "examine how ecological materiality *impacts* actors' sensemaking" (p. 892, emphasis added), which is a dualistic framing, they also at times seem to imply that ecological materiality has agency in terms of what sensemaking looks like and how it unfolds (e.g., "Material objects shape human interpretation and action"; ibid., p. 905), which hints of an entanglement perspective. Yet in elaborating their findings, the authors only go so far as to elucidate the processes through which human actors make sense of (i.e., "notice, bracket, make, and select connections and act on spatial and temporal cues"; ibid., p. 905) *external* ecological phenomena. The assumption is that ecological materiality is 'out there,' waiting to be discovered and made sense of 'in here,' and a key issue that the authors discuss is how much external ecological materiality actors will 'notice' and 'bracket' within their sensemaking, and in turn interact with. This assumption of an interior-exterior relationship between ecological materiality and ecological sensemaking leads to questions of how well that external materiality is represented internally in sensemaking processes. This question of the representational quality of ecological sensemaking is implied in such key findings as "The *acuity* with which ecological sensemaking is done is likely to affect outcomes such as survival and resilience" (ibid., p. 893, emphasis added), and "ecological embeddedness facilitates more *accurate* ecological sensemaking because it enhances the relevance of prior enacted environments and increases opportunities to bracket and *accurately* interpret local topography and ecological processes over time" (ibid., p. 906, emphases added).

According to Whiteman and Cooper (2011), how well ecological sensemaking works is a question of the verisimilitude of its internal human representations of external ecological materiality. Questions of the verisimilitude of representations naturally lead them to the argument that the quality of such representations is *mediated* by how embedded a sensemaker is in the ecological phenomena in which his or her sensemaking is occurring. The authors define 'ecological embeddedness' as "the degree to which a manager is rooted in the land—that is, the extent to which the manager is on the land and learns from the land in an experiential way" (Whiteman & Cooper, 2000, p. 1267). Whiteman and Cooper state that "Human understandings of—and responses to—the natural world are *mediated*" (ibid., p. 905) and argue that how ecologically embedded actors are shapes the relationship between ecological sensemaking and ecological materiality, such that the greater the extent of embeddedness, the more accurate that representations of ecological materiality should be within an ecological sensemaking process. Thus, greater representational accuracy, mediated by ecological embeddedness, increases the acuity of ecological sensemaking.

Discussions of mediation, acuity, and accuracy are hallmarks of a representational approach to understanding, studying, and managing experience (Barad, 2007; Hacking, 1983, Rouse, 2002). Representationalism is the assumption of 'the independently determinate existence of words, pictures, measurements, or some other values, and the things they refer to' (Barad, 2007, p. 195). Thus, at the heart of representationalism are the self-contained, non-relational entities of metaphysical individualism (ibid.). Barad further elaborates how representationalism relates to metaphysical individualism, as well as mediation, in the following:

> The idea that beings exist as individuals with inherent attributes, anterior to their representation, is a metaphysical presupposition that underlies the belief in political, linguistic, and epistemological forms of representationalism. Or to put the point the other way around, representationalism is the belief in the ontological distinction between representations and that which they purport to represent; in particular, that which is represented is held to be independent of all practices of representing. That is, there are assumed to be two distinct and independent kinds of entities—representations and entities to be represented. The system of representation is sometimes explicitly theorized in terms of a tripartite arrangement. For example, in addition to knowledge (i.e., representations), on the one hand, and the known (i.e., that which is purportedly represented), on the other, the existence of a knower (i.e., someone who does the representing) is sometimes made explicit. When this happens, it becomes clear that representations are presumed to serve a mediating function between independently existing entities ...
>
> *(Barad, 2007, p. 46–47)*

Figure 1.1 presents the 'tripartite arrangement' that, as Barad argues, is at the heart of representational perspectives of knowledge processes, whether those processes involve mere observing, something more complex like measuring, or even

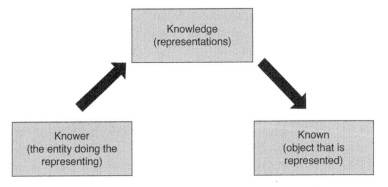

FIGURE 1.1 Diagram of Barad's 'tripartite arrangement' that is at the heart of representationalism.

sensemaking. In this arrangement the knower seeks to know the separate, external object, but, because they maintain their individuality throughout the process, the knower only has access to the object through an intermediary, which involves making or attaining representations, such as images, concepts, mental maps, of or about it. Representations that were formed in past experiences are stored as knowledge, and re-emerge when the object, or something similar to it, is re-engaged (whether just mentally or both mentally and physically). Thus, in Figure 1.1, the object exists as a stand-alone, independent entity awaiting the interactions of the knower; the knower interacts with the object in some sort of knowledge-seeking practice, through which the knower obtains information about the object, as an individuality. If the knowledge process disturbs the object, then the knower must be able to subtract that disturbance out of information that he or she gains and therefore know the object as it existed prior to the interaction (which relies on the assumption that the object can exist as a stand-alone entity). For this knowledge process to work, it must be metaphysical: the knower and the known are each constituted, at least in part, by non-relational boundaries, properties, and meanings, which persist prior to and throughout their interaction, whose separate individualities can be represented by abstract concepts, theories, etc., that can exist independent of the particular object or knowledge process (Barad, 2007).

A couple of additional aspects of the tripartite arrangement are important. First, note that in order for the knowledge that the knower obtains to be about the object alone (and not about the knower or the knowledge process), which is a basic premise of traditional Western science, the object must not only exist in an 'observation-independent reality' (Barad, 2007, p. 107), but its boundaries and properties must be relatively continuous. The maintenance of a certain level of continuity is the only reason the knowledge obtained is useful; if the object changes in some significant way throughout the process, then the knowledge obtained can neither be a property of the object as it existed prior to the interaction, nor can it serve as something useful for subsequent knowledge processes. Second, an implication of both the independence and continuity of the object is that the creation and internalization of representations *must* come by way of mediation. Mediation allows information to be transferred across stand-alone entities, which helps maintain the necessary independence and continuity of those entities (along with processes in which interaction effects are subtracted out). Mediation is needed to meet the goal of the metaphysical method, which is to obtain some values or characteristics that are intrinsic to the object of inquiry alone, and separate from the knowledge process. Also note that in this arrangement, that which is known might be active, and might initiate the interaction, but it is is a passive recipient of the meaning-making activity; if it were not, we would run the risk of violating the rule that the entities are independent.

As Figure 1.1 implies, in the representational understanding of knowledge processes there is an 'ontological gap' between the knower and the object to be known. This ontological gap logically leads to concerns of representational accuracy, and in turn the acuity of the knowledge-seeking process. As Barad's quote above continues:

This taken-for-granted ontological gap generates questions of the accuracy of representations. For example, does scientific knowledge accurately represent an independently existing reality? Does language accurately represent its referent? Does a given political representative, legal counsel, or piece of legislation accurately represent the interests of the people allegedly represented?

(Barad, 2007, pp. 47)

Figure 1.2 depicts this 'ontological gap' and the concern with accuracy that it engenders.

Returning to our current understanding of ecological sensemaking, Whiteman and Cooper's findings boil down to a representational approach in which the ecological sensemaker exists in a tripartite arrangement with ecological materiality and ecological embeddedness. In this process the knower, engaging in ecological sensemaking, is ontologically separate from ecological materiality, or that which the sensemaker is attempting to know. The gap between the two is mediated by ecological embeddedness, which is the breadth of one's knowledge of ecological materiality. Whiteman and Cooper describe this mediation in the following: "Our two cases suggest that ecological embeddedness facilitates more accurate ecological sensemaking because it enhances the relevance of prior enacted environments and increases opportunities to bracket and accurately interpret local topography and ecological processes over time" (p. 906, citing Fazey, Proust, Newell, Johnson, & Fazey, 2006; Whiteman & Cooper, 2000). Thus, ecological embeddedness is constituted by representations derived from past experience in the ecological context, which link the sensemaker to external ecological materiality (see Figure 1.3). The mediating function that ecological embeddedness serves between the ecological sensemaker and ecological materiality is the reason Whiteman and Cooper propose that one's extent of embeddedness, which they differentiate into categories of 'expert-driven,' 'fragmented,' and 'disembedded,' impacts the accuracy of one's ecological sensemaking. Though Whiteman and Cooper cite and quote Barad

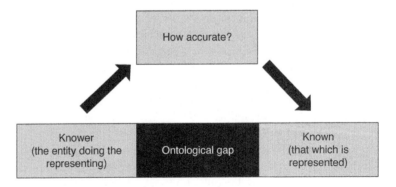

FIGURE 1.2 Barad's 'tripartite arrangement,' emphasizing the 'ontological gap' and its relationship with interests in accuracy.

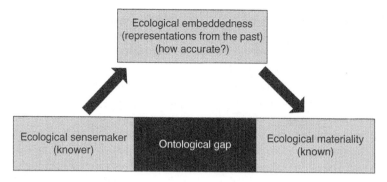

FIGURE 1.3 Whiteman and Cooper's (2011) findings interpreted through Barad's 'tripartite arrangement,' including the ontological gap that leads to questions of accuracy.

(2003) in support of their arguments, those arguments embody the very representationalism, and its embedded assumption that relations between humans and nature need to be mediated, that Barad rejects (e.g., Barad 2003, 2007). For example, Barad had this to say about this sort of mediation:

> The ubiquitous pronouncements proclaiming that experience of the material world is "mediated" have offered precious little guidance about how to proceed. The notion of mediation has for too long stood in the way of a more thoroughgoing accounting of the empirical world.
>
> *(Barad, 2003, p. 823)*

Elsewhere Barad argues that

> the notion of mediation—whether through the lens of consciousness, language, culture, technology, or labor—holds nature at bay, beyond our grasp, generating and regenerating the philosophical problem of the possibility of human knowledge out of this metaphysical quarantining of the object world.
>
> *(Barad, 2007, p. 375)*

Whiteman and Cooper's elegant work has moved the organization and management literature far forward in extremely important ways. Yet, our understanding of ecological sensemaking cannot be that it is solely a process through which the extent of ecological embeddedness mediates the gap between the ecological sensemaker and ecological materiality, for the approach is ontologically paradoxical in that it depends on the fallacious nature-culture dualism. Weick in fact warns us against depending on such dualisms in our understanding of sensemaking in various works, including his 1995 sensemaking treatise, *Sensemaking in Organizations.* For example, in drawing on Mary Parker Follett to elaborate the sensemaking principle 'enactment' (see discussion above), Weick states, "To remain alert to the ongoing *codetermination* that occurs during sensemaking, we need to be especially careful of how we portray process ... If we begin to think about *sensemaking as relating*, several classical issues in organizational studies become recast" (Weick, 1993, pp. 32–33, emphases added). One such issue is the assumption of a clear separation between an organization and its environment. Yet such dualisms as organization-environment and human-nature have an insidious way of sticking around and shaping our thoughts, conversations, studies, and findings, perhaps due in no small part to their structural embeddedness in our language, practices, culture, and society. Ensuing chapters make the alternative case that ecological sensemaking is a meaning-, matter-, and organization-making apparatus that is constitutively embedded in (i.e., formed by and formative of) entangled human and natural phenomena; and, as such, it involves processes through which what we bound off as 'natural' phenomena materialize in and constitute (i.e., engage in boundary-, property-, and meaning-making activities within) what we bound in as 'human' sensemaking practices. A chief argument of ensuing chapters is that meaning, or sense, is inseparable from, constituted by and constitutive of, physical, 'environmental,' and 'natural,' materiality, and vice versa. As Bohr made clear in his analysis and elaboration of quantum mechanics, matter and meaning are mutually entailed; there is no tearing meaning away from matter, and there is no tearing matter away from meaning. In fact, both are unintelligible apart from the other. This book concerns how the mutual entailment of meaning and matter plays out in ecological sensemaking at the front-line of a commercial fishery, while paying particular attention to the physical matter, such as catch and bycatch, that emerges through such mutually constitutive, human-natural sensemaking.

No research has been conducted on the organizing processes through which frontline managers in natural resource extraction industries make sense of the natural systems they engage with on a day-to-day basis, and in turn how such sensemaking relates to good and bad outcomes of those practices. In elucidating how entangled human-natural organization emerges through sensemaking at the frontline of a resource extraction industry, this book bridges organization and management theory with the frontlines of natural resource extraction industries, contexts, and practices. This bridge is grounded in a theoretical and practical need for a richer and more realistic understanding of the processes through which industries organize with natural systems in order to extract resources from them, including the materializations (i.e., meanings and matter) that are part and parcel of those processes. This need is signaled by global issues like climate change, our transition into the Anthropocene, and broad calls to action like the United Nations Sustainable Development Goals. While there are studies of the behavior of managers in frontline resource extraction industries (e.g., Acheson, 2006; Branch et al., 2006; Carlsson & Berkes, 2005; Grafton et al., 2006; Hilborn, Orensanz, & Parma, 2005; Plummer & Fitzgibbon, 2004), these studies predominantly come from economics-based domains of scholarship. As such, they are steeped in rational decision making assumptions and frameworks, which, in their dependence on dualistic assumptions and frameworks, provide limited value in contexts characterized by indeterminate phenomena (Allison & Zelikow, 1999; Daft & MacIntosh, 1981; Scott & Davis, 2006; Weick, 1993; Weick et al., 2005), such as commercial fishing and other resource extraction industries. Sensemaking more generally, and ecological sneaking more particularly, in focusing on "vague questions, muddy answers, and negotiated agreements" (Weick, 1993, p. 636), and in being intended to "break the stranglehold that decision making and rational models have had on organizational theory" (Weick, 2003, p. 186), provide a lens that is capable of elucidating a much richer understanding of frontline organizing and management practices in resource extraction industries. And when coupled with Barad's agential realism, sensemaking more generally, and ecological sensemaking more particularly, is able to provide a rich and realistic understanding of the materialization of entangled human–natural organization, including its embedded material outcomes, such as bycatch, at the frontline of a resource extraction context.

Empirical problem: Fisheries bycatch and discard

This book does not examine ecological sensemaking and agential realism in the commercial fishing context in order to just improve our theoretical understandings; it does so primarily to help us understand one of the most important issues in natural resource extraction industries: bycatch. Bycatch involves catching or impacting flora or fauna that is incidental to the flora or fauna one is targeting and will retain for sale or use. Fisheries bycatch, in particular, is defined as "fish that are captured in a fishery but not retained for sale or personal use" (Patrick & Benaka, 2013, p. 470), and is widely considered a major threat to marine ecosystems and the human economies that rely on them, chiefly because most of what is bycaught is discarded and wasted (Abbott & Wilen, 2009; Patrick & Benaka, 2013; Lewison et al., 2011; Phillips et al., 2016).

Worldwide, the amount of fish that is discarded is anywhere from 8% (Kelleher, 2005) to 25% (Davis, 2002) of the total catch, which is estimated to be around 90 million tons, annually (FAO, 2018). In the US, annual estimates of discarded fish are around one million metric tons (Harrington, Myers, & Rosenberg, 2005; Kelleher, 2005). Discards, as Kelleher (2005, p.1) states, "are generally considered a waste of fish resources and inconsistent with responsible fisheries." In particular, discarding has been shown to have negative impacts on bird populations (Grémillet et al., 2008), to modify natural migratory patterns of birds (Bartumeus et al., 2010), as well as to more generally disrupt food chains and create pollution (Murawski, 1996) which can lead to localized anaerobic conditions (Chapman, 1981). Others suggest that discarded fish are more susceptible to predation, a factor which is not typically accounted for in estimates of discard mortality (Raby, Packer, Danylchuk, & Cooke, 2014). Diamond and Beukers-Stewart (2011) found that a Norwegian ban on discarding in the Northeast Arctic is associated with increases of stocks and economic performance of cod, haddock, saithe, and herring fisheries. As Harrington, Myers, and Rosenberg state more generally,

> By-catch, particularly discarded by-catch, is a serious conservation problem because valuable living resources are wasted, populations of endangered and rare species are threatened, stocks that are already heavily exploited are further impacted and ecosystem changes in the overall structure of trophic webs and habitats may result.
>
> *(Harrington, Myers, & Rosenberg, 2005, p. 351)*

Yet, as Kelleher (2005, p. 69) states, many ecological impacts of discarding remain unquantified. While the ecological soundness of discarding is questionable at best, scholars are largely in agreement that discarding is economically unsound (Alverson, Freeburg, Murawski, & Pope, 1994; Branch, Rutherford, & Hilborn, 2006; Diamond & Beukers-Stewart, 2011; Patrick & Benaka, 2013; Pascoe, 1997; Pulver & Stephen, 2019; Stokesbury et al., 2019). A key reason for the economic unsoundness of discard is the loss of the value of the discarded catch.

At sea, captains attempt to efficiently catch what they can sell, and, to the extent it is profitable to do so, avoid catching what they cannot sell. Captains work to turn potential catch into actual catch, but their actual catch may turn out to be something other than what they hoped it would potentially be. Captains in fishing industries around the world face increasing pressure to be more selective in terms of the material they extract from natural systems (Kelleher, 2005; Patrick & Benaka, 2013), while also being saddled with intense economic pressure to fill their vessels as efficiently as they can (Priour, 2009; Cheilari, Guillen, Damalas, & Barbas, 2013). Trawl captains, including the Gulf of Alaska trawl captains studied for this book, face intense pressure to make sense of what they might catch next, and to be quick about it. This book argues that attempting to extract certain natural resources while not extracting certain other natural resources requires ecological sensemaking, of which we know little about.

Overview of findings

Before I give a brief glimpse into what each ensuing chapter contains, I want to give an overview of the overarching contributions of the book. I believe there are three; readers, however, will find fragments here and there that, in the interest of actually finishing the book, have not been further developed, though perhaps they could if they meet with the right reader-embedded potentialities (this phrasing will make more sense later in the book). The first overarching contribution is a non-dualistic understanding of the organization of human and natural phenomena that forms at the frontline of a natural resource extraction industry. Thus, this understanding does not presume that humans and nature are first inherently separate, and that they then come together at certain times and in certain places, to certain effects. Due to our long-standing assumption of the metaphysical individuality of humans and nature, our awareness of their relations has been driven by perceived problematic impacts that humans have *on* nature. Such a problem-driven approach to understanding the relationality of human organization and nature, however, has been, by its very nature, nothing short of disastrous. If our research into, and regulation and management of, the relations that industries have with nature are chiefly inspired and driven by impacts that are *already* harmful, it is no surprise that our relations with nature are now, on a geological scale, highly problematic.

For decades organizational scholarship was concerned with activities that crossed organizational boundaries into 'the' environment, and in turn environmental activities that cross organizational boundaries into 'the' organization (e.g., Cyert & March,

1963; Lawrence & Lorsch, 1967; March & Simon, 1958). But this scholarship tended to take those boundaries for granted (as Weick has argued), overlooking key organizational activities that continually performed those boundaries, including those that occur between 'the organization' and 'nature.' Only after it became abundantly clear that organizations were one of the primary drivers of widespread environmental problems did scholars turn their attention to how organizational processes and structures might impact nature (e.g., Hoffman, 1999; King, 1995; Shrivastava, 1987, 1994; Starik, 1995). Currently there is growing interest in both understanding the relations that organizations have with natural systems and helping organizations understand how to account for them (e.g., Boons, 2013; Perey & Benn, 2015; Winn & Pogutz, 2013). Yet much of this work still takes dualism as a starting point, and therefore continues to overlook key practices, both human and non-human, through which boundaries 'between' organizations and nature are continually performed. As Barad argues:

> what is needed is an account not only of the materialization of 'human' bodies but of all matter(ings)/materializations, including the materializing effects of boundary-making practices by which the 'human' and the 'nonhuman' are differentially constituted. This must include not merely natural forces and social forces but the differential constitution of forces as 'natural' or 'social.'
>
> *(Barad, 2011, p. 124)*

Whitehead long ago similarly argued that such elision of the 'all-embracing relations' that encompass and pervade humans and nature, which both differentiates them and trouble such differentiations, is born of dualistic thinking. In Whitehead's 1919 treatise against the presumption of dualistic relationship between humans and nature, what he called 'the bifurcation of nature,' Whitehead speaks to the difficulty of working against our dualistic modes of thought, analysis, and understanding in order to identify such 'all-embracing relations':

> It may be that the task is too hard for us, that the relations are too complex and too various for our apprehension, or are too trivial to be worth the trouble of exposition. It is indeed true that we have gone but a very small way in the adequate formulation of such relations. But at least do not let us endeavour to conceal failure under a theory of the byplay of the perceiving mind. What I am essentially protesting against is the bifurcation of nature into two systems of reality, which, in so far as they are real, are real in different senses ... Another way of phrasing this theory which I am arguing against is to bifurcate nature into two divisions, namely into the nature apprehended in awareness and the nature which is the cause of awareness. The nature which is the fact apprehended in awareness holds within it the greenness of the trees, the song of the birds, the warmth of the sun, the hardness of the chairs, and the feel of the velvet. The nature which is the cause of awareness is the conjectured system of molecules and electrons which so affects the mind as to produce the awareness

of apparent nature. The meeting point of these two natures is the mind, the causal nature being influent and the apparent nature being effluent.

(Whitehead, 1919, pp. 30–32)

Whitehead's 'byplay of the perceiving mind' can be analogously understood as the 'byplay of the organizational boundary.' In this book I use the tools that Barad's agential realism provides to understand the entanglement of ecological sensemaking practices and natural phenomena in a particular natural resource extraction context. Those tools allow me to examine those practices without first presuming that they are separate from natural phenomena, and therefore not overlook the exceedingly important articulations through which entangled human organizing practices and natural phenomena emerge as 'separate.' The deployment of those tools in turn allows me to develop a non-dualistic understanding and framework of what I argue is *the* primary articulating process—ecological sensemaking—through which entangled human practices and natural phenomena are organized at the frontline of a natural resource extraction industry. The result of this development process, which spans Chapters 3–6, is a posthumanistic ecological sensemaking framework that involves Weick's sensemaking (and Whiteman and Cooper's ecological sensemaking), Whitehead's process philosophy, some ecological theory and findings, as well as Barad's agential realism. The purpose of the framework is to give future researchers a tool to study entanglements of ecological sensemaking, organizations, and natural phenomena, as well as to help regulators think differently about how they govern natural resource extraction businesses and industries.

Part of this contribution is another perhaps more fundamental offering. Various scholars across various disciplines argue that humans and nature are entangled, at the core of which is a 'strong relation' (Slife, 2004) or 'intra-action' (Barad, 2007), in which "Relationships are not just the interactions of what was originally nonrelational; relationships are relational 'all the way down.' Things are not first self-contained entities and then interactive. Each thing, including each person, is first and always a nexus of relations" (Slife, 2004, p. 159). Like two waves rolling across the ocean, being strongly related or intra-active means that there is both differentiation and lack of separation. Organization and management studies is one of those disciplines that has, as of late, become interested in the strong relationality of organizations and nature (e.g., Allen, Cunliffe, & Easterby-Smith, 2019; Boiral, Heras-Saizarbitoria, & Brotherton, 2019; Good & Thorpe, 2019). Yet no scholarship in this realm, and in most other realms (at least from my reading), tells us how we might analyze intra-activity/strong relationality. We are asked to understand that humans and nature are mutually constitutive, i.e., entangled, but we are not given a means of understanding what such mutual constitution among humans and nature looks like.

The posthumanistic ecological sensemaking (PES) framework provides one such means of understanding human-natural entanglement. It does so by using empirical data to theorize that, due to the entangled relationship between captains' practices and natural phenomena, captains face pervasive indeterminacy at sea, which demands ecological sensemaking (rather than rational decision-making); then the book argues that, due to that indeterminacy, ecological sensemaking is highly dependent on propositions (created through abductive processes), rather than expectations (as the current sensemaking literature argues), to move forward; then sensemaking depends on instrumental actions, particularly what are elaborated as 'agential cuts,' to physically enact determinacy in the form of distinct materialities (e.g., a spot on the fishing grounds, catch on deck); yet from there, indeterminacy emerges anew, and ecological sensemaking carries forth. This understanding of the process of ecological sensemaking is structured, drawing from Whitehead's process philosophy, by the actuality-potentiality dimension of entangled reality. In this dimension potentialities condition actualities, and actualities condition potentialities, such that "actuality is the exemplification of potentiality, and potentiality is the characterization of actuality, either in concept or in fact" (Whitehead, 1968, p. 70). What I argue is that the actuality of ecological phenomena co-constitutes the potentiality of fishing practice, and the potentiality of fishing practice co-constitutes the actuality of ecological phenomena; likewise, the potentiality of ecological phenomena co-constitutes the actuality of fishing practice, and the actuality of fishing practices co-constitutes the potentiality of ecological phenomena. While this understanding of organization-natural entanglement is quite dizzying this early in the book, what it comes to is that the actuality-potentiality dimension within human and natural phenomena is anchored across both, such that, due to their entangled natures, the potentiality of one is inseparable from the actuality of the other, and the actuality of one is inseparable from the potentiality of the other. This is one way to understand the mutual constitution of human and natural phenomena, and it is captured by the PES framework (see Chapter 6).

The final contribution is a human-sized manifestation of Bohr's central lesson of quantum mechanics (Barad, 2007). This is the lesson that "we are part of the nature that we seek to understand" (Barad, 2007, p. 247). According to Bohr, whether electrons or quanta of light are particles or waves depends on the mechanics of their measurement. This is because what 'they' are known as is entangled with the apparatus of knowing (or observing, measuring, manipulating, extracting, or merely engaging) them. Their determinate identities are enacted though the apparatus, particularly through the performative enactment of agential cuts; prior to such performances, there is only ambiguity (though the boundaries, properties, and meanings at the core of such determinacies, which are enacted in those performances, are always, at their own core, ambiguous). Of course phenomena exist outside our practices of knowing them, but the determinate nature of what materializes through those apparatuses are entangled performances, of which we and our processes of knowing are part. Determinacy comes by way of entangled knowledge practices, which are not solely, or primarily, human endeavors.

Importantly, Bohr came to the realization that what emerges as measured is inseparable from the apparatus of measurement through his examination of the role of concepts, such as 'wave' and 'particle,' in quantum mechanics (specifically in such apparatuses as the double-slit experiment) (Barad, 2007, 2011). Bohr's work with concepts in quantum mechanics should arouse the interest of any social scientist, for it speaks to an inherent inseparability of physical and conceptual phenomena; in other words, conceptual phenomena are 'relational all the way down' (Slife, 2004), and physical phenomena are 'relational all the way up.' According to Bohr, concepts are meaningful, i.e., unambiguous, to the extent that they are physically and exclusively articulated by a particular knowledge apparatus. Apparatuses that articulate light to be a wave cannot articulate light to be a particle; the articulation of one is exclusive of the articulation of the other—they are mutually exclusive. And, because the concepts of particle and wave, in terms of light, concern the same phenomena, i.e., light, they are complementary (hence Bohr's 'complementarity principle'). What Bohr's findings mean, according to Barad, is that "*the very nature of the entity—its ontology—changes (or rather becomes differently determinate) depending on the experimental apparatus used to determine its nature*" (Barad, 2011, p. 142; emphasis original). The determination of things, whether particles or waves, comes by way of the apparatus of knowing; the determination does not exist apart from it. Further, certain differentiations are required within the apparatus to arrive at a particular unambiguous, determinate, meaningful concept. Drawing on Bohr's work, Barad calls such differentiations 'agential cuts,' for they are agentially enacted through the apparatus—they do not exist outside of it. As opposed to the (fantastical) Cartesian cuts (e.g., culture/nature, ontology/epistemology, subject/object, word/world), agential cuts are not separations that are inherent to the phenomena of interest. The determination of light as a particle, or alternatively as a wave, is dependent on certain agential cuts being performed through the apparatus of knowing the phenomena of light; and the agential cuts that articulate light as a particle cannot also articulate light as a wave.

The physical articulation of determinate meaning has direct application in the context of commercial trawl fishing. I demonstrate here that the physical articulation of determinations of the composition of trawl catch is performed through the apparatus of knowing that captains perform at sea. I argue that this apparatus is best understood as ecological sensemaking (as opposed to some form of rational decision-making), and demonstrate that captains must perform the agential cuts of towing and then examining the catch in order to arrive at an unambiguous, determinate meaning of what it is that they were entangled with at sea. Thus, the meaning is not just out there to be represented inside the practice of fishing; it must be agentially performed through the apparatus of ecological sensemaking. Captains repeat the axiom, 'You never known until you tow' as a way to characterize their practice at sea, and I provide a quantum mechanics- and ecological sensemaking-based explanation as to why this axiom is true (it would, I believe, be difficult to find a pithier rendering of the quantum mechanical workings of industrial practices than this axiom). Captains can make good guesses, or propositions (as they are elaborated here), but, due to the entangled nature of their fishing practice, in which it is mutually constituted by human and non-human phenomena, they still never know until they perform the agential cut of towing.

This finding, that (due to the quantum mechanics of ecological sensemaking) captains cannot perform the determinate meaning of what they are articulating with until they perform the agential cut of towing has important implications for bycatch management (see Chapter 7), as well as for our understanding of ecological sense-making in particular, and sensemaking more generally. Though there is a growing interest in the materiality of sensemaking (e.g., Cornelissen, Mantere, & Vaara, 2014; Neukirch et al., 2018; Stigliani & Ravasi, 2012; Whiteman & Cooper, 2011), the current literature largely still maintains that making sense is primarily a human endeavor, which is performed primarily through narrative processes, depends largely on cognitive maps, and in turn is quite conceptual (e.g., Brown, 2000; Cornelissen, 2012; Gioia & Chittipeddi, 1991; Maitlis, 2005; Weick et al., 2005; Sonenshein, 2010). While previous studies demonstrate how sense is made in conjunction with material artifacts or ecological materialities, they have yet to demonstrate, at least to my reading, how the 'sense' of sensemaking is always a physical articulation. Thus, rather than being a chiefly conceptual phenomenon, as well as primarily relegated to the minds of people, sensemaking is, at its core, a physical apparatus that is con-stituted by and constitutive of human and non-human materiality. There is no sense without the boundary-making performed by physical phenomena, but there is non-sense; non-sense is conceptualizations that are not physically articulated. Thus, it makes little sense to bifurcate sensemaking into two realities, the human and the non-human; the physicality of sensemaking renders is a posthumanistic process. This is how it is articulated in this book.

Roadmap to the rest of the book

This study investigates the relationship between ecological sensemaking and fisheries bycatch and discard through a grounded theory-based analysis of front-line practices in a commercial trawl fishing industry operating in the Gulf of Alaska (GOA). Day-to-day operations in this fleet put relations between human and natural phenomena front and center, for managers in this context (i.e., vessel captains) continually wrestle with understanding and extracting material from the (non-human) natural phenomena that they are entangled with. This study focuses on the GOA trawl fleet in particular due to my prior work experience in Alaskan commercial trawl fisheries, which gave me the legitimacy I needed to gain access, as well as my desire to study a relatively modern fleet whose captains lived near the area in which they worked (Kodiak Island) (which would reduce access hurdles). While multiple communities in Alaska met this criteria, Kodiak is per-haps the most accessible, modern, and largest of the lot. A much more elaborate description of the GOA trawl fleet, my reasons for choosing them, and my method of studying them, is given in Chapter 2.

In Chapter 3 I first make the case that the type of natural resource management system that regulates fisheries in federal GOA waters is rational systems manage-ment (Scott & Davis, 2006); such a management system is based on the assumption that fishing practices at sea can play out in rational decision-making fashion. Then I empirically and theoretically demonstrate that because of the indeterminacy that pervades fishing practices, processes at sea cannot play out as both rational decision-making theory assume they do. The chapter ends with an elaboration of the source of the indeterminacy that prevents at-sea fishing practices from aligning with rational decision-making frameworks, and thus fitting into rational systems management approaches. This source is the entanglement of fishing practices and the natural phenomena that captains are seeking to know and extract material from.

The outcomes of Chapter 3 set the stage for Chapter 4, which makes the case that due to the pervasive indeterminacy that captains face, ecological sensemaking is what actually occurs at sea. This chapter explores in detail what this ecological sensemaking looks like, and argues that, in the face of pervasive indeterminacy, ecological sensemaking is not so much driven by expectations, as the current literature argues (e.g., Maitlis & Christianson, 2014; Weick et al., 2005) as it is by indeterminacy (and that the two are different). Then the chapter argues that ecological sensemaking, in being indeterminacy-driven, takes on a propositional functionality, and that because of this, the process needs to be understood as involving abduction. Chapter 4 then ends by the applying the lessons from Chapters 3 and 4 to an empirical bycatch event. This application further deepens our understanding of where much of the indeterminacy that captains face comes from, namely the inherent ambiguity of boundaries within phenomena at sea. This chapter also provides strong evidence that supports Bohr's 'central lesson of quantum mechanics' mechanics,' namely that concepts gain their meaningfulness not from abstract deliberation but from their articulation by physical phenomena (Barad, 2007). Thus, this application demonstrates why the concepts such as particular species and bycatch are only determined, or made unambiguous, through the physical activity of hauling up the catch and depositing it on the back of a vessel for further inspection. Sense comes not solely by mental acuity, but also, and perhaps primarily, by the boundary-making performances of physical activity. Both before and during the process of towing, such concepts are not meaningfully articulated by the entanglement of captains' practices and natural phenomena.

Chapter 5 takes one of the key lessons from Chapter 4, that ecological sensemaking takes on a strongly propositional nature in pervasively indeterminate conditions, as a window into Whitehead's process philosophy. The purpose of doing so is to use Whitehead's extensive work on propositions to produce a framework that can be used to study, analyze, and further understand ecological sensemaking. This framework is based on Whitehead's contention that propositions function to move one through the actuality—potentiality dimension of experience. Thus, a primary outcome of this chapter is an actuality—potentiality-based framework of indeterminacy-driven ecological sensemaking. In turn the chapter also explores more of the functionality of ecological sensemaking through the framework. The argument is that the abductive part of ecological sensemaking, as elaborated in Chapter 4, moves the actor from (potentiality-conditioned) actuality to (actuality-conditioned) potentiality through the production of a proposition, and the more physically active part of ecological sensemaking (i.e., 'instrumental action') moves the sensemaker from (actuality-conditioned) potentiality to new (potentiality-conditioned) actuality, and that all of this occurs recurrently. The chapter ends by making the empirical argument that in order for the propositions of ecological sensemaking to be actionable, i.e., to foster instrumental action, they must offer an efficient way forward, they must be plausible, and they must be strategic.

Through Chapter 5 the book explores and elaborates what ecological sense-making looks like in a context in which human and natural phenomena are inherently entangled, but primarily in terms of the indeterminacy that such an entanglement engenders within human affairs (i.e., captains' fishing practices). Thus, the book explores how ecological phenomena play a role in captains' eco-logical sensemaking, but primarily in terms of being a source of indeterminacy due to being entangled with captain' practices. Thus, indeterminacy is the voice of natural phenomena. This means that, through Chapter 5, the book is not quite posthumanistic. Chapter 6 attempts to rectify this by elaborating more directly how captains' practices and ecological phenomena not only mutually constitute what materializes at sea through ecological sensemaking, such as target catch and bycatch, but that captains' practices and ecological phenomena are *already* entangled prior to any sort of materialization. Thus, what materializes through ecological sensemaking, such as a particular fishing spot or a certain composition of catch on deck, is mutually constituted by captains' practices and ecological phenomena, which are entangled prior to any such materialization. This chapter demonstrates, using the indeterminacy-driven ecological sensemaking framework developed in Chapter 5, how the framework can be used to understand natural phenomena alone, as well as how human and natural phenomena are entangled. Thus, Chapter 6 demonstrates how the indeterminacy-driven ecological sensemaking framework is also a posthumanistic agential realist framework. The product of the chapter is the PES framework.

And finally, Chapter 7 applies the PES framework to an extreme bycatch event that took place in a GOA trawl fishery in 2010. This was perhaps the largest bycatch event on record in Alaskan fisheries, which has changed how bycatch is regulated in the GOA. The purpose of this application is to put the framework into action as a way to gain a better understanding of the entangled and nature of ecological sensemaking at sea, and to help diagnose how deleterious outcomes such as bycatch materialize, and what can be done about them. Much of the chapter is devoted to recommendations as to how the federal fisheries management system can help captains who are at sea make sense of, and in turn reduce their catch of, bycatch. These recommendations focus on shifting to a catch share system and requiring full retention (with some exceptions). The goal of the chapter is to demonstrate how the PES framework can help us see things differently, with the hope of regulating and managing them more economically and ecologically sus-tainably, and to provide a sort of initial example of a mode of analysis that future researchers to improve upon.

Notes

1 My own language will undoubtedly violate my protestations and arguments against taking the separation of humans and nature for granted. Given that our entity-based language and our cultural and educational systems (particularly those that are Western in orientation) are grounded in, and continually uphold, Cartesian dualisms, I can hardly avoid doing so. Barad herself notes that "It would be surprising" if her own discussions did not "fall prey" (Barad 2007, p. 428) to the alluring simplicity and human tendency to talk, think, and write using the ease of a language of metaphysical individualism. Wanda Orlikowski and Susan Scott, elaborating the idea of 'sociomateriality,' which is largely drawn from Barad's agential realism, offer a similar disclaimer: "Part of the difficulty in discussing this perspective is that our language makes it difficult to express indissolubility. We are used to dividing, separating, and distinguishing. Thus, even terms such as 'mutual constitution', 'entanglement', 'assemblage', and 'relationality' allude to separateness, even as they try to move beyond it" (Orlikowski & Scott, 2008, p. 468).
2 Sensemaking is retrospective in that we are always making sense of experience that has passed, or that has been considered as something that may come to pass; we are never making sense of experience before it has passed or has been envisioned to pass; as Alfred North Whitehead stated, "There is no holding nature still and looking at it. We cannot redouble our efforts to improve our knowledge of the terminus of our present sense-awareness; it is our subsequent opportunity in subsequent sense-awareness which gains the benefit of our good resolution" (Whitehead, 1919, pp. 14–15).
3 'Cues' are bracketed and extracted portions of experience, such as a rushing river (Whiteman & Cooper, 2011), a storm off in the distance (Kayes, 2004), a fire jumping across a gulch (Weick, 1993), facial expressions (Patriotta & Spedale, 2009), innovative designs (Stigliani & Ravasi, 2012), or even gaps in the sensemaking of others (Maitlis & Lawrence, 2007).
4 Sensemaking is about telling ourselves and others a good story in the interest of getting on with our organizational practices, rather than telling the 'one' true story (whatever that even means). See Weick et al., 2005).
5 'Enactment' is another term for action, but it differs in that it captures the creative side of action; thus, a bill is *enacted* into law. 'Enactment' is commonly used in such a context because it captures both the act of passing the bill and the creation of a new reality that is the law and its radiating effects; the use of 'enactment' instead of 'action' in sensemaking is intended to emphasize that all actions are really enactments—they are not only active, but also creative (Weick 1995).

2

CONTEXT AND METHODOLOGY

Context

This study helps expand management and organizational theory by incorporating frontline resource extraction practices, the first link in many supply chains, within its purview. Its findings are derived from an ethnographic study of the Kodiak, Alaska trawl fleet. Kodiak is the second largest island in the US (behind Hawaii's 'Big Island'), and has a population of around 14,000. It houses one of the top five fishing ports in the US in terms of the value and weight of the catch that crosses its docks. The commercial fishing industry "has long been the primary economic activity of Kodiak" (Kodiak Chamber of Commerce, 2013, p. 33), and the trawl feet is a primary component of that activity. For example, in 2012, 382 million pounds of fish was delivered to Kodiak's docks, worth $178 million. About 75% of the total catch was 'groundfish,' which includes pollock, rockfish, flatfish, Pacific cod, sablefish, and lingcod (yet excludes salmon, Pacific halibut, crab, and Pacific herring, which are classified under different categories of commercial species). This groundfish catch was worth about $57 million in ex-vessel value (prior to being processed and shipped to market), which was about half of the value of all the fish caught in 2012. Multiple fleets, including trawl, pot, and longline, fish for groundfish, which makes it difficult to determine how much of this fish was delivered by trawlers; yet we do know that only the trawl fleet fishes for pollock and rockfish, which accounted for 50% of the groundfish delivered to Kodiak in 2011, worth $23 million in ex-vessel value (Kodiak Chamber of Commerce, 2013). We can also safely assume the trawl fleet delivered a large portion of the remaining 49%.

This book focuses on how the Kodiak trawl fleet makes sense of natural processes in order to extract the catch that helps drive Kodiak's economy. These at-sea operations are embedded in regulatory structures and management processes that are aimed at ensuring that the fleet overshoots neither their target quotas nor their bycatch limits. Thus, to understand how the Kodiak fleet operates we have to understand characteristics of the fleet and the broader regulatory system it is embedded in. This chapter discusses nine common, yet not exhaustive, characteristics of the Kodiak trawl fleet. As discussed below, the Kodiak trawl fleet fishes under the same regulatory authority, with the same type of gear, using the same type of vessel, with the same organization structure, under the same quota allocation regimes, in mostly in the same fisheries, for the same species, are managed the same in-season agency management processes, and often create their own management structures.

Fishing under the same regulatory authority

The regulatory structure of the at-sea fishing processes are enacted by a federal body known as the North Pacific Fishery Management Council (NPFMC). There are eight Regional Fishery Management Councils in the US, each regulating fisheries within the federal waters that extend from 3 to 200 miles off the US (Figure 2.1). These councils were created by the Magnuson-Stevens Fishery Conservation and Management Act (MSA), which was passed in 1976. The MSA is the 'organic act' for all fisheries in US federal waters, and charges the councils with creating fishery management plans (FMP), which, when implemented, will meet the ten National Standards that are enumerated in the MSA. These standards state that conservation and management measures shall:

1. prevent overfishing while achieving optimum yield;
2. be based upon the best scientific information available;
3. manage individual stocks as a unit throughout their range, to the extent practicable; interrelated stocks shall be managed as a unit or in close coordination;
4. not discriminate between residents of different states; any allocation of privileges must be fair and equitable;
5. where practicable, promote efficiency, except that no such measure shall have economic allocation as its sole purpose;
6. take into account and allow for variations among the contingencies in fisheries, fishery resources, and catches;
7. minimize costs and avoid duplications, where practicable;
8. take into account the importance of fishery resources to fishing communities to provide for the sustained participation of, and minimize adverse impacts to, such communities (consistent with conservation requirements);
9. minimize bycatch or mortality from bycatch; and
10. promote safety of human life at sea.

The NPFMC has created, and continually amends, groundfish, shellfish, and salmon fishery management plans that are aimed to meet these standards, as well as other regulations (e.g., Marine Mammal Protection Act, Endangered Species Act) for the major fishing areas within Alaskan waters: The Bering Sea and Aleutian Islands, the Gulf of Alaska (GOA), and the Arctic Ocean. The agency that

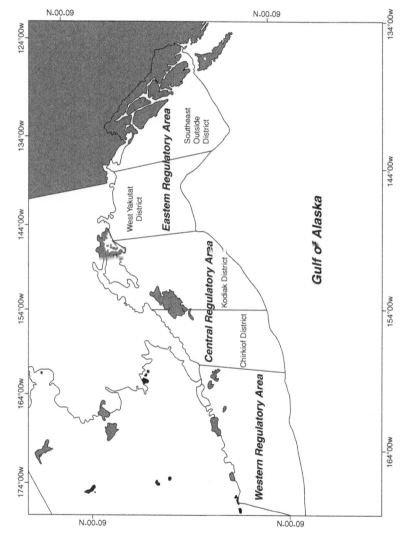

FIGURE 2.1 Regulatory fishing areas in the Gulf of Alaska.
Source: NPFMC (2019, p. 10)

implements fishery management plans is the National Marine Fisheries Service (NMFS). Regulators who sit on the NPFMC, including members representing the states of Alaska, Washington, and Oregon, as well as fishery stakeholder representatives, depend on input from fisheries scientists, deploy NS 2 (the best scientific methods), to set catch limits for NS's 1 (preventing overfishing and attaining optimal yield) and 9 (reducing bycatch), which are structured according to NS 3 (managing according to population units).

One of the primary duties of the NPFMC is balancing the competing demands of Standards 1 and 9: encouraging the "optimum yield" of target species, while also minimizing the bycatch that is caught along with target species. 'Target species' are "those species primarily sought by the fishermen in a particular fishery" (NOAA; 2006, p. 53), and bycatch is species caught incidental to target species, which may be retained or discarded. "Optimum yield" is "The harvest of a species that achieves the greatest overall benefits, including economic, social, and biological, considerations" (ibid., p. 34). The tension involved in aiming for both optimum yield and bycatch minimization is due to the common occurrence in which species other than those being targeted are perceived as engaging in similar temporal and spatial patterns of behavior to those being targeted. When captains cannot differentiate species in their fishing practices, they end up catching both when only targeting one, or sometimes the wrong species altogether (this is a detail that will be discussed in great detail in later chapters).

Fishing with the same gear

The Kodiak trawl fleet is foremost defined by the type of gear they deploy to catch fish—trawl nets. Trawling involves using a large net to catch fish that are located either on the bottom or in the water column. The largest of these nets approaches a mile around, typically with an opening of around 80 ft. high by 240 ft. wide, mesh as big as 120 feet at the front, "large enough to drive a car through" as one captain commented, tapering to about five inches at the back of the net, in a section called the 'codend' (see Figure 2.2). The codend is where caught fish collect as the captain tows and hauls up the net onto the back of the vessel. Codends are

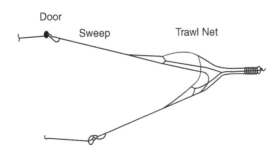

FIGURE 2.2 Diagram of a trawl net.
Source: Rose, Munk, Hammond, & Stoner (2010, p. 1)

typically 120 feet around and anywhere from 60 feet to over 1200 feet long, varying with the type of fish targeted. The larger codends in the Kodiak fleet hold as much as 100 tons of catch.

To trawl, a captain must locate schools of fish and overtake them with a net, in contrast to more static gear that uses an attractant, such as bait, to draw fish to it (e.g., hook and line, pots). Once the captain set the gear behind the vessel, he steams forward at two to three knots per hour, pulling two large rectangular and concave metal 'doors' that are connected to either side of the front opening of the net. Each door has about 60 square feet of surface area and weighs around 1500 to 3000 pounds in the water. When the vessel steams forward, the concavity of the doors pushes against the density of the seawater, creating hydrologic resistance that opens the mouth of the net. At this point the net is fishing (i.e., capable of catching fish), and the captain will work to maintain it at a depth that aligns with the school he is attempting to catch, and, depending on how rocky the bottom is, at a depth that avoids hitting the bottom and tearing the net. To know where to trawl, captains rely on a sonar to 'see' the bottom and schools of fish both upon the bottom and in the water column. Depending on the variability of the bottom topography and the location of schools of fish, trawling may require ongoing adjustment of the net's vertical location in the water column.

To fish with a trawl net is to conduct a tow, which is the basic event of a trawl fishing operation. Tows add up to a trip and trips add up to a season and seasons add up to a year. The tow starts with setting the net and ends when the captain hauls the net up and the crew dumps the codend either straight into the fish hold or onto the trawl deck for sorting. Individual tows constitute a fishing trip, which is the period from when a vessel leaves the dock, heads out to the fishing grounds, fishes either until its fish holds are full (or until some other factor ends the trip), and returns to the dock to unload its catch. Individual trips are conducted within fishing seasons, which last either until the quote is caught (discussed below), a prohibited species bycatch limit is reached (also discussed below), or simply until the season is scheduled to close according to its regulatorily defined time frame. The length of a fishing season tends to be a factor of the size of the quota, the extent of fishing effort aimed at catching it, and the nature of natural systems in which captains are fishing—primarily how much target fish are aggregated and how amenable the weather is to fishing. If the natural conditions are ripe for trawling, then fishing will likely be "fast," and the season will be relatively short.

Fishing with the same types of vessels

Commercial fishing fleets in Alaska are categorized by several factors, one of which is whether they deliver their catch to a shoreside or floating processing plant or instead process it onboard. The Kodiak trawl fleet is constituted almost entirely by catcher-vessels (CVs), in which they deliver their catch to one of the handful of processing plants that are situated along Shelikof St. The alternative to catcher-vessels is catcher-processors, which house their own processing plants on board.

Catcher-vessel and catcher-processor fleets tend to be regulated differently, even if they use the same type of gear and fish for the same species. For example, CPs are not allowed to fish for pollock in the GOA, while they are allowed in the Bering Sea.

The Kodiak fleet consists of a stable core of CVs that primarily fish in the Central Regulatory Area of the GOA, as well as a group of more transient vessels that move from the GOA to the Bering Sea to the coasts of Washington and Oregon, as well as in the Western Regulatory Area of the GOA. While the size of the fleet fluctuates with how lucrative local fisheries are as compared with fisheries in other areas, the fleet is typically around 35 vessels. About 25 vessels homeport in Kodiak, and the remainder homeport primarily in Washington and Oregon. Approximately 15 vessels are owner-operated, which means the owner runs the vessel for some part of the year, while several owners own multiple boats. Corporations that own fish processing plants also own a few boats in the Kodiak fleet, and the number of "corporate boats" (as stated by several Kodiak trawl captains) appears to be increasing every year.

Vessels in the Kodiak trawl fleet range in length from around 58ft to around 125ft, with an average length of around 80ft feet (see Figure 2.3 for examples). While vessels vary in how much fish they can carry in their fish holds, about half of the fleet meets or exceeds their regulatory fishing trip limit of 300,000 pounds, while the other half holds anywhere from 150,000 to 280,000 pounds (this trip limit is one of the 'Steller Sea lion Protection Measures,' which are discussed

FIGURE 2.3 Photograph of Kodiak trawl vessels, taken while they are docked together at a processing plant.
Source: Photograph taken by the author

below). The trip limit means that even though a vessel may hold more than 300,000 pounds of fish, it can only bring 300,000 to port in a 24-hour period. The fleet as a whole, limited by trip limits, holds about 3,800 tons of fish.

Fishing with the same organization structure

Each Kodiak vessel is an organization in that each is constituted by "social structures created by individuals to support collaborative pursuit of specified goals" (Scott & Davis, 2006, p. 11). All Kodiak vessels have the same goals—to fish profitably, safely, and legally, and all employ the same general organizational structure to accomplish these goals, which is constituted by a captain, first mate, engineer, and one or two deckhands. Each of these roles comes with its own generic rules, procedures, and contributions to the overarching operation. The first mate usually works on deck with the deckhands, helping with and managing their work as they conduct the hundreds of interlinked maneuvers, adjustments, and connections required to set a trawl net into the water, haul it back on board, and dump its contents. The engineer is responsible for all vessel mechanics, from maintaining the one or two diesel engines employing anywhere from 500 to 1200 horsepower (most of the fleet operating at around 900 horsepower, which is twice the average horsepower of a semi-truck), to operating the hydraulics as they pull the net on board, to fixing a malfunctioning toilet. The captain oversees the first mate, deckhands and the engineer, while also determining where to fish, and, once he finds a place to fish, determining how to catch them. Vessels usually have two captains who alternate running the boat throughout the year, and most crew alternate as well.

The captain is also responsible for everyone's safety and overall compliance with the numerous regulations a vessel has to follow while at sea. These regulations include which fish can be sorted from the catch once it is dumped on the deck, what type of trash can be tossed at sea, which areas the vessel can fish in, or even 'transit' in, and so on. Two captains, while interviewing them in their wheelhouse, waved a thick book of regulations at me, emphasizing the complexity and magnitude of regulations they have to abide by at sea. This book is issued by NMFS. The local NMFS manager charged with enforcing those regulations also waved this book at me in his office, also emphasizing it size and complexity.

Fishing in the same fisheries

A fishery is the merging of a quota, a management structure defining the timing and location in which the quota can be fished and the types of vessels that can do the fishing, and fishing effort. A quota is an amount of a certain population unit that regulators decide, based on recommendations from fisheries scientists, captains can annually extract and attain optimal yield without overfishing. Thus, a fishery is the integration of relatively abstract management structures and relatively concrete fishing activity, in which that effort is limited to certain vessels, bounded in time and space, and focused on a particular species (or group of species). The Kodiak trawl fleet engages in pollock, Pacific cod, various flatfish, and various rockfish fisheries.

GOA trawl fisheries are spatially structured. This spatial structuring is based on three progressively smaller boundaries. First, with the passage of the MSA in 1976 came the Exclusive Economic Zone (EEZ). For the preponderance of the resource management era prior to the MSA, the US's territorial waters extended a mere three miles offshore. Then in 1966 Congress added a nine-mile contiguous fishery zone adjacent to its territorial waters. This relegated the three-mile zone to state control, and the adjacent nine miles to federal control. The MSA expanded the US's federal waters, now the EEZ, to 200 miles offshore. While trawling is allowed in the EEZ, most state waters are closed to bottom trawling year-round, with a small number of areas open to pelagic (mid-water) trawling (e.g., Prince William Sound, Middleton Island winter fisheries). Second, federal waters in the EEZ around Alaska are further divided into the Arctic Sea, the Bering Sea, the Aleutian Islands, and the GOA. And third, the GOA is divided into regulatory areas (610, 620, 630, 640) (see Figure 2.1). Each of these areas, in turn, has its own fisheries. The Kodiak trawl fleet primarily operates in the Central Gulf, which encompasses areas 620 and 630, and sometimes crosses into areas the Western Gulf (610) and the Eastern Gulf (640). The neighboring Sand Point trawl fleet primarily operates in the Western Gulf, while sometimes crossing into the Central Gulf.

Fisheries are further spatially bounded within these areas, largely as a result of the 1990 listing of the Steller Sea Lion (SSL), which is a large pinniped whose males grow a mane of hair around the neck, under the Endangered Species Act. Since the SSL's listing, the NMFS has enacted multiple rules, i.e., 'protection measures,' designed to control the relationship between fishing and steaming activity and SSL breeding and feeding activity. These spatial closures, known as "haulouts" and "rookeries," often change in size depending on the time of year. Rookeries are "terrestrial areas used by adult Steller sea lions during the breeding season"; haulouts are "terrestrial areas used by adult Steller sea lions during times other than the breeding season and by non-breeding adults and subadults throughout the year" (NMFS, 2010, p. 96). There are 79 area-based closures that impact pollock fishing in the GOA, and 77 that impact cod fishing. The size of each area tends to vary depending on whether it is a haulout or a rookery, the type of fishing gear a vessel might use, and time of year. As stated in the most recent Endangered Species Act SSL Biological Opinion, SSL area closures are a "complex" and "complicated" "mosaic" of temporal and spatial closures, which make it "impossible to easily sum these various closures and determine how much of the area is closed to fishing" (NMFS, 2010, pp. 59–60).

Various other measures also impact where captains can choose to fish, adding to the complex and complicated mosaic of closures. There are eight areas closed to protect red king crab rearing and breeding around Kodiak Island, some of which are closed for part of the year, others for the entire year, and still others are contingent on biological 'recruitment events' of specific populations of red king crab. Other closed areas intended to protect crab stocks include the Cook Inlet Non-Pelagic

Trawl Closure Area and the Southeast Outside Trawl Closure. In 2010 the NPFMC created additional tanner crab closures near Kodiak Island, which closed some areas to trawling. In addition, there are several Essential Fish Habitat closures in the Gulf (Coral Habitat Protection Area; Alaska Seamount Habitat Protection Areas; Slope Habitat Protection Area), and there is the Sitka Pinnacles Marine Reserve.

A similar regulatory framework shapes when captains can fish, which divides fisheries into fishing seasons. Much of this temporal framework is also born of the SSL protection measures. One of the key aspects of the protection measures is that they are "intended to temporally disperse pollock catches in the [GOA]" (NMFS, 2010, p. 62), meaning that they are designed to distribute fishing effort across time in order to limit the extent to which it impacts the life history traits of SSLs. Starting in 2001, the protection measures required trawl fishing start each year on January 20 rather than January 1, which is when non-trawl Gulf groundfish fisheries begin. The protection measures also require annual pollock and cod quotas to be split throughout the year into pre-defined seasons. The annual pollock quota is now divided equally among four seasons: two winter seasons (A, B), and two fall seasons (C, D). Each regulatory area (610, 620, 630) has an A, B, C, and D season, resulting in 12 pollock fisheries in the Gulf each year. A and B seasons span January 20 to the end of May, and C and D seasons run from August 25 to November 1.

While these protection measures structure the pollock, cod, and, to a lesser extent, the flatfish fisheries, the timing of the rockfish fisheries is determined by a different regulatory framework. This fishery is structured to provide income to vessels, shoreside fish processing plants, and the secondary businesses that rely on fishing activity, during what was previously an annual lull in employment and commercial activity in Kodiak.

One of the key factors in the complexity of trawl fishing in the GOA is that fishing seasons overlap in time and space. Due to the overlapping seasonal structure, vessel owners tend to construct annual fishing plans. Fishing plans outline which season a vessel will be fishing in at any given period throughout the year. These plans are based on the overarching trawl business model that is to always be fishing, and to do so in the most profitable manner that is also safely and legally possible. Kodiak owners tend to structure their fishing plans around the regulatory start dates for the most lucrative Central Gulf fisheries— cod, pollock, and rockfish, in between which they may target flatfish, or they may fish in other areas. Some vessels, depending on where they are permitted to fish, go north to fish in the Bering Sea, while others often head south to fish off the US Pacific coast.

The Kodiak fleet tends to fish in the same fisheries at the same time, collectively moving from one fishery to another, with some individual variation. This fleet-level movement is based on an attempt to organize fishing operations to align with ecological phenomena of trawl target species, but under the constraints imposed by seasonal structures, as well as other regulations.

Fishing under the same quota allocation schemes

Captains, mates, and deck crew use catcher vessels and its trawl gear to fish for species that they have been allocated quota to catch. In the GOA trawl fisheries, quotas are allocated either at the fleet or vessel levels. When quotas are allocated at the fleet-level, all the vessels in that fleet fish for the same quota. For example, 100% of the pollock quota is allocated to the catcher-vessel fleet, and is divided into regulatory areas (e.g., 610, 620, 630). Any vessel that belongs to the catcher-vessel fleet and has a permit to fish for pollock in a regulatory area can fish for same pollock quota. This type of management structure is known as a 'race,' 'derby,' or 'Olympic-style' fishery; the race fisheries the Kodiak fleet engages in are pollock, cod, and flatfish.

The length and competitiveness of a race fishery varies greatly. Though they open on regulatorily defined dates, how long they stay open depends on the size of the quota, the extent of fishing effort, how aggregated the target fish are, how plentiful those aggregations are, and how amenable the weather is to towing through those aggregations. If we assume amenable weather and plentiful fish, when vessels are fish under the same quota there will likely be high levels of competition. This means that the amount of fish one captain catches may detract from the amount of fish another captain has the potential to catch. Thus, how much income captains make is dependent on how fast they can get out from the docks, find fish, tow, fill their vessel, steam to the dock, offload, and get back out fishing. Captains race one another to catch as much as they can before together they exhaust the quota; such fisheries tend to only last for a few days, closing much earlier than their regulatorily defined closing dates. Some fisheries are open for a day or less. For example, from 2002 to 2008 a winter pollock fishery in area 630 was open for as few as two days and as many as 26 days, with an average of 10 days. Like all fisheries, this fishery opens on a date that is defined by regulation, yet sometimes sits open while the fleet fishes for cod. When the fleet turns its attention to this fishery, however, it typically closes within one to two days. In conditions of plentifully aggregated pollock, vessels usually get in one to two trips before the fishery closes. Yet, if a vessel is faster than other vessels, it may get lucky and complete three trips in this fishery.

A different type of fishery structure involves percentages of a quota being allocated to individual entities, such as a community, cooperative, vessel, or person. In such fisheries, captains fish for predetermined amounts of fish (their 'share'). This means that the amount that one vessel catches does not detract from the amount another has the potential to catch. These types of management structures are known as 'privatized' or 'rationalized' fisheries, and include such management structures as catch shares and individual fishing quotas. In addition to reduced competition, another aspect of the privatized nature of this quota allocation scheme is that the length of a fishery typically aligns with regulatorily defined opening and closing dates. Captains can typically fish at their leisure within those dates, presumably operating much more efficiently and comfortably. The only privatized trawl fisheries in the GOA thus far are the Central Gulf rockfish fisheries, which were rationalized in 2007. From 2000 to 2006, this fishery opened around July 1 and tended to close around July 10. Since 2007, however, vessels have had their own rockfish shares (a % of the total quota), and can catch them any time between May 1 and November 15. Thus, the Kodiak trawl fleet has experience fishing in both rationalized and race fisheries, and do so within the same year as they shift from pollock, cod, and flatfish in the winter to rockfish in the summer and back to pollock, cod, and flatfish in the fall.

Fishing for the same target species, bycatching the same non-target species

The Kodiak fleet is a multi-species fleet. Unlike the catcher vessel trawl fleet in the Bering Sea, which fishes almost solely for pollock, Kodiak trawl vessels target pollock, Pacific cod, several species of flatfish, and several species of rockfish. A target species is created when regulators assign a quota to a species, the amount of which is derived from on a combination of scientific recommendation and regulator opinion, and in turn allow fishing to occur for that species. All non-target species are 'bycatch' (NOAA, 2006), but not all bycatch species are created equally. Some species are rendered bycatch because there is no market for them or because captains or processing plants do not retain them for technical reasons (e.g., too big to bring on board, too small to be processed), while others are rendered bycatch by regulatory prohibition. Although captains cannot retain certain bycaught animals due to other laws (e.g., marine mammals, birds), a particular group of fish species has been designated as 'prohibited species' in Alaska groundfish fisheries. Prohibited species can neither be targeted by trawl captains nor retained if caught while targeting other species; thus, they cannot be sold by trawlers even if there is a market for them—and the species that are 'prohibited' in the GOA trawl fisheries are some of the most valuable in Alaska. Prohibited species in the GOA trawl fisheries consist of tanner ('snow') crab, king crab, Pacific herring, Pacific Halibut, steelhead trout, and Pacific salmon, which, in terms of the Gulf, refers to Chinook and chum salmon.

Two prohibited species have a profound impact on how GOA trawl fisheries unfold. In GOA trawl fisheries, Pacific halibut and Chinook salmon have prohibited species catch limits, and can have such impact. While halibut limits have been in place since 1985, the limit for Chinook bycatch in the Gulf pollock fisheries was an outcome of an extreme catch of Chinook salmon (est. 50,000 fish) that occurred in the GOA in 2010, which violated the Endangered Species Act (due to the high number, it is likely that some of the salmon caught were from endangered Chinook salmon from Washington, Oregon, and California). Prior to that event there was no in-season management limit on how much Chinook salmon, or any salmon for that matter, could be bycaught in GOA trawl fisheries. This event is used as a case study in Chapter 7.

Target species have quotas, and bycatch species typically have limits. The difference between a limit and a quota is that the term 'quota' is used for a target species in a specific fishery, while 'limit' is typically used for prohibited species, and tends to apply to all fisheries in which that species is caught over a certain period. When a prohibited species limit is reached, all open target fisheries in which that species might be bycaught close, and they do not re-open until more limit becomes available—even if there is target species quota remaining. Currently, the prohibited species Pacific halibut and Chinook salmon have catch limits in GOA trawl fisheries (king crab also has a type of catch limit). Pacific halibut catch limits tends to impact Pacific cod and flatfish fisheries, and Chinook salmon limits catch primarily impacts pollock fisheries. Prohibited species catch limits function as a bank account for target quotas—they are used to fund fishing for target species. Once prohibited species catch funds are spent, NMFS managers will close which-ever fisheries the prohibited species is typically bycaught in, and they remain closed until more limit becomes available. The halibut limit is divided and released four times a year, while the full Chinook limit is released at the beginning of the year.

Fishing within the same in-season management structure

In-season management is the control of fishing effort, primarily based on quotas, limits, and seasonal structures, to meet the National Standards of preventing over-fishing of target species and minimizing bycatch, while also achieving optimum yield. In-season management is conducted by NMFS employees. At the time of this research, there were two employees charged with managing all federal Alaskan fisheries. They describe their work as follows:

> [We] have quotas that we make sure are not exceeded. If people want to fish they have to follow what we say. But we also want to maximize the alloca-tions once they are set … If the fleet wants to do something, it's our job to make sure they don't go over their allocations. We don't like to see negative numbers on the catch reports … When we make closures we know they are affecting people, that it affects their pocketbooks, and we don't close fisheries without keeping that in mind.

A fishery closes on noon of a particular regulatorily defined day, unless in-season managers have closed it early in order to avoid seeing negative numbers on weekly catch reports (which state the percentage of quota that remains, and when a quota is exceeded a negative percentage is given). A fishery 'closure' means that all fishing activity for a particular species in a particular fishing area must cease. In-season managers close fisheries early for one of two reasons: they predict a fleet will catch its target quota or reach its prohibited species catch limit prior to the regulatory end date of the fishery.

The process in-season regulatory managers go through for closing a fishery early is largely the same for both a target quotas and prohibited species catch limits. First they monitor and track target species and prohibited species catch amounts. From these data, in-season managers formulate target and prohibited species catch rates, which enables them to predict when a fleet will exhaust a quota or reach a limit, accounting for predictable changes in fishing effort or weather.

The catch data that in-season managers rely on come from the catch delivery accounting that processing plants conduct and NMFS fisheries scientists placed on fishing vessels and in processing plants, who are called 'fisheries observers.' NMFS fisheries observers are government-contracted biologists who work onboard fishing vessels and within processing plants whose primary duty is to enact data based on a vessel's catch. This data is the foundation of how NMFS managers manage fisheries in season, and how NPFMC regulators regulate fisheries out-of-season. Thus, the work of NMFS fisheries observers is the lifeblood of Alaska's federal regulatory management system, as is stated in the NMFS *Observer Sampling Manual*:

> The Bering Sea and Gulf of Alaska Fisheries are among the best managed in the world, in large part due to the data collected by observers. Statisticians and fisheries managers rely heavily on observer data and also rely heavily on the assumption that these data have been collected a specific way.
>
> *(NMFS, 2013, p. 2-18)*

The GOA Fishery Management Plan also indicates how important data generated by observers are:

> The Council and NMFS must have the best available biological and socioeconomic information with which to carry out their responsibilities for conserving and managing groundfish resources. The purpose of the Observer Program is to verify catch composition and quantity, including those discarded at sea, and collect biological information on marine resources. Used in conjunction with reporting and weighing requirements, the information collected by observers or electronic monitoring systems provides the foundation for inseason management and for tracking species-specific catch and bycatch amounts. Scientists use information collected by observers or electronic monitoring systems for stock assessments and marine ecosystem research.
>
> *(NPFMC, 2019, p. 60)*

The primary function of the fisheries observer is to transform fisheries catch into 'scientific data' through statistical sampling procedures. While there are several legitimate sources of data that in-season managers use to track *total* catch weights (e.g., captains' estimates, processing plant weights), observer-derived data are the only legitimate source of information for determining the *species composition* of catch. To provide data on catch composition, observers use statistical sampling protocols to turn catch into pre-determined discrete categories (e.g., species, quantity, weight). In-season fisheries managers in turn take observer data sampled from a tow and extrapolate it to the entire tow, and then from multiple tows to the entire trip. Because roughly only about 30% of fishing effort in the GOA trawl fisheries is observed, in-season managers extrapolate observer data from observed vessels to unobserved vessels, using total catch weights provided by processing plants to do so. From the combination of total catch weights and observer-based catch compositions, in-season managers, and out-of-season regulators, are able to track and assess how much captains are catching vs. how much they are allowed to catch in terms of quotas for target species and limits for non-target species.

In addition to using catch delivery accounting and observer-based data, in-season managers will also reach out to industry managers, owners, and captains to get a more concrete understanding of fishing effort. Yet in-season management is, however, somewhat abstracted from at-sea fishing processes. Managers often receive catch data collected by processing plants one to three days after it was caught, and prohibited species catch data a week or more after it was caught. The further behind fishing activity that in-season management process are, the further into the future they have to predict when a quota or limit will be reached, and thus the less precise such predictions may be. In-season managers discuss this predictive process, and how their detachment from fishing activity influences it, in the following:

> Fisheries are different every year, every season. You don't expect it to be the same ... We have to re-learn how a fishery will react every season. We have to learn how the weather is going to affect things, moon phases, I mean just about everything affects these fisheries. But we have learned over time what to look for, but we are still learning ... The dynamics are always changing, and our reception of fishing activity data is always behind what is actually happening, so we have to project for that ... If we [close a fishery] a day under or a day over depending on catch rates, that can be a big deal. If we are a day under, we might then have to re-open the fishery.

Not only do in-season managers have to predict days in advance due to delays in getting catch data, they also have to project around the Federal Register. This is because all fishery closures must be publicly announced in the Federal Register. It takes several days to do so, more if a weekend or holiday is approaching, as an in-season manager elaborates in the following:

> We are beholden to the Federal Register ... If we have to close a fishery, we will pick a closure date, send it to headquarters in DC, it gets some review there, then we send it to the Federal Register. But the Federal Register isn't open on the weekends or on holidays, so we have to project. With holidays we have more days to project to determine a closure, and if the holiday is in the middle of the week we have to project differently.

Captains operate according to the whims of the weather and the unpredictability of ecology, on weekends and on holidays, while in-season managers operate according to the predetermined bureaucratic schedules of the Federal Register.

Fishing in the same fleet-generated structures

The Kodiak fleet's movement from one fishery to the next is shaped by ecological and weather conditions, sizes of quotas and values of species, the actions of in-season managers, and an fleet-level logic that each vessel should have fair access to shared, fleet-level quotas. Yet fishing seasons overlap, which means that situations can arise in which one group of captains, or even just one captain, fishes from a quota in one fishery, while another group of captains fishes for a quota in another fishery. When this situation occurs, the captains fishing in different fisheries at the same time diminish each other's opportunity to catch as much as they can of both quotas. For instance, in the winter, pollock and cod fisheries open on January 20, enabling the fleet to contemporaneously fish for both quotas. This means that some captains could fish for pollock, others could fish for cod, and both groups could diminish one another's opportunity to fish for the other quota. To prevent situations in which captains contemporaneously diminish one another's opportunity to have fair access to a quota, they work together to create fair access in what they call 'fleet agreements.' Fleet agreements must be signed by all members of the fleet.

The most common fleet agreements are the 'fair start' and the often accompanying 'stand down.' In these agreements, captains delay their fishing effort ('stand down') and start fishing on a chosen date that is typically after the regulatory-defined start of the season ('fair start'). These agreements structure fishing operations in order to maintain fair access to quotas as captains move from one fishery to another. Returning to the instance above of the cod and pollock fisheries, in most years the fleet agrees to stand down in the pollock fishery when it officially begins on January 20 in order to first fish for the cod quota, and then start fishing for pollock on a pre-selected date that is after they predict they will have caught the cod quota. These agreements mean that captains cannot go fishing for pollock and "catch the quota out from underneath" captains who went fishing for cod.

Captains also create fleet agreements in order to align their fishing operations with life history traits of their target species, primarily the timing of aggregating or schooling behavior, and often for roe development in pollock. Harvesting roe from female pollock, and selling it to overseas markets, is the most lucrative part of the pollock fisheries. Therefore, captains attempt to adjust the timing of their fishing efforts to the timing of roe development in pollock populations. In the following a captain gives reasons during a fleet meeting (in which he is addressing other captains) for delaying fishing effort for pollock in the winter seasons in relation to roe development:

> The longer you delay any [winter pollock] season, the better off the fleet is. The last time we had a big roe year was 2007 when B season came and we sat because of weather. It was 10 days after [the season started],when we left the dock and we had big numbers ... There is no downturn about it. So, I think we should come up with a plan everyone likes, and go from there. The longer we postpone it the better off we all are truthfully.

When setting out to fish, captains search for a place to fish, with the time in which they go fishing being largely predetermined—either by regulation or fleet agreement.

Another important type of fleet agreement is the voluntary catch share. This structure is also intended to create fair access, often in cases in which in-season managers have determined that there is too little quota available, in relation to potential fishing effort, to open a race fishery. By regulation, fisheries must be open for at least a 24-hour period, but in some cases, the fleet will likely overfish the quota in that period, before the in-season managers have a chance to track fishing effort and close the fisheries to prevent overfishing. In 2010 in-season managers started allowing the Kodiak fleet to self-manage certain fisheries by creating fleet agreements and then monitoring and controlling their own catch amounts (while overseeing such efforts by tracking catch data and fishing effort). Evidence indicates that this sort of arrangement allows great precision in terms of reaching, yet not exceeding, quotas. For example, from 2010 to 2013 Kodiak captains have engaged in this sort of management scheme for all the A and B 630 pollock fisheries, and caught an average of 95% of the 630 A and B quotas. From 2003 to 2009, however, the 630 A and B pollock seasons were enacted as traditional race fisheries, resulting in either the 630 A or B quotas being overfished each year, with captains catching an average of 128% of the fish they were allowed to catch; in one B season the fleet caught 323% of the quota. Further, in two of those years in-season managers did not open the 630 B season at all in order to compensate for the overfishing that occurred in the A season. As an in-season manager commented, "A fishermen can come in on their quota a lot better than we can project."

Research methodology

I collected qualitative data from the Kodiak trawl fleet due to its sensitivity to individuals' interrelations and activity sequences, as well as to contextual elements and processes (Langley, 1999; Lofland, Snow, Anderson, & Lofland, 2006). My primary data collection occurred in Kodiak, Alaska, and spanned January through May of both 2011 and 2012 as the Kodiak trawl fleet enacted the same seasons each year: a winter Pacific cod season, four winter pollock seasons, and part of their annual flatfish and rockfish fisheries. Primary data sources included participant observation, observation, semi-structured interviews, and archival data. The following describes each of these methods.

Observation

Observations included multiple public fisheries-oriented meetings, from a local multi-sector fisheries advisory group called the Kodiak Fisheries Advisory Committee, to the Kodiak City Council, to the Federal fisheries regulatory body known as the North Pacific Fishery Management Council. It was private meetings, however, that were the most informative in terms of my research question. These were meetings of the Alaska Whitefish Trawlers Association (AWTA), which is an industry group of Kodiak trawl vessel owners and operators. The purpose of the AWTA is to formulate fishing strategy at the fleet-level, primarily in terms of when and where members will fish for certain target species, as well as to negotiate with processing plants for fish prices. I also observed meetings of the Alaska Groundfish Data Bank (AGDB), which is an industry group of both trawler vessel owners and fish processing plant managers. The purpose of the AGDB is to monitor and disseminate fishing effort and catch information, formulate fleet-level fishing strategies, as well as create political strategies in relation to State and Federal fisheries regulatory bodies. During my time in Kodiak (in both 2011 and 2012), I observed 15 AWTA and AGDB meetings, each of which lasted from one to three hours.

Participant observation

I conducted participant observation in primarily two settings. The first involved one day of observation on board vessels conducting non-fishing, industry-organized research. In 2011 approximately five vessels 'steamed' (i.e., drove, navigated) out to the fishing grounds to test equipment that would help salmon escape their nets when fishing for pollock; I collected data onboard two of these vessels, for approximately eight hours of participant observation. The participant nature of these trips consisted of filming the activities for the fleet, while also helping out with equipment while on board. The second setting was onboard two vessels during two fishing trips, which were conducted in 2012. Each trip lasted about three days. One vessel targeted flatfish, the other rockfish. The participant nature of these trips included helping to sort the catch and various other activities, such as a "wheel watch" (i.e. sitting in the wheelhouse to make sure nothing untoward occurs when the vessel is on autopilot and the rest of the crew is sleeping).

Semi-structured interviews

I conducted semi-structured, conversational interviews with multiple participants of the Kodiak commercial fishing industry. While I made contact with one key person who works for the Kodiak trawl fleet prior to arriving in Kodiak, I had the good luck of timing my arrival with a Board of Fish meeting (which is the State of Alaska version of a fishery management council), in which many fishing groups were gathered in the same building for a multi-day event. This coincidence enabled me to make contact with several captains and key actors in the trawl fleet. Ultimately I conducted 54 interviews using a snowball approach within a targeted group of actors (e.g., trawl captains, processing plant managers, industry management consultants, regulatory managers). These interviews included 26 Kodiak trawl captains, four Kodiak-based fish processing plant managers, seven salmon and Pacific halibut captains, 11 fishing industry management consultants, and six government managers. Interviews typically lasted between one and two hours, with the longest lasting over four hours and the shortest about half an hour. Kodiak captains had an average of about 25 years of experience at the helm of a fishing vessel, with a range of 16 to 41 years.

Archival data

To complement my research that focused on the human side of the frontline of commercial trawl fishing in the Gulf, I analyzed scientific assessments of populations of trawl target species, what are called Stock Assessment and Fishery Evaluation (SAFE) reports. National law requires SAFE reports to be produced annually for all federal fisheries. They "are intended to summarize the best available scientific information concerning the past, present, and possible future condition of the stocks and fisheries under federal management" (A'mar et al., 2013, p. 3). These assessments are based on statistical ecological surveys conducted at sea by government scientists, outside of regular fishing activity, while also depending data from fishing activity. Two types of surveys are conducted—surveys using trawl vessels are conducted every two years, and surveys using sonar are conducted annually. Vessels drawn from the trawl fleet, also employing vessel crew, are used for the trawl surveys, while government vessels are used for the sonar surveys. SAFE reports inform fisheries regulatory decision-making, such as the amount of fish that can be removed at a certain time from a certain population while maintaining the health of the population, which are known as quotas. I analyzed SAFE reports of primary trawl target species (arrowtooth flounder, dusky rockfish, Pacific Ocean perch, flathead sole, northern rockfish, rock sole, pollock, Pacific Cod), for a five-year period—2012 through 2016—focusing on sections that described behavioral patterns. In my analyses I sought to establish relations between these ecological behavioral patterns and the behavioral patterns of trawl captains. In addition, I also analyzed NPFMC discussion papers and analytical regulatory documents related to groundfish fisheries in general, and issues concerning Chinook salmon bycatch in particular (est. 300 pages).

Analytical approach

I analyzed the data derived from these methods according to grounded theory principles (Glaser & Strauss, 1965). First, using the Nvivo analytical program, I conducted line-by-line coding in order to identify 'informant-centric' concepts, from which I developed, through recurring comparison of those concepts to the academic literature, theory-informed themes (Gioia, Corley, & Hamilton, 2013, p. 18). I began this process with interview data from vessel captains, after which concepts relating to human organizing with natural systems quickly emerged; such concepts include 'searching for aggregations,' 'Chinook salmon bycatch,' 'dealing with the weather,' and 'tearing nets on the bottom.' After several interviews, concepts began to group themselves into themes. Such themes included 'avoiding bycatch,' 'interacting with ecological processes,' and 'interacting with other captains.' After I finished coding interviews I moved to the observational and participant observational data, and continued to discover new concepts and themes, while existing concepts and themes organized subsequent data. Yet, while coding helped to organize the data, the number of concepts and themes I had amassed in Nvivo exceeded 300, suggesting that I had exhausted that mode of analysis.

To impose different structure on the data, I shifted from coding raw data to crafting narratives. 'Narratives,' as used here, refers to the use of concepts and themes to describe an individual event (e.g., captains accidentally fishing in a closed area), a repeated phenomenon (e.g., difficulty avoiding Chinook salmon bycatch), types of actors (e.g., captains), or types of locations (e.g., a fishing spot). While nearly all of the narratives involved captains organizing with natural systems, the one that seemed to address the research question most directly, completely, and repeatedly was the story of a fishing trip. The fishing trip is the locus of direct mutual constitution of captains' fishing practices and natural processes, and analyses of fishing trip observations and interview data concerning fishing trips offered a rich resource for understanding how human–natural organization emerges in this context.

After the transition to the trip as my focal event I began crafting different theorized storylines (Golden-Biddle & Locke, 1997) to explain it, which involved exploring different domains of organizational theory (e.g., sensemaking, institutional logics, routines, sociomateriality). After several iterations of drafting different domain-based storylines (and getting feedback on them), I settled on a storyline that, as perhaps put best by Pratt (2000, p. 462), "I believed offered a strong contribution to theory without doing undue violence to [my] experience." The following analytical chapters elaborate that storyline.

3

(NON)RATIONAL DECISION-MAKING AT SEA

This book is focused on answering the following questions:

- How do frontline managers in a commercial fishing industry make sense of, and in turn organize with, natural phenomena?
- What does that sensemaking mean in terms of material outcomes of fishing, such as target catch and bycatch, and in turn how resource extraction practices should be regulated and managed?

A key outcome of answering these questions is a framework that can inform our understanding of the processes through which frontline managers in resource extraction industries determine what to do *next*, using fishing vessel captains in the Gulf of Alaska (GOA) trawl fleet as a case study. By 'framework' I mean an abstracted sketch of recurring phenomena, grounded in both theory and practice, that in turn acts as a tool for understanding, studying, regulating, and managing such phenomena. This framework focuses on how managers determine what to do *next* because "the problem about what will come next" is not only "perhaps the fundamental problem of ordering and organizing" (Cooper & Law, 1995, p. 242), it is also a key part of the practice of commercial fishing. As past research has indicated, a fishing captain's primary duty is making sense of which spot on the fishing grounds to steam to and which space beneath the vessel to tow through *next* (Gatewood, 1984; Gezelius, 2007; Orth, 1987), and it is those sensemaking processes that this chapter, and ensuing chapters, brings to the surface, teases apart, and puts on display. The goal of this demonstration is to reconfigure our understanding, and ultimately our regulation and management, of frontline resource extraction practices in terms of how they *actually* occur, not how outdated and ill-suited models say they *should* occur.

While I develop this framework throughout the next several chapters, I start here by examining how the regulatory system that governs organizing practices in federal Alaskan waters, often called the best fisheries management system in the world, assumes that trawl captains determine what to do next. I demonstrate below that GOA trawl captains are assumed to engage in rational decision-making processes at sea as they determine where on the fishing grounds to steam to, and where beneath the vessel to tow through, next. While explaining what rational decision-making is, I use qualitative data, which I collected while studying the GOA trawl fleet *in situ* (see Chapter 2 for an elaboration of my research methods and data), to identify which aspects of the rational decision-making framework hold up in this context, and which do not. The data show that captains' processes of determining what to do next are entirely sensible, but due to the pervasive role that indeterminacy plays in them, they are not rational—at least in terms of how rationality is understood in academic and regulatory circles. Through this examination the mismatched relationship between the federal Alaskan regulatory management system on land and fishing practices at sea becomes apparent. In the next chapter I begin to elaborate an alternative framework for understanding the processes through which captains determine what to do next, which offers a tighter coupling between how we understand, study, and regulate what occurs at sea, and what actually happens there.

A rational approach

Let's start with an example of a captain determining what to do next during a fishing trip targeting flathead sole, which is a type of flatfish (flatfishes include flounders, soles, halibuts):

RESEARCHER: Why are we heading there to fish?
CAPTAIN: I'm going over here for three reasons. I'm going over here because I have a feeling that there's gonna be some flathead over here, and if that's true I think I'll get a jump on the rest of the fleet, they are gonna mill around town, take a day off, whatever … so I want to look at that. It's gonna be better weather over here … And I don't really know, the only other option for me right now would be to go someplace where I could just load this boat in a day with arrowtooth [flounder], but I think that fishing has come and gone. We've had some really good arrowtooth fishing, we've had three full loads of arrowtooth in the last 15 days, we've pulled a lot of arrowtooth out of the water, and so fishing drops off after that and bycatch goes up. So I don't really want to go someplace where we've pulled a million pounds of arrowtooth out of the water.
RESEARCHER: When you say you have 'a feeling,' what do you mean?
CAPTAIN: You know, in the spring they spawn, and I've been seeing flathead my last three trips, some nice flathead with some eggs in them. There is a volume, there is quite a bit of flathead over here all the time, it's just whether or not they are together enough to make a living fishing for them.

At the heart of this determination of where to fish next is the relationship between knowledge and action, and there are two overarching ways of understanding it: In the first, actors assume that what will come next is determinable, i.e., can be known, before taking action, and therefore they work to gain the knowledge they need to make such a determination. After making that determination, which takes the form of an expectation of what will come, they take action. If what was determined to come next in fact does *not* come next, then they must deal with the unexpected. In the second way of understanding the relationship between knowledge and action, actors assume that the future is not determinable, i.e., cannot be known, before taking action. Thus, in this relationship between knowledge and action, actors take action in order to understand what 'next' is.[1] If these actors expect anything, it is to learn what will happen next only after acting to bring 'next' into actuality. The first way of understanding the relationship between knowledge and action describes acting knowingly; the second describes acting inquiringly. The first assumes a determinable future; the second assumes an indeterminable future. The first is more akin to rational decision-making; the second is more akin to sensemaking (Weick, 1995). The first is what Alaskan regulatory management systems assume occurs at sea; the second is what actually occurs at sea.

The current approach to federal fisheries management in Alaska assumes that the captain above engaged in, or at least was capable of engaging in, rational decision-making. Rational decision-making (often called 'rational choice' or 'economic decision-making') is at the heart of the venerable academic domains of political science and economics, holds great sway in other areas like ecology and evolutionary biology, and has long enjoyed immense influence in the practical realms of business, regulation, law, and natural resource management (Ferraro, Pfeffer & Sutton, 2005; Ghoshal & Moran, 1996; Raworth, 2017). Economics, as stated by economist Kate Raworth, "is the mother tongue of public policy, the language of public life, and the mindset that shapes society" (Raworth, 2017, p. 6). Or as management scholars Fabrizio, Pfeffer and Sutton put it:

> There is little doubt that economics has won the battle for theoretical hegemony in academia and society as a whole and that such dominance becomes stronger every year. This dominance is especially strong in Western countries, particularly the United States, but is spreading rapidly over the globe.
>
> *(Fabrizio, Pfeffer & Sutton, 2005, p. 10)*

The 'theoretical' part of the 'hegemony' that these scholars speak of is the assumption that actors are always, to a greater or lessor extent, engaging in some form of rational decision-making. To be rational is to be intentioned, reasoned, and goal-directed (Mumby & Putnam, 1992); being rational involves optimizing one's activities in order to gain the most benefit for the least cost; and, at its core, rationality is the assumption that actors can make the right or best choice of action in terms of what will occur afterward (i.e., what will come next) (Allison & Zelikow, 1999; Elster, 1989; Simon, 1979). According to the theory, an actor's choice of which activity to engage in involves an analysis of a suite of alternatives, which is produced from a range of information about how entities will interact to produce future events. Such a choice tends to involve 'satisficing' (i.e., sufficing + satisfying), in which actors use rules of thumb, or decision-making heuristics, to select a particular option to act on (Simon, 1979, 1983).

Fisheries management is one of the sectors of academia and regulation where rational decision-making assumptions and frameworks enjoy hegemony. As several scholars describe (e.g., Gezelius, 2007; Holland, 2008; Jentoft, 2006; Jentoft, McCay, & Wilson, 1998; Ostrom, 1998), the lion's share of research examining fishing and fisheries management implicitly or explicitly takes a rational decision-making perspective (e.g., Acheson, 2006; Condie, Grant, & Catchpole, 2014; Eliasen et al., 2014; Gillis, Peterman, & Pikitch, 1995; Grafton, Kompas, & Hilborn, 2007; Grafton et al., 2006). Eminent fisheries management scholar Ray Hilborn, in an essay reflecting on how fisheries should be managed, exemplifies such a perspective:

> Quite simply, fishing fleets can be thought of as a rational economic entity, that will, in aggregate, make decisions to maximize their well-being within the constraints of the legal and institutional incentives that are imposed on them. This provides a powerful framework for predicting the consequences of incentives.
>
> *(Hilborn, 2007, p. 288)*

According to this way of thinking about how captains operate, outcomes of fleet-level practices can be pre-determined by using incentives to shape individual-level decision-making. Thus, individual-level rational decision-making aggregates, when guided by incentives and structured by regulatory institutions, into a collective-level 'rational economic entity.' Such incentives and institutions include catch limits, spatial closures, and temporal seasons, as well as 'bycatch' avoidance schemes (see Chapters 2 and 7 for discussions of 'bycatch'), such as those that the make a captain's ability to fish for a particular target species dependent on not catching certain amounts of particular bycatch species. The broader idea is that because individual-level practices of determining what comes next can unfold in rational decision-making fashion, governance of those practices, and their embedded outcomes, can be top-down, allowing regulatory bodies on land to use rational decision making-based frameworks and tools determine what outcomes occur at-sea. The success of such a rational approach assumes, however, that at-sea practices *can* play out in rational decision-making fashion. As we will see, this assumption is, at best, questionable.

Before we look closer at the questionable nature of using a rational decision-making approach to manage at-sea fishing practices, we need to first dive deeper into what rational decision-making entails. Rational decision-making starts with a clearly defined place where a decision needs to be made (a fork in the road), and ends with clearly determined outcomes of that decision. In between is a common set of parts that articulate in recurring, predictable ways. These parts include discrete options, clear outcomes, determinate relationships between discrete options and clear outcomes, a preference structure for choosing among discrete options and their clear outcomes, and incentives for choosing a certain option and its outcome (Allison & Zelikow, 1999; Elster, 1989; Simon, 1979). Options may be things, such as a particular species to target or a type of fishing gear to use, or they may be instrumental actions. Instrumental actions have significant impacts on how practices unfold; for example, a captain may choose the instrumental action of steaming to a certain spot (rather than steaming to a different spot, or even not steaming at all) or towing in a particular space (rather than towing in another space, or not towing at all).

The next part of a rational decision-making process is the 'preference structure.' Preference structures work to arrange or prioritize options in some pre-determined way. They can provide criteria for evaluating alternatives, such as ranking potential fishing areas in terms of how much fish was caught at each area in the past, or they can define decision rules, such as choosing whichever fishing spot is closest to town. These tools tend to concern the attainment of immediate goals, such as moving to the next stage in a process (from steaming to towing), as well as adherence to more universal norms, such as enacting efficient, fair, and safe practices. And finally, incentives are the parts of rational decision-making processes that influence how the other parts are crafted and articulated. Ultimately, they are factors that motivate the decision maker to select a certain desired option in order to produce a certain determinate outcome. Critically, adding or manipulating incentives is the primary way that people outside of a decision-making process tend to influence how it plays out (Elster, 1989). Reward and punishment are perhaps the most prominent types of incentives, with rewards including such factors as pay, food, and various forms of pleasure, and punishment including such things as loss of potential rewards and various forms of pain.

Having worked through the parts of a rational decision-making process, let's look at the example at the beginning of the chapter through a rational decision-making lens. From what we can tell, the captain generated two options for what to do next, namely the one he chose, which was to go to a particular spot to fish for flathead, and the one he did not choose, which involved fishing for a type of flatfish called 'arrowtooth flounder.' Based on his recent fishing experiences (e.g., "I've been seeing flathead my last three trips"), as well as on more abstract knowledge of his target species' biological and ecological characteristics (e.g., "You know, in the spring they spawn"), the captain attached certain bycatch-based outcomes to those options. We can assume that the second option, i.e., fishing for arrowtooth, involved the potentiality of catching too much bycatch, which was, in this case, Pacific Halibut (e.g., "fishing drops off after that and bycatch goes up. So I don't really want to go someplace where we've pulled a million pounds of arrowtooth out of the water"). At least partly due to regulatory bycatch incentives (which are explored in more detail below and in Chapter 7), the captain chose the option that he thought would generate less bycatch. Thus, the captain made his particular choice between two options because (1) he thought that he would find his target fish (flathead sole) in one spot, and (2) the bycatch-based incentive meant that fishing for arrowtooth at the other spot, and catching too much Pacific halibut bycatch while doing so, would jeopardize his and his fleet's ability to catch the full quotas of their target species in subsequent fishing trips and seasons. So we can look at the event using a rational decision-making framework. But was this actually a *rational* decision?

A defining characteristic of rational decision-making is that the process is "endowed with reason" (etymonline.com), such that it is intentioned, determinate, and goal-directed (Mumby & Putnam, 1992). When the relationship between options and outcomes is determinate, meaning that outcomes can be known, predicted, or calculated prior to taking action (Elster, 1989; Rudolph, Morrison, & Carroll, 2009), and when the creation of options and the making of a choice is intentioned and goal directed, then choices should be obvious and automatic (Elster, 1989). Further still, the intentioned, determinate, and goal-directed nature of rational decisions opens the door to assessments of quality in terms of how optimal a choice, and how efficient the process, was. Yet such assessments depend on the relationship between choices and outcomes being determinate. When the condition of determinacy between options and outcomes is met, and when the process is intentioned and goal-directed, people with similar experiences, knowledge, and training who are dropped into similar situations and roles will, as the theory goes, make similar decisions; which means that, because the process is deterministic, they will produce similar outcomes (Scott & Davis, 2006). Thus, 'rational' means that how a decision-making process unfolds from choice to outcome is not tied to the individualities of actors or to the idiosyncrasies of their particular contexts; actors with similar experiences, knowledge, and training can be interchanged across similar contexts without significantly changing the outcomes (Scott & Davis, 2006). The intentioned, determinate, and goal-directed nature of rational decision-making in turn endows people with the ability to look back upon decision-making events and judge them for their quality, i.e., their rationality. In many domains of life past decision-making events, and the people in them, are regularly adjudicated as being either 'good' (i.e., rational) or 'bad' (i.e., irrational). And in many of those domains, people attempt to regulate and manage events such that past 'bad decisions,' understood through their outcomes, are not repeated by the same, or similar, people.

In rational decision-making processes, choices can be pre-determined, actions can be standardized, and outcomes can be known prior to actions being taken (Elster, 1989). This way of understanding organizing practices assumes a prospective determinism, in which future events can be known if people are just smart, willing, and hard-working enough to do so. 'Determinism' means that events unfold in a cause-and-effect, before-and-after fashion, such that if one can know the 'before,' one can know the 'after.' Thus, what one can know about the future is only limited by the quality of one's knowledge practices. Rational decision-making's determinism has deep roots, signaled by its overlap with the 'strict determinism' of Newton's classical physics. Barad describes this sort of determinism in the following:

> The hallmark of Newtonian physics is its strict determinism: given the 'initial conditions' (i.e., the position and momentum of a particle at any one instant in time) and the full set of forces acting on a particle, the particle's entire trajectory (i.e., its past and future) is determined.
>
> *(Barad, 2007, p. 107)*

Both the physicist and the rational decision-maker can know the 'initial conditions' that shape how phenomena will unfold (in which 'unfolding' is the movement of either a particle or an individual process through space and time); the decision-maker's knowledge of how a decision-making process will unfold through time and space is dependent on his or her knowledge of all the things that will impact that unfolding, which is akin to the physicist's ability to measure, and therefore know, the 'full set of forces' that will impact the particle; further, the decision-maker can know where the decision will land him or her in the future (as well as how past decisions have brought him or her into the present), which is analogous to the physicist determining 'the particle's entire trajectory (i.e., its past and future).' Both rational decision-making and classical physics involve an object, i.e., a particle, outcome, or an individual, that can be separated from its context, such that the object and the context can be measured as distinct entities, from which one can then determine how they will impact or act on one another through time and space. Such impacts or inter-actions can then be analyzed and determined prior to their actual occurrence.

The similarity of rational decision-making and classical physics is not surprising, for both are constructed with Cartesian dualisms (see Raworth, 2017 and Barad, 2007 for discussions of the role of Cartesian dualisms in economics and in classical physics, respectively). Dualisms assume an inherent separability between inside and outside, subject and object, mind and body, humans and nature, word and world, and so on, in which entities, phenomena, or other objects on either side of an inherent, absolute boundary or divider have their own rosters of intrinsic, non-relational properties (Barad, 2007; Farjoun, 2010). What such dualistic thinking leads to, and is surreptitiously premised upon, is humans, in deistic fashion, existing as separate from a world that they look down upon in order to know, manage, and control it. In separability lies determinism, in determinism lies foreseeability, and in foreseeability lies control. Rational decision-making and Newton's classical physics lie upon the same troubled and troubling foundation, but while Newton's classical physics has been 'superseded' by quantum mechanics (Barad, 2007; Wendt, 2015), rational decision-making continues to reign supreme outside of quantum physics departments and journals, even as numerous scholars have argued that it be superseded as well.[2]

Thus, the extent to which the captain's decision above was rational is largely a question of whether or not other people with similar knowledge and experience, dropped into a similar situation, would choose a similar option, and in turn— because the process is deterministic—produce similar outcomes. Such an assessment only makes sense, however, if the assumption that the process is deterministic (i.e., that relationships between options and the outcomes that will follow are, for the most part, knowable at the outset) holds. If the relationship between options and outcomes is indeterminate, then the process is not, well, deterministic. And if the process is not deterministic, it makes little sense to judge it as a rational decision-making process, for a recurring decision could be deemed rational based on other criteria (perhaps because it is intentioned and goal-directed), yet continually produce deleterious outcomes due to the foreseeable indeterminacy between its options and its outcomes. If determinism between options and outcomes is not necessary for a decision-making process to be rational, then decision-making processes that recurrently produce unwanted outcomes could still be deemed 'rational.' Taken to the extreme, we face with the illogical situation in which decision-making that continually harms, or even kills, its decision makers, destroying its own basis for recurrence, can be deemed rational simply because it met other criteria for rationality. Thus, the decision-making would be self-defeating, yet 'rational.' For practices to be regulated and managed as rational decision-making processes, they must, at the least, be deterministic—they must involve the situation in which outcomes can be known, predicted, or calculated prior to actions being taken (Elster, 1989; Rudolph et al., 2009). This requirement, as we will see, is not met in the GOA trawl context (and is very likely not met in many contexts in involving relations among human organizational and natural phenomena).

The North Pacific Fishery Management Council's rational decision-making approach

The assumption that rational decision-making processes are what actually occurs (or at least can occur) at sea is at the heart of the North Pacific Fishery Management Council's (NPFMC's) rational approach to regulating commercial fisheries in Alaskan waters, including the GOA trawl fleet (the relationship between the NPFMC and the GOA trawl fleet is detailed in Chapter 2). By 'rational approach,' I mean that the NPFMC's strategy focuses on shaping how rational decision-making plays out at sea, which of course is premised on captains actually being able to engage in rational decision-making as they enact their fishing practices.

The NPFMC's approach to regulating what they call 'prohibited species catch' exemplifies their rational approach. According to regulations created by the NPFMC, vessels fishing for groundfish[3] must discard (i.e., toss overboard at sea either immediately after catching it or after first delivering it to a processing plant and then transporting it back out to sea) certain non-target species that they catch in the process of capturing their target species. The particular non-target species that captains must discard include all salmonids (i.e., king/Chinook, silver/coho, red/sockeye, chum/dog/keta, pink/humpy), Pacific halibut, Pacific herring, king crab, and tanner or 'snow' crab. Thus, while captains regularly catch an array of non-target species (what is known, once it is caught, as 'bycatch'), non-target species that they catch but are not allowed to retain are called 'prohibited species' (which, once caught, are called 'prohibited species catch,' or PSC). Prohibited species are themselves the target species of other fisheries that are governed by other political bodies (i.e., the State of Alaska and the International Pacific Halibut Commission).

Although the NPFMC does not allow GOA groundfish captains to retain and sell prohibited species, the vast majority of the prohibited species they catch, save 20% of crab and 33% of Pacific halibut (NPFMC, 2007, 2014) is dead when brought on board a trawl vessel. This discard requirement means that thousands of tons of fish and crab are wasted every year in the GOA (e.g., for just Pacific halibut, an average of 1,292 tons were caught and wasted each year over the six year period from 2013 to 1018),[4] even though these are some of the most valuable species that are caught in Alaskan waters (or any waters for that matter). The NPFMC's logic for requiring such vast amounts of natural resource waste is twofold: First, they reason that doing so removes an incentive for captains, operating in rational decision-making fashion, to purposefully catch, or to at least not actively avoid catching, prohibited species as they pursue their target fish; Second, having to discard certain species means that trawl captains cannot bring lower-quality individuals of those species to market (as compared to fish that are caught through fishing practices that are tailored to those particular species, such as Chinook salmon captains who target and catch Chinook salmon using seine nets, after which they use specially tailored onboard equipment to transport them in pristine condition). Lower quality fish would, theoretically, have a negative impact on the market value of the species as a whole. Using this logic, trawl-caught Chinook salmon, being of lower quality than seine-caught Chinook salmon (due in large part to more extensive bruising caused by a trawl net), would bring down the market value of all Chinook salmon. These reasons are exemplified in the following excerpts from the Gulf of Alaska Groundfish Fishery Management Plan, which is the NPFMC's chief regulatory document that guides the management of groundfish fisheries in the GOA:

> The PSC of Pacific halibut, crab, Pacific salmon, and Pacific herring has been an important management issue in the commercial fishery for more than twenty years. The retention of these species was first prohibited in the foreign groundfish fisheries, to ensure that groundfish fishers *had no incentive* to target on these species.
> (NPFMC, 2019, p. 89; emphasis added)

> Except as provided under the prohibited species donation program [see Chapter 7 for a discussion of this program], retention of prohibited species captured while harvesting groundfish is prohibited to prevent covert targeting on these species. The prohibition *removes the incentive* that groundfish fishers might otherwise have to target on the relatively high valued prohibited species, and thereby, results in a lower incidental catch. It also eliminates the market competition that might otherwise exist between halibut fishers and groundfish fishers who might land halibut in the absence of the prohibition.
> (NPFMC, 2019, p. 41; emphasis added)

The idea behind this incentive is that by not allowing captains to retain PSC, captains will not 'target on' those species. This incentive is assumed to function within decision-making processes by influencing captains to avoid towing where they will catch prohibited species to such an extent that fishing becomes inefficient; these inefficiencies stem from the crew having to spend time sorting PSC from the catch, as well as from PSC occupying space in the net that salable fish could occupy. One may question whether this incentive functions as intended, i.e., if it has an appreciable effect on captains' decision-making of where and when to tow next; but as we will see below, the more important question is whether it *can* have the intended effect, namely to force at-sea decision-making to be more rational, such that the amount of prohibited species that are caught, and therefore wasted, in the Gulf trawl fisheries is reduced.

The function of indeterminacy

Though captains' determinations of what to do next fit certain rational decision-making characteristics, their fishing practices depart from rational decision-making in one profound way. Namely, in resource extraction contexts such as commercial trawl fishing, particular outcomes of choosing and taking particular instrumental actions cannot be determined prior to making such choices and taking such actions. The captain's answer in the opening quote of "I have a feeling" when asked why he chose to steam to a particular spot on the fishing grounds exemplifies this departure. As this phrase suggests, there was an indeterminate relationship between actions and outcomes within the captain's deliberation of what to do next. In other words, there was a void in the captain's understanding of what he would find at his next fishing spot, which is further evidenced by his statement, "whether or not they are together enough." This phrase indicates that the captain did not know how aggregated his target fish would be in his chosen spot until *after* he arrived there. Due to this unknown relationship between instrumental actions and their outcomes, the captain also did not know if he and his crew would be able to "make a living" fishing at his chosen spot before steaming there, and they would likely not know the answer until after fishing there well.

Indeterminacy, according to Merriam-Webster (www.merriam-webster.com), is the "quality or state of being indeterminate," and 'indeterminate' means "vague; not known in advance; not leading to a definite end or result." In terms of the academic literature, indeterminacy is a primary way in which processes fail to be rational (Elster, 1989; Rudolph et al., 2009). The data show that when resolving the issue of where to fish next, captains face recurring indeterminacy regarding the relationship between options, in the form of various places to steam to or tow through next, and their outcomes in terms of what they will find at a certain fishing spot and what the species composition of their catch will be after fishing there. Such indeterminacy between options and outcomes is on prominent display in the captains' axiom, "You never know until you tow." When captains repeat this axiom they are communicating that they are never quite sure what the species composition of their catch will be (particularly in terms of weights and numbers of prohibited and other bycatch species and weights of target species) until after they have steamed to a fishing spot, used their sonars to examine the material beneath the vessel in that spot, towed there, hauled up their net up from the depths, and either dumped its contents onto the back decks of their vessels for sorting by species or emptied it directly into their fish holds for delivery to a fish processing plant (where the catch is then sorted by species and the results are communicated back to captains). The following quotes from interviews with GOA trawl captains exemplify this axiom:

RESEARCHER: What was the first clue that boats were catching a lot of salmon bycatch?
CAPTAIN: When I hauled back and had an assload of salmon in my net.

RESEARCHER: What was your approach to avoiding Chinook salmon in the pollock fisheries this year?
CAPTAIN: There's no rules whatsoever in terms of whether you will catch salmon here or you won't catch them there, or time or whatever, everything is so fluid you just have to go about it cautiously.

RESEARCHER: How do you deal with salmon bycatch?
CAPTAIN: Just try to look for them and move, they are hard to see. One thing about the salmon you got to realize is, people talk about these huge numbers of salmon, but when you look at the numbers of pollock that are being delivered you know, it's like one salmon per metric ton, and that it's not a lot. And so they're hard to see when we are dumping fish. I mean, you just try to stay in touch with people and if somebody says there's a lot of salmon you try to do something different, move, go to a different spot. Last year we had a rockfish trip, and we were catching them fast, and in rockfish you just didn't think you could catch that many salmon, but it was pretty bad. So then the next trip [the plant] wanted some more [Pacific Ocean perch rockfish] so we ran right past that spot, where the fishing was killer, to another spot like 20 or 30 miles away, and I don't know, I think maybe it was better, it had less salmon, but still a lot. They really are a problem. You can't have the attitude that you just don't care, but you try to, I don't know, I don't know that anybody really has the answer to that one.

RESEARCHER: Are you going to set [the net] back in the same place?
CAPTAIN: I don't know, it looked like they almost lifted off the bottom, but it didn't look quite right either ... if I didn't catch it I wouldn't find out what it was. But I don't know what I am going to do next. Make sure the net is in one piece. I can see how any kind of weather is no good for this.

RESEARCHER: How do you watch out for salmon?
CAPTAIN: For me, you really can't tell if there is any salmon or not until you haul back.

RESEARCHER: So what has your approach been to chinook bycatch?

CAPTAIN: I don't know, like down south when I'm hake fishing I pay attention to it. I've been doing pretty good, but I think the last trip of my hake season I caught something like 40 Chinook you know, and before that I might have had 40 Chinook for the year. And just all of a sudden they showed up in this spot where I had been fishing for trip after trip after trip, and they just kind of (snaps fingers) moved in.

Indeterminacy is prominent in situations in which managers face unknown, hidden, or missing cues as to what is happening or will happen next (Weick, 2006, 2010). And as these quotes attest, frontline managers in the GOA trawl fishing industry face pervasive indeterminacy.

Part of indeterminacy's pervasiveness is its perpetual recurrence. Even as captains gain a better understanding of the properties of natural phenomena in a particular fishing spot after they arrive and tow there, every tow is always a *next* tow, and indeterminacy emerges anew as captains transition from one fishing spot, and/or one tow, to the next. While indeterminacy's perpetual nature is implicit in the 'never' part of the axiom 'You never know until you tow,' the following example illustrates it more vividly:

RESEARCHER: Do you still see things on your sonar that you are not sure what they are?

CAPTAIN: All the time, you are never sure what it is until you put your net down in it. Last year I drove out [to the grounds] and I saw this sign (i.e., object on the sonar display that suggests the presence of fish beneath the vessel) and I made a short tow because I didn't know what it was and I had caught mackerel there like two weeks before. I hauled back, and got straight pollock, and I said, 'All right!' So I went and threw it back out, pulled it up and it was like 50% mackerel that time—same spot, same sign. I mean what the hell are you supposed to do? It was pretty frustrating.

Indeterminacy continually re-emerges in this context because knowledge of what will come next, whether it is knowledge of what one will find at a fishing spot or what one will haul up from the depths, only materializes through captains' acts of doing next. What will come next can only be known after captains act and bring 'next' into existence. All captains have before acting, due to the indeterminacy between their options and their outcomes, are propositions regarding which actions might allow them to tell the stories they want to tell about what *came* next. Chapters 4 and 5 elaborate the propositional nature of captains' practices in much more detail; for now, our concern is the indeterminacy that renders captains' deliberations incapable of knowing what will come next, before taking action, to the level of exactitude required by regulators, markets, and other stakeholders.

The data make it clear that determinacy is born of captains' instrumental actions of steaming to a particular spot on the fishing grounds, or towing in a particular space beneath the vessel, and taking a 'measurement' of what is in that particular spot or space. In the axiom 'you never know until you tow,' captains do not know what the composition of their catch will be after they perform the 'measurement' of towing; yet the data also indicate that captains do not know what they will find at their chosen fishing spots, until after they steam there and take a look around. Captains can only determine what they will find at a certain fishing spot by steaming there, and they can only determine what they will tow in that spot after towing there. As quantum mechanics teaches us, determinacy is a product of the act of 'measuring' (which includes observing, experimenting, or engaging in some other way); prior to the act, there is nothing determinate to know regarding the particular outcome that will materialize in that particular process (Barad, 2007).

So what is indeterminacy in this context? Where does it come from? What will become clear in the ensuing chapters is that indeterminacy in this context (and perhaps in any context) is not so much about people's inability to know something that is dynamic and obscured from view. Indeterminacy is not simply a question of being able to accurately represent a 'separate' thing within one's practices; it is not just about representation. Instead, indeterminacy is born of the mechanics of knowing the 'separate things' one is inherently entangled with. I will address some of the basics of these mechanics here; the chapters to follow elaborate how these mechanics both call for and shape captains' ecological sensemaking, and in turn the human-natural organization that continually forms at the frontline of the GOA trawl fishery.

In contexts plagued by indeterminacy, knowledge of what comes next emerges through 'measurement' activities. Yet no action occurs in a vacuum. There is no isolated, individual action, and there is no activity that captains enact in their at-sea fishing practice that is not entangled with natural activities, such that they have separately determinate boundaries and properties. If you attempt to conceive of an isolated action, occurring solely of its own accord, with its own roster of non-relational properties, you will inevitably run into other actions—including your own—that the 'isolated' action is inseparable from, that are part if 'its' constitution, and therefore the very individuality you are seeking to understand; the action's isolated-ness is born of both 'its' boundary-making effects and the boundary-making effects of other activities, including your own boundary-making attempts to isolate it. Attempts to isolate the action create separation, but this is only a 'local' form of separation, not the sort of separation that is assumed by metaphysical individualism (see Chapter 1). Your attempts to isolate it create separability within your engagement with the action, but it is only a contingent 'exteriority,' a differentiation that is performed within entangled activities (Barad, 2007). Such exteriority is, as Barad argues, an 'agential separability,' for it is an enacted boundary, not an ontological state. Further, the action's isolated nature is also constituted by what is cut away from it by the boundary-making intra-activity, what Barad calls 'constitutive exclusions.' All of these activities co-articulate the boundaries that circumscribe 'the' action, which create material conditions for certain ideas, concepts, and theories to make sense, to the exclusion of others. Thus, 'the' action is inherently entangled with differentiating activities, all of which are both making 'it' what 'it' can be, as well as what 'it' cannot be. Put succinctly, the measurement activities, the boundaries they perform, and what is bounded away from them, are entangled physical practices that create the conditions for certain meanings and senses of experience to materialize.

The construct of 'entanglement' is central to the arguments outlined in the chapters to follow (also see Chapter 1 for another discussion of entanglement). To be entangled, according to Barad (2007, ix), "is not simply to be intertwined with another, as in the joining of separate entities, but to lack an independent, self-contained existence." Entangled actions, and in turn entities (e.g., atoms, people, processes, organizations, systems) lack individually determinable and isolatable boundaries, properties, and meanings, instead gaining such qualities through the activities that constitute them, and which they help constitute. From an entanglement perspective, actions can never be isolated in and of themselves, or to one entity, but rather function to perform the boundaries from which 'separate' actions and entities take form and attain individuality. The fact that the boundaries, properties, and meanings that constitute and define entities emerge through activities is the reason that our knowledge, which is inherently entitative (meaning it relies on discrete, separate categories, labels, concepts, etc.), only follows action. While indeterminacy emerges at sea as captains act their way into knowing, or determinacy, the source of that indeterminacy is the entanglement of captains' actions with the natural phenomena they are attempting to know. Put in terms of agential realism, this entanglement is the inseparability of objects at sea, such as what captains will find at a particular fishing spot or after they haul up their catch from the depths, and apparatuses of observation, which are the broader fishing practice through which such 'measurements' are performed.

To better understand entanglement, let's look further at the relation at its core. This relation is Barad's '*intra*-action.' The 'intra' of 'intra-action,' and alternatively the 'inter' of 'interaction' are the relational aspects of action, but in which 'intra' and 'inter' signify fundamentally different understandings of those relations, and in turn of action (and from there, reality). An 'inter' type of relation means that actions are ontologically separable, even if they intermittently, or even almost continually, impact other actions or things. An 'intra' type of relation, however, means that actions are only epistemologically and semantically separable; we cut them apart as we attempt to gain clarity of thought, intention, communication, and action, but they are ontologically inseparable, and thus retain an inherent ambiguity. Barad explains the difference in more detail in the following:

> The neologism "intra-action" signifies the mutual constitution of entangled agencies. That is, in contrast to the usual "interaction," which assumes that there are separate individual agencies that precede their interaction, the notion of intra-action recognizes that distinct agencies do not precede, but rather emerge through, their intra-action. It is important to note that the "distinct" agencies are only distinct in a relational, not an absolute, sense, that is, *agencies are only distinct in relation to their mutual entanglement; they don't exist as individual elements.*
> (Barad 2007, p. 33)

'Inter' is the relation in which action adds two or more things together, while 'intra' is the relation that differentiates action into two or more things. Intra-actions are boundary-making relations, while interactions are connection-making relations. Understanding human and natural phenomena as separate entities, constituted by distinct actions, means that they involve interactions, such that human phenomena act on natural phenomena, and natural phenomena act on human phenomena, yet they are ultimately separable. Understanding human and natural phenomena as constitutive of one another means that they involve *intra*-actions, such that human and natural phenomena only differentiate from one another through their intra-actions. Thus, 'intra' and 'inter' are mutually exclusive understandings of reality— actions are either inseparable or separable, intra or inter; they cannot be both.

Another way to understand for the 'intra' of 'intra-action' is the phenomenon of 'superposition.' 'Superposition' is inherently quantum mechanical (Barad, 2007); it is what happens when waves overlap. While there is no wave in isolation, that exists separate from the material that constitutes the wave and its action, or from other waves that are formed from the same material, there are obviously differentiated waves. Yet when differentiated waves overlap they do not merely *impact* or *act on* one another; they do not displace or dislodge one another, and the change in one wave cannot be measured as a reaction to the other. There is no cause and effect, at least in terms of how cause and effect is classically and traditionally understood, i.e., as the action of one thing impacting another. Rather, in the case of superposition, when two waves overlap their amplitudes combine into one. Depending on the nature of the two amplitudes, the resulting new aptitude may be larger, smaller, or even reduced to zero. The waves, which are already part of the same broader phenomenon, and therefore already intra-related, intra-act to articulate something new; they mutually constitute the materialization of a newly differentiated wave. The newly differentiated wave is born of the entanglement of waves, as were the waves that intra-acted to form it.

The phenomenon of superposition is also called 'interference' or 'diffraction.' These concepts capture the nature of any one wave, as well as multiple waves, as being both differentiated and superpositioned, such that the differentiation of waves is the result of superposition, and superposition only occurs through differentiation. When multiple waves occur they form interference or diffraction patterns. When you toss two pebbles into a pond and watch the waves that emanate from the places where the pebbles entered the water, you are looking at a diffraction pattern that is formed by the superposition of waves. The diffraction pattern is a series of superpositions, which are intra-actively created.

So what is the significance of superposition for our purposes? New materialism scholars (e.g., Karen Barad, Donna Haraway), drawing from various fields, including quantum mechanics, argue that all entities, including all boundaries, are superpositions, articulated by intra-acting differentiations; entities do not exist outside one another, on either side of a clear dividing line, allowing for a geometrical relationship, whereby one can be mirrored or represented by another. As stated by Haraway:

> Diffraction does not produce 'the same' displaced, as reflection and refraction do. Diffraction is a mapping of interference, not of replication, reflection, or

reproduction. A diffraction pattern does not map where differences appear, but rather maps where the effects of difference appear.

(Haraway, 1992, p. 300, cited in Barad, 2014)

Intra-acting differentiations are always performing superpositions, co-articulating the materialization of new differentiations. In terms of GOA trawl captains, my argument is that, just as your reading of this text involves the co-articulation of differentiation and superposition, captains' 'readings' or 'measurements' of natural phenomena, whether done through the trawl net or the sonar or each other, involve the ongoing articulation of both differentiation and superposition, and this is the reason they 'never know until they tow.'

Quantum mechanics, through Barad's agential realism, teaches us that all phenomena are born of the ongoing articulation of differentiated entanglements, within which are differentiated superpositions, and that all entanglements are phenomena. Entanglements are formative of phenomena, and phenomena are formative of entanglements. Particular entanglements make particular phenomena, whether human or natural, physical or conceptual, possible, different, meaningful, effective, ineffective, included, excluded, and so on. Thus, particular entanglements act as apparatuses (see Chapter 1 for more discussion of apparatuses), which perform particular *inclusive* outcomes of interest, i.e., superpositions, which depend on, and are inseparable from, particular *exclusive* outcomes, i.e., constitutive exclusions (Barad, 2007). What is excluded from a particular superposition of interest, or from any materialization, is just as important to it is as what is included. Constitutive exclusions are essential to what makes anything a thing (Barad, 2007; Whitehead, 1967b); they play a constitutive role (i.e., performing boundary-, property-, and meaning-making relations) in making catch, or a spot on the fishing grounds, or any other outcome of a knowledge process, what it is, and, equally importantly, what it is not. Further, what is excluded tends to comes back, shaping the articulation of ensuing superpositions. As Barad puts is, "That which is determinate (e.g. intelligible) is materially haunted by—infused with—that which is constitutively excluded (remains indeterminate, e.g., unintelligible)" (2014, p. 178). Particular apparatuses perform particular superpositions and constitutive exclusions due to the particular boundary-, property-, and meaning-making activities of their entangled phenomena. Such activities include those that function to differentiate phenomena into 'human' and 'natural' categories, creating the constitutive exclusions that we see as the separation of humans and nature. The world articulates itself differently—into differently entangled boundaries, properties, meanings—but not separately (Barad, 2007), and what materializes from such articulation is a function of particular differentiating, superpositioning, and constitutive excluding.

Once we see that humans and nature are inherently entangled, i.e., that we are both differentiated and superpositioned, it is not difficult to see Bohr's 'central lesson of quantum mechanics,' namely, that "we are part of the nature that we seek to understand" (Barad, 2007, p. 247) at work in the GOA trawl fishing context. As ensuing chapters make clear, the source of captains' indeterminacy at sea, or the reason they cannot know until they tow (or steam), is the fact that they are part of the nature they seek to understand, and that nature is part of them and their process of understanding (or, as later chapters make clear, their ecological sensemaking); and, further, the intra-actions of *both* captains and nature constitute what materializes through their entangled activities, as well as what does not. Indeterminacy lies in the superposition of captains' practices and the ecological phenomena that they seek to understand, as well as in the entanglement of what materializes through captains' practices and ecological phenomena (e.g., a particular place to tow and a particular composition of catch), and what is constitutively excluded from it. Thus, as Chapter 6 argues in greater detail, not only is what materializes through the apparatus that is captains' fishing practices an entanglement of human and natural phenomena, but captains' fishing practices and natural phenomena are *already* entangled prior to any individual materialization. In other words, captains' fishing practices and natural phenomena are entangled 'all the way down' (Slife, 2004).

What entanglement, intra-action, constitutive exclusion, and superposition come to, in terms of the indeterminacy that pervades captains' fishing practices, is this: Indeterminacy continually re-emerges at sea due to the entanglement of captains' activities and natural phenomena, such that for captains to know something definitive about natural phenomena, they must take some sort of boundary-making, exteriority-creating, constitutive-excluding measurement action (such as arriving at a particular fishing spot and examining what is there through the sonar, or hauling up the catch and disaggregating it into numbers and weights of species-based, target and bycatch groupings). Yet, because the natural phenomena that materializes in captains' practice is entangled with, and therefore co-constituted by, captains' activities, what materializes through captains' practices of towing, or steaming to a certain place on the fishing grounds, or some other knowledge process at sea, is always a particular differentiation (e.g., what a captain finds in a fishing spot, the composition of a tow), as well as a superposition of the potentialities embedded in the included and excluded intra-actions that were part of that apparatus. Captains cannot 'know before they tow,' or before they arrive at a fishing spot, or take any sort of 'measurement' of natural phenomena, because what they come to know, as a thing with its own individual boundaries, properties, and meanings, *does not exist* before they take the boundary-making actions that are necessary to cut a particular array of entangled activities together, and a particular other array of entangled activities apart; yet that thing that materializes, whether catch on deck, a spot on the fishing grounds, or something else, is constituted not just by the captains' boundary-making activities, but also the boundary-making activities of the array of human and natural phenomena the captains' practices are constitutively embedded in, both in the present and throughout the past. What captains come to know is always a differentiation within the particular entangled activities of that particular knowledge process, which is constituted both by what was included in and excluded from that materialization, and what was included in and excluded from previous materializations. That differentiated materiality is in turn a superposition of both included and excluded, contemporary and historical, human and natural, potentialities.

Entanglements are always in a state of becoming. Materialization, superposition, differentiation, constitutive exclusion, do not stop. Fishing practices are always embedded in entangled seas of ocean life occurring within, beneath, above, around, and through them. Such entanglements of ocean life are actualities born of the potentiality that ocean life has for enacting activities that foster ongoing persistence, such as breeding and feeding; these entanglements is the manifestation of a certain type of actuality, embedded in which is a certain array of potentiality. Such activities are constituting captains' practices, and captains' practices are constituting them. What captains can know after, and therefore before, they tow is determined by the dynamic boundary-, property-, and meaning-making activities that constitute their fishing practices, which are entangled with the dynamic boundary-, property-, and meaning-making activities of fish beneath their vessels, of the weather above their vessels, of the currents around their vessels, of their past practices, of their current and potential future practices, of other vessels' practices, of regulatory practices, of management practices, and so on. Natural activity is in motion, human activity is in motion, they are in motion with one another, they are enacting boundaries and differentiations between and among one another, they are constituting one another, they are changing one another. In the process of knowing what they towed captains change the nature of what they towed through, what they towed through changes its nature, captains change the nature of their entanglements within broader phenomena, while broader phenomena change the innumerable entanglements that constitute it, captains, and nature. Entanglements of human and natural activities are perpetually becoming because they are always being formed and re-formed as their constitutions change with every new human and non-human intra-action, including various types of 'measurement' activities. What captains know after they tow is the superimposed human-natural materialization of differentiation within the ongoing and roiling entanglement of their practices and natural phenomena. Captains never 'step in the same river twice' (i.e., never steam to the same spot, or tow in the same space, twice), because the phenomena they tow and steam through are perpetually becoming something new, as are captains' fishing practices, which are constitutively entangled in those phenomena. 'The river' cannot be known before stepping in, or taking some other measurement of, it.

Yet we must be clear that this is not simply an issue of uncertainty. It is not just, or even primarily, about the dynamic nature of what captains are attempting to know, or their extent of embeddedness in the contexts in which they are operating; it is not simply the case that captains cannot know before they tow because 'the ground is in motion' (Emery & Trist 1969,p. 249), and their knowledge processes can't keep up. The idea that captains *can* know before they tow indicates that there is some 'thing' to know, that exists apart from their practices of knowing, whose pre-measurement individuality can be known if their knowledge practices are good enough. The problem with this uncertainty-based perspective is that it is based on metaphysical individualism, and relies on a logic of representationalism (Barad, 2007) (see Chapter 1 for a discussion of these concepts and their problematic nature).

Indeterminacy is different from, and perhaps incompatible with, uncertainty (Barad, 2007). The relationship between indeterminacy and uncertainty in quantum mechanics (see Barad, ibid., pp. 115–118 for a richer elaboration) is much the same as it is in commercial trawl fishing. Werner Heisenberg's famous 'uncertainty principle' states that, due to the mechanics of measurement, the pre-measurement position and momentum of light cannot be simultaneously known; what can be known is limited by the discontinuity of what is being measured, which is caused by the act of measuring. Bohr's indeterminacy principle, however, argues that there is no determinate *thing*, no discrete momentum or position, to know prior to the act of measuring. Instead, the act of measuring, including the relatively simple act of observing, is part of a broader apparatus, which also includes the 'external' phenomena of interest, through which the 'thing' one measures emerges with its 'thingness.' As Barad explains, Heisenberg makes an epistemological argument—that we *could* know what is out there, apart from us, as it exists in its determinate individuality, if our measuring apparatuses were just good enough (which includes the ever-present ability to subtract out the effects of our measurement activities on the external thing). Bohr's 'indeterminacy principle' (as Barad calls it) instead makes an ontological and semantic argument—that what we are attempting to know only exists as a separate thing, with its own determinate boundaries, properties, and meanings, through our knowledge (or other measurement) processes, which are intra-active with 'it.' It is in those processes that we identify superpositions as boundaries and separate properties and meanings (in which we perform disambiguating 'agential cuts') (Barad, 2007). Uncertainty essentially comes down to the notion of disturbance, such that our knowledge is limited by the disturbance that our knowledge processes cause to the thing we are attempting to know; indeterminacy, however, comes down to the notion of entangled emergence, such that what we come to know emerges in the process of knowing, and is bounded and constituted by the entangled phenomena of what is being known and the processes of knowing. Thus, for indeterminacy, the issue is not the limitation of knowledge, it is being clear about what the referent of the knowledge process is—namely, entangled phenomena and their superimposing and constitutively excluding intra-actions. Disturbance is important, but entanglement is paramount.

Captains' practices of towing certainly disturb what they are towing through; what was beneath the vessel is not the same after towing as it was prior to towing. But if it were just an issue of disturbance, then captains could know what they were going to tow through prior to doing so, if they could just find the tools needed to eliminate their uncertainty, and to know the separate ecological phenomena in their individuality. Such an understanding, however, relies on the fundamental separation of human and natural phenomena, and depends on a faulty representational view of reality (Barad, 2007; Hacking, 1983; Pickering, 1995; Rouse, 2002). Not only is catch a superimposed materialization, but, as Chapter 6 argues, captains' knowledge practices are *already* entangled with ecological phenomena, prior to knowing 'it.' Bohr's indeterminacy principle says that there is no separate individuality to know, and that what we deem to be separate properties and meanings is the result of both entangled human and non-human phenomena and the cuts, the boundary-making intra-actions, that we enact into them, creating 'exteriority within.' Thus, each mass of catch on deck, each fishing spot, is a superposition, and what is known as an individual thing, occupying its own location in time and space, such as a fishing spot or catch on deck, is formed through the materializing entanglements of fishing practices and ecological phenomena; each particularly articulated 'one' does not exist prior to such entanglements. Captains cannot know before they tow because there is no separate *thing* to know.

Yet, in the hegemonic view that underlies rational decision-making, and in turn rational management systems, humans and nature are inherently distinct, even if they often act on one another. In this way of understanding reality, Cartesian dualisms are the foundational structure of existence, enabling us to operate as if there are inherent, unambiguous distinctions among entities. Examples of such dualisms include subject/object, mind/body, culture/nature, organization/environment, word/world, and so on. Within a dualism, entities on either side of the division are self-contained and opposing (Farjoun, 2010). The use of dualistic terms, such as 'interacting,' 'inter-dependent,' 'impacting,' 'connecting,' and 'acting on,' when used to discuss relations among entities, either demonstrates an actively dualistic approach to enacting and understanding reality, a more passive approach, or, at the very least, a lack of attention to the nature of how the entities are related (and therefore formed). Regardless of the intentions of their users, dualisms work to give them the ability to think of themselves as engaging with something that is separate from them (Barad, 2007). Separation in turn allows the users of dualisms, including regulators, managers, and scholars, to act as if one can control that separate thing, and in turn determine what it is and is not, can be and cannot. And due to its inherent individuality, the effects of controlling and determining the thing can be isolated to that thing. This ontology is prevalent in humans' long-standing approach of 'managing nature' (as well as in other egregious ways that humans have treated forms of life that are not their own). The reality, however, is that there is no such thing as humans and nature that can be studied or managed apart from one another, in which they 'impact' or 'act on' one another; such separations, and in turn their interactions, are instead products of our dualistic thinking within inseparable human-natural phenomena. Humans and nature certainly shape what each other is and is not, but we need to rid ourselves of a fantastical understanding of how such shaping occurs.

Dualisms assemble as they divide; they are constitutive parts of the 'separate' phenomena they purport to depict. Rather than describing reality, dualistic thinking is an exemplar of the boundary-making that humans perform within entangled human-natural phenomena. In other words, they perform 'constitutive exclusions,' creating 'exteriority within' entangled phenomena (Barad, 2007). The differentiation of us from nature, and of nature from us, belongs neither to 'us' nor to 'nature,' but rather emerges as 'differentiation within' our entangled relationality (Barad, 2014). Such differentiations are a far cry from dualisms, as any glance at a species and its environment or niche will make clear—they mutually constitute and define one another's activities, morphologies, and genes (Lewontin, 2000). Yet we routinely, and often inadvertently, graft dualism onto differentiation, and then in turn treat the dualism as if it is foundational to differentiation. The reality is that what is differentiated, and the act of differentiating, are always mutually constituted. We are always part of whatever it is that we seek to differentiate ourselves from, and it is always part of us.

Yet, it is fundamental to rational decision-making that the outcomes of instrumental actions are known, or at least is calculable, *prior* to taking them (Rudolph, Morrison, & Carroll, 2009, p. 734). Such a relationship between knowing and acting clearly does not hold in this context, for the captains in the examples above determined that they must steam to a certain fishing spot and/or tow from a certain space beneath the vessel in order to *then* know what materializes, and in turn what it means in terms of moving on to next steps in their fishing practice. Thus, captains' knowledge of relationships between choices, instrumental actions, and outcomes continually emerges (and continually becomes outdated) *through* their boundary-, property-, and meaning-making activities, which includes steaming and towing, rather than before them. It is clear that, due to trawl fishing practices in the GOA being entangled, and therefore perpetually laden with indeterminacy, a rational decision-making framework does not capture what is happening. What is needed is just what Bohr argued was required to understand the outcomes of experiments in quantum physics (Thomas Young's double-slit experiment in particular): "a radical reworking of the classical worldview, including a new quantum epistemology that does not take the Cartesian subject-object dualism for granted" (Barad, 2014, p. 173).

There are decision-making processes in actuality, and then there is the use of rational decision-making frameworks for studying, understanding, judging, and managing that actuality. And quite often the two do not align. In such cases the reaction has predominantly been to deem processes (and the people in them) that fail to align with rational decision-making frameworks 'irrational.' Once the label of irrationality is attached, the all-to-common scholarly and regulatory next steps involve attempting to change the concrete processes so that they fit abstract frameworks. Thus, upon finding a mismatch between rational decision-making frameworks and actual practices, the approach has not been to ask if one is using the appropriate framework to understand actual practices, instead the approach has been to ask how to make the practices fit the framework. In other words, the approach is not to ask if one has the right tools for the job, but instead to make the job fit one's tools. The relationship between knowing and acting elaborated above, due to the pervasive indeterminacy that is born of an inherently entangled sea of human and natural activities, demands a different framework for studying, understanding, judging, and regulating resource extraction practices. Ecological sensemaking, which is taken up in the next chapter, move us closer to such a framework.

Notes

1   Because such an understanding is retrospective (according to the sensemaking literature—see Chapter 1), captains learn what their particular 'next' *was* at the same time they are learning what it *is*.

2 Academic readers will undoubtedly complain that criticizing economic decision-making is old hat; I implore them to visit perhaps any regulatory meeting in out in the real world, and they will find that what they presume to be a cowering, atrophied feature of scholarly life is not only alive and well, but thriving, shaping individual human lives and, in a very real way, how sustainable our society can be.

3 Groundfish species that are targeted in trawl fisheries include walleye pollock, Pacific cod, shallow and deep water flatfish, rex sole, flathead sole, arrowtooth flounder, northern rockfish, dusky rockfish, Pacific ocean perch, skate; other groundfish that are caught alongside target fish and are at times retained to be sold to a processing plant include sablefish; still other groundfish that are caught alongside target fish, but are routinely discarded include shortraker/rougheye rockfish, 'other slope' rockfish, pelagic shelf rockfish, demersal shelf rockfish, thornyhead rockfish, Atka mackerel, sculpin, octopus, shark, squid.

4 See NOAA Fisheries fisheries catch and landings reports at www.fisheries.noaa.gov/ala ska/commercial-fishing/fisheries-catch-and-landings-reports#goa-prohibited-species.

4

ECOLOGICAL SENSEMAKING AT SEA

The previous chapter detailed how Gulf of Alaska (GOA) trawl captains' processes of determining what to do next are presumed by regulators (and many academics) to occur at the frontline of commercial trawl fishing in the Gulf of Alaska, namely in rational decision-making fashion. Then the chapter demonstrated that a rational decision-making perspective is not an appropriate way of understanding how GOA trawl captains *actually* determine where to steam to or tow through next due to the indeterminacy that plagues their fishing practices. The chapter argued that this indeterminacy is due to the pervasive and unavoidable entanglement of human and natural phenomena at sea, such that captains can only know how their relations with natural phenomena are unfolding after they have already unfolded. Put more succinctly and contextually, captains 'never know until they tow,' for each tow. In light of the mismatch between the rational way in which at-sea operations are assumed to play out, and how they actually play out, this chapter begins to make the case for a different perspective for thinking about, studying, understanding, and ultimately managing and regulating at-sea organizing processes.

This chapter starts by outlining the reasons why 'ecological sensemaking' is a better perspective for understanding how GOA trawl captains determine what to do next. It explores empirical data from an ecological sensemaking perspective, and in doing so demonstrates that this perspective provides a tighter fit between our (on-land) understanding of fishing practices and how they actually unfold (at sea). Yet, in doing so, the chapter also argues that ecological sensemaking itself needs to be amended to better account for the inherently entangled nature of human and natural phenomena, and the indeterminacy it engenders. This amendment involves infusing the notion of 'abduction,' as primarily elaborated by philosopher of science Charles Sanders Peirce, into ecological sensemaking, for doing so provides a more comprehensive and realistic account of how captains organize their entanglement with natural phenomena in the face of indeterminacy. Through abduction, ecological sensemaking takes on a decidedly conjectural flavor, in which captains take a leap of faith into the unknown, with the goal of landing where they need to be next. Finally, after elaborating the abductive nature of ecological sensemaking, this chapter takes a deeper dive into the source of indeterminacy in ecological sensemaking, namely the inherent ambiguity of differentiations within ecological phenomena, and demonstrates how this indeterminacy requires the propositions that (it argues) are one of ecological sensemaking's key attributes.

Sensemaking

Ecological sensemaking is a subset of the broader domain of sensemaking. As elaborated in Chapter 1, sensemaking is both an organizing process and a process through which organization emerges (Weick, 1979, 1995; Weick et al., 2005). More particularly, it is defined as a process "through which people work to understand issues or events that are novel, ambiguous, confusing, or in some other way violate expectations" (Maitlis & Christianson, 2014, p. 57). Sensemaking involves the social processes (in which 'social' is the actual or imagined presence of others) through which actors use their identities, experiences, knowledge, logics, mental maps, etc., to derive meaning from and to enact meaning into their past, present, and future experiences and to strategically carve out a place for ensuing action, all while shaping their practices, their sensemaking, and themselves. In terms of its relationship with organizing processes, as well as broader organization, it is through sensemaking processes that organizational activities like as "managing, coordinating, and distributing" continually emerge and have a major influence on what the organization is and is not, can be and cannot (Weick et al., 2005, p. 411).

Sensemaking analyses tend to focus on the relatively broader processes through which people make *sense* rather than on the more narrow processes through which they make *decisions*. This is because people spend much of their lives working to understand what is happening in actuality, and what may come next in potentiality, and then attempting to turn certain potentiality into desired actuality; they spend much less of their lives engaging in clear-cut rational decision-making events. Like the woman changing jobs due to financial needs, the man entering a hospital for the treatment of a terminal disease, emigrants fleeing persecution and violence in their home countries, teenagers lashing out at parents who just don't 'get it,' most of the time what we call a 'decision' is really a continuation of ongoing processes that are embedded in an entangled assemblage of individual and collective, novel and established, processual and institutional, planned and random, human and non-human, conceptual and physical, cultural and natural activities and events. Outside of formally structured, deliberative decision-making bodies, the last thing people often have is the temporal, financial, and informational resources required to carry out their lives in rational decision-making fashion. The pervasiveness of the idea of 'having a choice,' and the academic and political fetishizing of 'making *the* right decision,' is often the outcome of the privileged few presuming how the under-privileged many should live.

A dialogue in the movie *Mission Impossible 4: Ghost Protocol*, for example, contains a discussion that demonstrates some of the key differences between sensemaking and rational decision-making. In this dialogue, the movie's protagonist, Ethan Hunt (played by Tom Cruise), a top special agent for an imaginary high-level spy agency, and a counter-intelligence analyst (played by Jeremy Renner), have just escaped their ill-intentioned pursuers. The analyst was thrown into his first combat event, while such an event was much more of a common occurrence for Hunt. Their pursuers had wrecked the vehicle that Hunt and the analyst were in, causing it to crash into a river, which rendered the two underwater targets of machine gun-wielding bad guys from a bridge above. Hunt engineered their escape through the inventive coupling of a flare and a dead body, in which he attached the flare to the body and then pushed both through the water in the opposite direction from which they would swim to their escape. The moving assemblage of body and flare diverted the attention of their pursuers, enabling Hunt and the analyst to reach safety. The two then discussed the previous events:

ANALYST: Why would that work?

HUNT: Why would what work?

ANALYST: The flare on the body, why would that work?

HUNT: It did work.

ANALYST: Yeah I know, but why? I mean, how did you know that would draw their fire?

HUNT: I didn't, I played a hunch.

ANALYST: OK, alright, so what was your scenario? So there's a guy being shot at in the water and all of a sudden you just decide to light up a flare and swim around [speaking with obvious skepticism]? I mean, what did you assume they would be thinking?

HUNT: [stops walking, turns to face the analyst, looking exasperated] Thinking?

ANALYST: Yeah.

HUNT: I didn't assume they would be thinking, I just assumed they would be shooting at anything that moved and I just gave them a target. Look these guys aren't Rhodes scholars, you know?

ANALYST: [shaking his head] This is really happening isn't it?

Once we shake ourselves free of a hyper-focus on decision-making, processes such as sensemaking come into sharper relief (as they did for the analyst). Hunt did not go through a rational decision-making process (see Chapter 3 for a description of such processes), in which he analyzed different choices in the form of scenarios, for he did not have the temporal or informational resources to do so; any attempt to do so would have in fact been deadly. Instead, he 'played a hunch'—he placed a bet, made a conjecture, he took instrumental action based on mere proposition. Hunt acted his way into a sense of what was happening, for doing so, as compared to rational decision-making, was the more efficient, effective, and safer way forward. Even in more mundane contexts it is likely that the easier, faster, and more efficient process of sensemaking is the more pervasive and influential organizing process; yet rational decision-making remains the overwhelmingly favored topic of academics, managers, and regulators. Herbert Simon's 'satisficing' (1979, 1983), which argues that people make decisions based on rules of thumb and other mental shortcuts, gets rational decision-making closer to what people really do; yet it does not take it far enough, for it merely modifies the traditional framework. Organizing processes may be speckled with salient decision-making events, but those events are floating in, and their trajectories are largely determined by, a vast sea of sensemaking: "Decision making is incidental, sensemaking is paramount" (Weick, 2003, p. 186). Decision-making necessarily involves sensemaking, and sensemaking necessarily involves decision-making (Rudolph et al., 2009), but to be sensible one need not be, and often one cannot be, what academics and regulators would call 'rational.'

Ecological sensemaking

Once we move from decision-making to sensemaking we are able to see and explain more of what is actually happening, not just what economic theory proclaims *should* be happening. And, as elaborated in Chapter 1, to talk of sensemaking in natural resource contexts is to talk of 'ecological sensemaking.' 'Ecological sensemaking' is "the way actors notice, bracket, make, and select connections and act on spatial and temporal cues arising from topography and ecological processes" (Whiteman & Cooper, 2011, p. 905). Whiteman and Cooper's work draws heavily on Weick's (1993) study of the disastrous efforts made by 'smokejumpers' to fight a woodland forest fire in Montana in 1949 (in what was perhaps the first ecological sensemaking study), an event first told by Normal Maclean in the book *Young Men and Fire* (Maclean, 1992). According to their work, ecological sensemaking occurs over large swaths of time and space, and the extent of one's embeddedness in an ecosystem influences which aspects of that ecosystem that one notices and incorporate into his or her sensemaking, how one interconnects those aspects into a sense of what was happening, what is happening, and/or what will happen, as well as what sense one retains for future sensemaking. Both Whiteman and Cooper and Weick studied crisis events, and their research makes it clear that there was no singular decision that determined the outcomes those crises; in fact, if either Whiteman and Cooper or Weick had focused on a particular decision, or even on a particular series of decisions, they would have missed much of the story. Research into ecological sensemaking, while exceedingly scant, provides salient evidence as to why "sensemaking implies that key organizational events happen long before someone realizes that there is some sort of decision they have to make" (Weick, 2003, p. 186). Ecological sensemaking, like more generalized sensemaking, may involve salient decision points, but it has historical, social, cultural, technological, and ecological depth and breadth that expand beyond decision making.

Chapter 1 went into detail about one of the facets of our current understanding of ecological sensemaking that this book addresses, namely its representationalism. 'Representationalism' assumes that knowledge, or one's sense of an object of observation or engagement, is about the correspondence between independently existing words, and other forms of likeness, and things, in which pre-existing words mirror, depict, characterize, or in some other way attach meaning to pre-existing things. Taking a representational view of knowledge naturally leads to concerns about the quality, or accuracy, of the correspondence between words and the things they represent (Barad, 2007). In its insistence on the inherent separation of words and things, representationalism runs counter to an entanglement-based perspective, in which there is no such inherent separation of words and things, or any*thing*. Whiteman and Cooper (2011) argue that to understand how people make sense of ecological materiality when embedded in natural phenomena, we have to account for the depth and breadth of their experience in such phenomena, i.e., their 'ecological embeddedness.' What ecological embeddedness offers ecological sensemaking is a "*repertoire* of examples, images, understandings, and actions" (Whiteman & Cooper, 2011, p. 892, citing Schön, 1983, p. 138; emphasis original) that sensemakers use to bracket and attach meaning to ecological materiality. 'Ecological materiality,' in turn, is "the interaction of dynamic biological and biophysical processes and organic and inorganic matter over space and time" (Whiteman & Cooper 2011, p. 892). In this view, ecological embeddedness is the storehouse of 'words' that sensemakers use to make sense of ecological materiality, or 'things.' Presenting a representational 'tripartite arrangement' (Barad, 2007) view of ecological sensemaking (see Chapter 1 for a broader explanation of this understanding of Whiteman & Cooper, 2011), Whiteman and Cooper argue that ecological embeddedness mediates the relationship between the sensemaker and the separate ecological materiality he or she is making sense of. Thus, the breadth and depth of one's ecological embeddedness mediates how accurate one's ecological sensemaking of external ecological materiality is (making it either 'expert-driven,' 'fragmented,' or 'disembedded').

This book's elaboration of ecological sensemaking takes a different approach. This approach is grounded in an entanglement perspective, and attempts to elaborate how entangled human and natural phenomena articulate the organization that is the frontline of a commercial fishery, including particular not-so-sustainable outcomes that are part and parcel of that articulation, i.e., bycatch. A key part of this elaboration is a framework of the entangled ecological sensemaking apparatus that both emerges through and helps articulate that organization. The following begins this elaboration.

Ecological sensemaking in the GOA

Let's start with a brief ecological sensemaking-based reinterpretation of the conversation that opened the previous chapter, which we explored through a rational decision-making lens. From the view of organizations as interpretive systems, ecological sensemaking, as it is in all sensemaking, it is by way of action that people answer the questions, "what's the story here?" and "now what should I do?" (Weick et al., 2005, p. 410). Thus, to engage in ecological sensemaking people who are embedded in ecological contexts take action in order to "interpret what they have done, define what they have learned, solve the problem of what they should do next" (Daft & Weick, 1984, p. 284). Their ensuing interpretations of their relations with ecological phenomena are influenced by "such things as the nature of the answers sought, the characteristics of the environment, the previous experience of the questioner, and the method used to acquire [that experience]" (ibid.). Thus, in ecological sensemaking, knowledge of one's relations with ecological phenomena follows action. Based on this rather simple understanding of ecological sensemaking, let's look again at the conversation:

RESEARCHER: Why are we heading there to fish?

CAPTAIN: I'm going over here for three reasons. I'm going over here because I have a feeling that there's gonna be some flathead over here, and if that's true I think I'll get a jump on the rest of the fleet, they are gonna mill around town, take a day off, whatever ... so I want to look at that. It's gonna be better weather over here ... And I don't really know, the only other option for me right now would be to go someplace where I could just load this boat in a day with arrowtooth [flounder], but I think that fishing has come and gone. We've had some really good arrowtooth fishing, we've had three full loads of arrowtooth in the last 15 days, we've pulled a lot of arrowtooth out of the water, and so fishing drops off after that and bycatch goes up. So I don't really want to go someplace where we've pulled a million pounds of arrowtooth out of the water.

RESEARCHER: When you say you have 'a feeling,' what do you mean?

CAPTAIN: You know, in the spring they spawn, and I've been seeing flathead my last three trips, some nice flathead with some eggs in them. There is a volume, there is quite a bit of flathead over here all the time, it's just whether or not they are together enough to make a living fishing for them.

The ecological sensemaking displayed here starts with the captain's need to determine what to do next, particularly to conjecture that a certain place on the fishing grounds will give his practice the potentiality it needs to conduct a profitable tow. In terms of the framework outlined above, to make such a conjecture the captain drew on previous experience (e.g., "There is a volume, there is quite a bit of flathead over here all the time"), the method he used to acquire that experience (e.g., "I had caught mackerel there like two weeks before"), current characteristics of the environment (e.g, "in the spring they spawn"), and the nature of the answers sought (e.g., "it's just whether or not they are together enough to make a living fishing for them"). The nature of the answers sought, namely their indeterminacy, meant that the captain knew he would gain determinacy as to what will happen next only *after* taking the instrumental action of steaming to a certain spot on the fishing grounds, whereupon he could use his sonar to see how aggregated the fish were in that spot (i.e., if "they are together enough"). In turn, the indeterminate nature of the answers sought demanded that the captain, rather than formulating determinations of what would come next at his next fishing spot prior to taking action, formulate propositions of what action to take next in order to plausibly bring a desired 'next' into existence. The best the captain could do was exclude certain actions from his ensuing practice, namely the action of fishing for arrowtooth (creating what Barad would call a 'constitutive exclusion'); he could not determine what he would find at his chosen spot, for what he would find next must be articulated through the boundary-, property-, and meaning-making apparatus that is his fishing practice. Until such an articulation, there is nothing determinate to know.

Thus, the captain's process was not so much a rational evaluation of alternatives and then a determination of what will come next, rather it was a conjectural process due to the inherent indeterminacy of what 'next' might be. The captains' determination of what to do next is not a distinct decision point but a continuation of ongoing practices that are *constitutively embedded* in an evolving assemblage of entangled natural, historical, technological, social, and regulatory boundary-, property-, and meaning-making intra-activities, all of which help articulate what 'next' is, and, of equal importance, what it is not.

The captain's *constitutive embeddedness* in the ecological phenomena he was 'organizing with' (or put more relationally, 'entangling with') is key to under-standing his sensemaking. Much like Bohr argued in terms of the mechanics of measurement practices, the captain's practices are part of the nature he seeks to understand and extract material from (see Chapters 1 and 3 for more discussion of Bohr's 'central lesson of quantum physics'). In commercial trawl fishing, the targets of fishing effort, and the ecological phenomena those targets are constitutively embedded in, are inseparable from those efforts. The answer to the question 'What's next?' is never determined before the action of producing 'next' is taken. Just as it is with measurements in quantum mechanics, prior to the 'measurement' that is seeing what is in a particular fishing spot through the sonar or sorting the catch by target and bycatch, the 'thing' that is seen or understood through the measurement (e.g., sonar-based indications of fish, or fish segregated into distinct categories) does not exist in any determined state (Barad, 2007; Hollin et al., 2017). While this view of how such 'measurement' practices play out seems unproblematic alone, it is highly disruptive when viewed alongside our current approach to understanding, studying, regulating, and managing fishing practices. For if captains physically cannot 'know until they tow,' for each tow, what does that mean in terms of regulating them in order to be more selective before they tow? That is *the* underlying question of the book, whose answer begins to be articulated here.

Indeterminacy vs. expectation in ecological sensemaking

Our current understanding of ecological sensemaking, and sensemaking more broadly, largely overlooks the issue of indeterminacy (despite Weick, 2006, 2012, alerting us to its significance), and in turn focuses little on the conjectures or pro-positions that such indeterminacy calls for. Instead, we understand ecological sensemaking to be centered on, and trigged by, issues related to expectations. The modest amount of ecological sensemaking research (e.g., Linnenluecke, Griffiths, & Winn, 2012; Tisch & Galbreath, 2018; Whiteman & Cooper, 2011; Weick, 1993) conducted thus far largely concerns the surprises, shocks, and jolts that stem from violated expectations, which fits snugly into understandings of sensemaking more generally, in which sensemaking is explicitly defined as 'triggered by violated expectations' (e.g., Maitlis & Christianson, 2014; Maitlis & Sonenshein, 2010; Weick et al., 2005). As stated by Weick et al. (2005, p. 414), "we expect to find explicit efforts at sensemaking whenever the current state of the world is perceived to be different from the expected state of the world." This prevailing expectation-based understanding of sensemaking is likely related to the fact that much of the formative sensemaking research focused on organizational crises (e.g., Brown, 2000; Gephart, 1984; Weick, 1988, 1990). Organizational crises are 'low-probability, high-impact events that threaten the viability of the organization' (Pearson & Clair, 1998, p. 60). Such events tend to emerge from situations in which people realize that what they *expected* to happen is in fact not happening, often with potentially or actually disastrous consequences. I call this more traditional sort of sensemaking, 'expectation-driven sensemaking.'

But expectation-driven sensemaking is not, for the most part, the type of sensemaking that is indicated in the preceding conversation (as well as in the quotes provided in Chapter 3). Instead of finding himself immersed in sensemaking that was triggered by violated expectations, the quote indicates that the captain was *expecting* to not know what the next stage in his fishing practice would entail until *after* he took instrumental action, arrived at his chosen spot out on the fishing grounds , and used his sonar system, as well as his own positioning and movement of the vessel, as an instrument of observation to investigate (or 'measure') the spot for aggregating fish. In expectation-driven sensemaking, people experience a loss of sense and then find themselves asking the sensemaking questions, 'What's the story here?' and, 'Now what do we do?' (Maitlis & Christianson, 2014; Weick, 2003; Weick et al., 2015) The violated expectation triggers uncertainty, and the actions that produce answers to the sensemaking questions result in a new expectation of what will come next, i.e., certainty, which enables normal practice to carry forth (Maitlis & Christianson, 2014; Weick, 1995; Weick et al., 2005). Yet as the data indicate, the sensemaking that GOA trawl captains engage in as they determine what to do next does not tend to concern an unexpected loss of sense, but rather an expected gap or interlude in sense. Instead of making sense by answering the sensemaking questions *before* getting back to engaging in their normal practice, GOA trawl captains make sense *through* their normal practice. In this context, sense, for captains, materializes through their ongoing, every day practice, which is a variously-articulated entanglement of a sea of human and non-human intra-activities; it does not stand outside of or precede it. Captains' sense of what to do next emerges as 'after-the-fact' materializations within various stages in the progression of each tow, and in turn each trip, and they often function to end such stages and trips.

Ensuing examples and discussions in this chapter and in the chapters to follow help make the case that each stage of a fishing process begins with a question of what's next and ends with a story of what came next. In between are propositions as to what one needs to do in order to be able to, at the end of the stage (such as arriving at one's chosen fishing spot and determining where to tow, hauling up the net and ending the towing process, evaluating the composition of the catch), tell a good story about what happened (such as a determination of its profitability). Captains' propositions regarding what to do next foster instrumental activities that can ideally help bring desired stage-ending storytelling into actuality. Such activities include steaming to a particular spot on the fishing grounds, towing in a certain space beneath the vessel, and examining the catch on deck. These activities also, however, include an important class of actions called 'agential cuts' (Barad, 2007). 'Agential cuts,' according to Barad, are divisions or differentiations within phenomena, but they are not absolute separations or absolute boundaries; they are not 'Cartesian cuts' in that they are inherently part of our ontology, already there waiting to be discovered (these are the fantastical separations that encourage us to think and operate according to metaphysical individualism, see Chapter 1). Rather, agential cuts are enactments of differentiations that mark boundaries between mutually exclusive-yet-complementary physical articulations of meaning, which enables one to form a determinate sense of what is happening. Thus, agential cuts create exteriority-within-phenomena, performing the material conditions needed to articulate disparate properties and meanings, while also holding them together (Barad, 2007, 2014, p. 177). Agential cuts create contingent and local determinacies, which function to 'resolve' ontological indeterminacies (i.e., the lack of separately determinate boundaries, properties, and meanings); yet they are intra-actions, and therefore do not, rather cannot, disentangle the relationality of the world. Where and when cuts are generally made is often defined by the broader (knowledge, extractive, measurement, etc.) apparatus, such as the practice of fishing, of which they are part and parcel; yet differences in the spatio-temporal emplacement of agential cuts are also often, depending on the broader apparatus, possible, or even necessary for the ongoing adaptation to local conditions (which is to say, sedimentations of entangled arrays of other intra-actions). Thus, agential cuts are 'agential' because they are enacted rather than ontological, yet their possible variation is why they are also performances. Further, in being intra-active, they cannot be isolated to one thing, person, or entity; they are always mutually constituted.

While GOA trawl captains enact multiple agential cuts as each stage of a fishing process unfolds, there is always a final cut that marks the end of a stage. It is the contingent determinacies created by these cuts that enable captains to tell stage-ending stories of what came next. Such cuts include choosing particular sign on the sonar as the target for towing (as distinguished from non-target sign) after arriving to the fishing grounds, hauling up a net full of fish from the depths (differentiating it from the ecological materiality beneath the vessel), and segregating the catch into mutually exclusive categories (dividing target fish from bycatch, and, depending on the species, fish that will be retained from fish that will be discarded). As these examples suggest, agential cuts separate 'objects of interest' from 'agencies or instruments of observation, measurement, extraction, etc.' (Barad, 2007). For captains, 'objects of interest' include aggregations of fish beneath the vessel, the trawl net and its catch, and the composition of the fish on deck or in the fish hold, and 'measurement instruments' include the sonar system, the captains' movements of the vessel, the towing process, and the act of separating the catch by species. Prior to the enactment of an agential cut, objects of interest and measurement instruments do not have separately determinate boundaries and properties; thus, their boundaries and properties, when looked at from the view of separate things, are ambiguous.

An agential cut works to disambiguate boundaries and properties, which in turn performs determinate meaning and fosters a clear sense of what has happened. Thus, where and when captains perform these cuts is one of the main outputs of their ecological sensemaking. After performing an agential cut, such as isolating sign on the sonar as a target to tow through or hauling up catch from the depths, there is 'agential separability,' which provides captains with the determinacy they need to tell a concrete story of what has happened. Thus, agential cuts create the possibility for certain concepts to be meaningful (e.g., target catch), while always providing the conditions in which other (mutually exclusive) concepts are not meaningful (e.g., bycatch). As ensuing discussions and data will indicate, much of captains' ecological sensemaking work focuses on figuring out where and when to enact the cuts that differentiate measurement instruments from objects of interest.

As we shift from expectation- to indeterminacy-driven ecological sensemaking, the nature of the sensemaking questions change. In expectation-driven sensemaking, the question 'What's the story here?' emerges from a settled state of affairs, i.e., certainty, that was upset by violated expectations, in which the determinate story of what will occur has not played out as it was told. What was certain became uncertain, and that uncertainty triggered sensemaking (Maitlis & Christianson, 2014; Maitlis & Sonenshein, 2010; Weick, 1995). After the transition from certainty to uncertainty, expectation-driven sensemaking in turn focuses on getting practices back on track by crafting a new and hopefully more accurate expectation as to what will come next in similar circumstances. This relationship between certainty and sensemaking is perhaps why sensemaking is considered by some to involve an interruption in rational decision-making (e.g., Maitlis & Christianson, 2014; Rudolph et al., 2009), for it is based on the assumption, which it shares with rational decision-making, that certainty is not only achievable, but is the baseline state of affairs. In this view, people can correctly 'the thing' that will actually occur, if their sensemaking is good enough. The quality of such sensemaking lies in the accuracy of the representations of future events that actors build up in the sensemaking process (Whiteman & Cooper, 2011), which they store as mental maps or schemata (Weick, 1995), and then transform into expectations when they find themselves in similar contexts.

In indeterminacy-driven sensemaking, however, the issue of what comes next (in contrast with what *came* next) keeps re-surfacing. This is because indeterminacy continually emerges anew as instrumental actions, including key agential cuts, and stories of what happened next deliver actors to the next stage of their processes, where new propositions of what to do next must be forged due to actors' constitutive embedd-edness in an ever-changing entangled array of human and non-human intra-activities. But this is not just a question of being able to know something 'out there' that is complex and changing; rather, it is an insistence on not ignoring the fact that, for any knower, human or non-human, there is no external some*thing* that can be known. Something of course is known, but the referent of that knowledge is not some*thing* that is external to the knowledge process. Instead, the referent of knowledge is the particular apparatus through which it was articulated, which is to say, the entangle-ment of boundary-, property-, and meaning-making activities that one is con-stitutively embedded in, through which that 'something' materialized. Indeterminacy emerges anew because there is nothing to know before one tows in a certain space, or before one steams to a certain spot, and enacts the agential separability (by way of agential cuts) through which unambiguous boundaries, properties, and meanings emerge. Because captains are constitutively embedded in the ecological phenomena they are organizing with, their instrumental actions and agential cuts shape the very nature of the ecological phenomena they can know (and as Chapter 6 argues, this goes both ways—the instrumental actions inherent in ecological phenomena are con-stitutive of the nature of captains' fishing practices). This constitutive embeddedness is the reason that indeterminacy-driven sensemaking does not so much involve the re-establishment of expectations as the ongoing creation of new hypotheses, propositions, wagers, gambles, bets, hunches as to how to enact a desired next materialization, such as a fishing spot that has a large aggregation of fish, or catch on deck that has little bycatch, into actuality.

Thus, indeterminacy-driven sensemaking is inherently conjectural. Captains make sense by asking 'Now what do we do?', by producing a conjecture of what to do next, and then by taking instrumental actions, which includes performing various agential cuts (e.g., setting the net according to certain sign on the sonar, hauling up the net, segregating catch by species). By making such cuts and pro-ducing objects with determinate boundaries, properties, and meanings (e.g., the size of an aggregation beneath the vessel, a certain composition target and bycatch), captains can then answer the question, 'What's the story here?' The answer to that question resolves the previous indeterminacy as to what's next. At the same time, however, the newly materialized sense and matter, due to the entangled human-natural assemblage that captains' practice is constitutively embedded in, has an indeterminate relationship with future actualities (such as a good fishing spot to steam to next or the composition of the next catch). And thus ecological sense-making carries forth, and captains again need to create a proposition of what to do next. We can see such an indeterminacy-based proposition in the following, in which a captain describes a past fishing event:

RESEARCHER: What still surprises you?
CAPTAIN: Oh, not much. Reading the meter still does. That's the sonar and down sounder. Here's an example, last fall me and another guy were out and there was this ball on the meter and we were both scared to death to set on it. What

if it was rockfish? Not only would we have to waste a bunch of rockfish, but then you have to spend hours cleaning the fish out of the gear. We were both looking at it and we were both like, "Should we?"

RESEARCHER: What did you do?

CAPTAIN: One guy did a quick dip. But most of the time we're pretty good about knowing what we're seeing on the meter. But then you might hit a ball of herring on the way up. I had that happen, that can ruin your day too. There are times when things can shut down an area for other guys. The big question in fishing is what you can't see with the instruments—those are all the flatfish, sablefish are hard to see, halibut, salmon, things that are in the feed bands.

As this conversation indicates, the captains proposed a way to bring 'next' into actuality, namely to do a 'quick dip,' a short tow, which would enable them to tell a story of what they caught. That story might be similar to the one they would later tell after they conduct a subsequent normal tow. Thus, by acting their way into understanding what they will catch when doing a quick tow, captains are in a better position to construct something of an expectation as to what they might catch if they towed in the same place immediately afterward. But even when their current extractive apparatus has changed relatively little (constituted by relatively the same entanglement of fishing practice and aggregation of fish, among other factors that have changed little), captains still 'never know until they tow' (as these captains suggest, and as much of the data presented in Chapter 3 indicate). The captains' sense of what they will haul up from the depths always materializes, or is made, after they take the instrumental action of towing and then performing an agential cut, at some point, in some place, that separates their fishing practice from the ecological phenomena beneath the vessel. In fact, the best captains can often do before towing is determine where they should *not* tow (enacting Barad's 'constitutive exclusions'); in the commercial fishing context, excluding certain potentialities tends to be much easier than pre-determining certain actualities. Thus, captains are not so much working in terms of expectations as to what the future would be as they are working to "narrow the range of 'might occurs'" (Weick, 1969, p. 40).

This is not to say that expectation-driven ecological sensemaking does not occur in the GOA trawl fishing context, or at the frontline of any resource extraction context, for it certainly does. One need look no further than the Exxon Valdez and Deepwater Horizon disasters to see stark examples of the workings of expectation-driven sensemaking. But this is to say that, on a day-to-day basis, where the practice of resource extraction is ongoing, indeterminacy-driven sensemaking, while typically more mundane, is commonplace because of the pervasive and expected nature of the indeterminacy of future actualities. Further, it is arguably more influential than expectation-driven sensemaking due to its widespread day-to-day impacts on ecological, social, and economic outcomes. Thus, while crisis events are flashier, it is the ongoing accumulation of day-to-day outcomes that is more likely to be the real danger. Violated expectations are incidental, indeterminacy is paramount.

Before we move forward I want to further explore the concept of the 'agential cut,' for, as previously stated, it is an important part and product of captains' ecological sensemaking. A key aspect of the agential cut is complementarity. For instance, the net with its catch can be an 'object of interest' and an 'instrument of extraction,' but it cannot be both at the same time (Barad, 2007). The two configurations of the extractive apparatus are mutually exclusive, yet complementary. Whether the net with its catch is an object of interest or an instrument of extraction depends on when and where in the fishing process the captain performs the cut that transforms it into one or the other. Thus, the fishing apparatus will either perform a configuration of intra-actions that articulates the net with its catch as an object of interest, or it will perform a configuration that entails the net with its catch as an instrument of extraction, but never both at the same time, for the apparatus has to configure itself differently for each.

The metaphor of the blind man and the cane, which Bohr used to explain his construct of complementarity (Barad, 2007), can help us understand the role of agential cuts. When the blind man holds the cane loosely as he explores his way around a room, the cane, bouncing in his hand in response to being tapped against physical objects, becomes an extension of those objects, and therefore is an object of interest; however, when the man holds the cane firmly and taps it against physical objects, he perceives are reverberations in his hand, up his arm, and perhaps further into his body. In this configuration, the cane is an extension of his body, and therefore is an instrument of observation. The knowledge apparatus that is the entanglement of the blind man, the cane, and the objects in the room can never be configured in such a way that the cane is simultaneously an object of interest and an instrument of observation, for each requires a different arrangement (one involving a tight grip, the other a loose grip). For the cane to become an object of interest, the man must perform an agential cut, creating 'exteriority within' the knowledge apparatus, which is the agential separability that enables the cane to transition from an instrument of observation to an object of interest. This is what captains do throughout their fishing practice, and it is part and parcel of their (posthumanistic) indeterminacy-driven ecological sensemaking.

The data indicate that ecological sensemaking in the GOA trawl context involves the transformation of indeterminacy into determinacy, recurrently. More particularly, the process moves from indeterminacy as to what comes next, to the ensuing creation of a proposition as to what story one might be able to tell after taking particular instrumental action, to the taking of that instrumental action, which includes the enactment of an agential cut that separates knowledge practices from the objects of interest, to the manifestation of new material outcome, and then to the telling of a story of what came next. Such a story solidifies what was made, fixing specific boundaries, properties, and meanings into experience, turning past indeterminacy into present determinacy. Yet a story of what has happened also involves the unearthing of new indeterminacy as the sensemaker, needing to carry on with organizational practices, looks toward a new future from a newly entangled present. And thus indeterminacy-driven sensemaking carries forth. The following story a captain told of a fishing trip exemplifies this indeterminacy-driven ecological sensemaking:

I've gone over [to the fishing grounds] the day before a [seasonal] closure and I've steamed back home empty because of the weather. I made a decision of safety over dollars, and that's the decision, and it's a tough one to do. I turned around five times, steamed, steamed back, shitty; steamed, steamed back, shitty; steamed, steamed back, shitty. Five times I did it, and I finally said, 'fuck it I'm going home, safety first,' and forfeited a load of fish.

At first glance this may seem like a story of decision-making, namely the "decision of safety over dollars." Thus, while this quote could be analyzed as a story about rational decision-making, doing so would not only leave out much of what happened, it would also give a false impression of the event. A key piece that would be missing involves how the captain carves out and interprets his environment, particularly how such interpretations are conditioned by ecological phenomena, how his interpretive processes and his relations with natural phenomena constituted one another through time and space, how those entangled boundaries, properties, and meanings in turn shaped the proposition the captain made regarding story he would be able to tell after arriving at his chosen fishing spot, how those processes were entangled with regulatory and market factors, how they all co-articulated what materialized at his chosen fishing spot, and in turn shaped his ensuing proposition to leave without fishing. In conducting such an analysis, the entangled human-natural factors that had agency in how the captains' fishing process unfolded would come to light, rather than leaving us with merely human factors. Thus, instead of focusing solely on the captain's decision-making, it would be more informative to focus on the entangled factors, such as the captains' practices, regulatory and market boundaries, the rough seas, and the aggregation of fish beneath the vessel, among others, and how they articulated what the captain conjectured to do next before and after arriving at his fishing spot, and what he found there.

At second blush the captain's process may seem like an issue of sensemaking that arose due to a violated expectation, namely the expectation of being able to fish in a particular spot. Such an understanding, however, confuses expectation with prognostication, and misplaces the location, and mistakes the temporal orientation, of the sense that was made. A different sort of sensemaking comes to light once we appreciate the agency that natural phenomena have in captains' conjectures of what comes next. One such phenomenon is the weather: When captains talk about where or when they will fish, their discussions usually involve a qualifier related to weather, such as the one stated in unison by three captains when, during a meeting, the fleet was asked when they were going to start fishing: "It depends on the weather." The following statement by another captain, also during a fleet meeting, drives home the same idea: "I've only been here for 27 years but I don't think any of us could call the weather on the 15th or 16th which is four days from now; I can't call the weather frickin' 24 hours ahead." Generally, if a captain is the first to steam to a certain spot, or is lacking information from captains who are already in a spot, he knows he cannot be sure what the weather will be like in that spot until after he is there; and even then the weather may soon change. In the example above the captain created a proposition as to what the range of 'might occurs' could be at his chosen fishing spot, all the time knowing that he could only tell if the proposition was true or false after arriving there. Rather than expecting a certain outcome at that spot, the captain expected to learn what the outcome would be through his instrumental action of steaming there and enacting the agential cut that determines a particular place as 'the spot.' Of course, natural phenomena existed at his destination prior to him arriving there, but the weather, with its particular boundaries, properties, and meanings, as it occurred in relation with the captain's sensemaking, did not; the weather only materialized through his ecological sensemaking apparatus.

Yet, the weather did not just materialize through the captain's activity. As Chapter 6 argues, natural phenomena are not mere passive participants in captains' ecological sensemaking process. One of the reasons the captain did not know until he arrived at his fishing spot was that the natural phenomena that constitute 'the weather' is inherent in captains' ecological sensemaking apparatuses, co-articulating certain boundaries, properties, and meanings, shaping the locations and timings of captains' agential cuts. In other words, natural phenomena, such as the entanglements we know as 'the weather,' have agency in captains' sensemaking.

While the captain undoubtedly engaged in sensemaking throughout his journey, it was only after arriving at his chosen spot that his sense of what the weather actually was materialized, or became determinate. Such sense, however, is largely about what *has* happened, not what *will* happen. In the face of ongoing, pervasive indeterminacy, the question of what to do next requires a conjecture, a proposition as to the sense one will be able to make after taking particular instrumental action. Captains move from one phase of their fishing practice to the next, from steaming to a certain place to towing in a certain space, and from towing in a certain space to steaming to a new place, *conjecturally*. They do not merely act with the bravado of expectation, but also, and perhaps predominantly, with the wisdom of ongoing prognostication, its elaboration through instrumental action, its determination through the strategic placement of agential cuts, and its retrospective elaboration into a story of what was happening; these are all boundary-, property-, and meaning-making intra-activities, which together constitute ecological sensemaking apparatuses. Apparatuses change as contexts change, and different apparatuses articulate different instrumental actions, including different agential cuts, and therefore different senses of what has happened. Captains know all too well that, at sea, where they have to carry out their practices while constitutively embedded in an entanglement of human and natural activity, 'ignorance and knowledge grow together' (Meacham, 1983, as discussed in Weick, 1993); in other words, indeterminacy as to what comes next is embedded in determinacy of what has happened, and determinacy of what has happened is embedded with indeterminacy as to what comes next.

While this more conjectural form of ecological sensemaking is apparent when captains make relatively major shifts to demonstrably different phases in their practice, it is also apparent on a much smaller scale. In the following a captain, describing 'three kinds of fishermen,' alludes to this smaller-scale prevalence of indeterminacy-driven ecological sensemaking:

See, there are three different kinds of fishermen here in the trawl fleet. You have the hunters. They hunt down their target. They make short little tows here and there in different areas where they know there are biomasses of the target that they are after. And once they make their short little tows and they find it, they will take a stroke on it, and they will go—these are the hunters—they will go a little further on one end and see if their halibut bycatch goes up or not. And if it doesn't they will turn around, they will dump it and they will make another tow, and they will tow a little further the other way where they found their target. Just a little bit. Just a little bit more on each end. They say, "Oh, OK it's still clean." Then, all of a sudden they will see it's a little harder bottom or a change in habitat or change in structure, and they will go "Oh, hey, we got a few more halibut," and they will go, "We had better not be going up in here," so they will turn around and take it a little further the other way. They are trying to stay with that target, and it's moving—they are trying to stay with that fish as it goes. Those are your hunters, and you are going to find that your hunters have a lot less bycatch than your gatherers.

OK, your gatherers are people who set the net, open up a book, tow four or five hours, something stupid, haul back, and go, "Oh God, I gotta get out of here." Everybody should be a hunter. Everybody should fish like hunters. They should narrow down their target, they should make a 20-minute tow, a 15-minute tow, a 30-minute tow, and say, "OK, here is my target." Gatherers are a bunch of [idiots].

OK, and then the third kind, these are savvy fishermen, these guys are really good. [They are] great fisherman, they catch a lot of fish and keep their bycatch numbers real low most of the time ... They are just uncanny, they are really good ... And they have been fishing for a long, long time too. They know where to go, they know what to look for, they know how to make their gear work in any different situation to its utmost potential.

It is clear that the hunters, and we can assume savvy fishermen as well, engage in a process involving creation and discovery, wisdom and ignorance, in which they do not presume to have an accurate depiction of what the future will be, or to expect to know what the 'correct' story is, but instead aim to make certain conjectures and to take certain actions that will imbue their practices with ever-increasing potentiality for telling certain desired stories about what happened. From the articulation of each story hunters and savvy fishermen can adjust ensuing con-jectures, instrumental actions, including agential cuts, in order to change their potential and hopefully tell better stories as they continue to shape how their practices materialize. Note that at the heart of this ever increasing potentiality are captains' placements of agential cuts between their objects of interest, such as the composition of the biomasses beneath their vessels, and their instruments of extraction, which are constituted by their sonars, trawl nets, vessel operations, and their own sensemaking (among other factors). In fact, it appears that what differ-entiates the hunters and savvy fishermen from the gatherers is how strategically they enact those agential cuts. The processes that captains undergo to make sense encompass inseparable conjecture and action, storymaking and storytelling, meaning and matter, sense and making. Captains do not so much expect that certain things will occur after taking certain instrumental action as they expect to learn what has occurred, and to then use that learning to produce conjectures that foster instrumental actions and that enable them to make agential cuts that allow them to get closer to telling the retrospective stories that they want to tell.

Abductive ecological sensemaking

I have argued that indeterminacy-driven ecological sensemaking is how trawl captains determine what to do next, the next step is to dive deeper into the propositional part of indeterminacy-driven ecological sensemaking.. To do so I first turn to two classic modes of inquiry for help: induction and deduction. When engaging in sensemaking, people act their way into understanding (Weick, 1995); when engaging in rational decision-making people understand their way into acting (Elster, 1989). Sensemaking, therefore, is more akin to induction, in which people create new knowledge through acting, while rational decision-making is more akin to deduction, in which people act based on what they already know. The inductive relationship between acting and knowing, in which acting fosters knowing, is at the heart of the sensemaking axiom, "cognition lies in the path of action" (Weick, 1988, p. 307), as well as the sensemaking 'formula,' "How can I know what I think until I see what I say?" (Weick, 1979, 1995, citing Wallas, 1926) Yet, in the examples provided thus far, captains are doing more than just acting inductively, for they must know *something* in order to produce propositions and take the instrumental actions of steaming to a particular place on the fishing grounds and towing from a particular area beneath the vessel. The examples indicate that captains also act deductively by drawing on past experience and established knowledge. Thus, captains' process of creating a proposition regarding what to do next in order to be able to tell a story they want tell involves both induction *and* deduction.

This glance at induction and deduction points us to a third mode of inquiry that incorporates both: abduction. Abduction is a process of "intelligent guessing" that produces propositions (conjectures, hypotheses, guesses) as to what will happen if certain action is taken (Peirce, 1931–1958, cited in Rescher, 1978,p. 42). As Charles Sanders Peirce (1839–1914), known as 'the father of abduction,' outlined, "deduction proves that something *must* be; Induction shows that something *actually is* operative; Abduction merely suggests that something *may be*" (Peirce, 1955, p. 171, emphasis original).[1] A deductive process tests the truthfulness of previous understandings; An inductive process identifies new contextual information; An abductive process draws from previous understandings and contextual information to produce a proposition that guides processes of inquiry forward. Thus, abduction, as stated by Rescher (1978, p. 47), "tells us where to shine the beam of inquiry's lamp. There is no point in researching, however carefully, in the wrong spot." In other words, abduction, drawing from previous experience and bounded, propertied, and given meaning by contextual relations (i.e., entangled natural, regulatory, social, technological, and market factors), provides the conjecture that feeds instrumental action, which together with agential cuts articulate the matter and the sense that materializes, such as a story of what is happening at a place on the fishing grounds, or what was hauled up from the depths after towing.

The relationship between sensemaking and abduction has been occasionally discussed (e.g., Jeong & Brower, 2008; Maitlis & Sonenshein, 2010; Weick, 2006, 2010, 2012), used as an analytical method (e.g., Cunliffe & Coupland, 2012; Kramer, 2007), and found to be embedded in empirical phenomena (e.g., Abolafia, 2010; Patriotta, 2003). As Weick describes, abduction comes into play when sensemaking requires "vocabularies of the invisible (e.g., faith, belief)" (2006, p. 1730). Patriotta (2003), studying 'breakdowns, interruptions, technical perturbations' on the shop floor of a car manufacturing plant, characterizes sensemaking as an abductive "detective process." Such a process starts with a detected anomaly, after which a search for an explanation ensues, which involves "the formation of conjectures based on the collection of evidence in the form of clues" (ibid., p. 368). Likewise, Abolafia (2010) found abduction to be a key part of the sensemaking that occurred in meetings of the Federal Reserve, in which abduction is "the means by which policy makers question their policy models in terms of their knowledge of the current environment. They compare the ideal relationship in the model to the real one represented by current events" (p. 353). In other words, members of the Federal Reserve produce "a conjecture that is tested by fitting it over the facts" (ibid., citing Polkinghorne, 1988, p. 19). Both of these studies of the abductive nature of sensemaking bear much resemblance to what captains do at sea: they face a mystery as to what they will find at a certain fishing spot, or what they will haul up from a space beneath the vessel, or what will change as they tow a little further one way or the other, and as a result act as detectives by formulating conjectures, which they in turn test by fitting them over the facts as they take instrumental action.

In addition to integrating abduction into sensemaking analyses, the previous studies also point to an overlap of abduction and one of sensemaking's core processes. Weick discusses this overlap in stating that "abduction incorporates a fundamental act of sensemaking, namely, the connection of a *cue to a frame*" (Weick, 2012, p. 148; emphasis added). By 'cue,' Weick means a physical or conceptual thing, an entity, that has been carved out of the sea of actuality one is constitutively embedded in, identified as meaningful, and brought to the foreground of experience. Thus, cues are conceptual or physical matters-of-fact that have materialized through boundary-making activities, such as conjecturing and taking instrumental action. And by 'frame,' Weick means the conceptual structures guide activities as they carve out and foreground cues, and organize and interrelate them into something that matters (i.e., materiality) (Weick, 1995).

The connection of a cue to a frame in the production of sense is implied in both the sensemaking and abduction literatures. In terms of the abduction literature, Harrowitz (1983, p. 190) states that abduction merges an observed fact (i.e., the cue) with an explanatory rule (i.e., the frame), and "the observed fact is read through the rule," which produces a new "case" (i.e., sense). Similarly, Schruz (2008, p. 205) characterizes abduction as consisting of the merger of "beliefs or cognitive mechanisms which drive the abduction" (i.e., the frame) with "evidence which the abduction intends to explain" (i.e., the cue). Meanwhile, parts of the sensemaking literature look much the same: Weick et al. (2005, p. 410) state, "To make sense is to connect the abstract [i.e., the frame] with the concrete [i.e., the cue]," while according to Mills (2003. p. 53), "In essence, everyday sensemaking involves a frame, a cue, and a connection"; Likewise, Jeong and Brower (2008, p. 230) argue that sensemaking is "a kind of combining process in which the cue is connected to a frame of reference, through which a state of affairs (meaning) of the cue is constructed," and according to Islam (2013, p. 34), people use stories to make sense by "relating the particular [i.e., the cue] and the universal [i.e., the frame]."

While all sensemaking incorporates abduction, when sensemaking is driven by indeterminacy rather than violated expectations, abduction takes on a defining role. This is because resolving indeterminacy involves the boundary-making activities of abducting a proposition as to what story one will be able to tell after taking certain instrumental actions, taking those instrumental actions, and then telling a story of what happened. These boundary-making activities function to articulate the sea of entanglements captains are constitutively embedded in a certain way, such that certain matter and meanings are physically articulated. In other words, they form a particular apparatus through which certain materials are performed. The ultimate product of such articulations is a newly materialized actuality, such as a new spot on the fishing grounds, a new sign on the sonar, a new space beneath the vessel to tow through, or new catch on deck. In this newly materialized actuality is new potentiality for enacting ensuing new actuality. Yet, due to the pervasive indeterminacy of being entangled with natural phenomena, the relationship between new and future actuality is indeterminate. From that indeterminacy, sensemaking re-emerges to abduct a new proposition of what to do next, to take instrumental action to bring that next into actuality, to perform a new agential cut that gives certain boundaries and properties to what is next, and then to tell a story of what that next is/was.

What this chapter to is that GOA trawl captains' processes of determining what to do next are not so much rational decision-making but ecological sensemaking; yet this ecological sensemaking is not so much defined by violated expectations as it is by indeterminacy; and in being defined by indeterminacy, ecological sensemaking takes on an abductive nature in that it relies on propositions to move processes forward into the undefined. To begin to close out this discussion, I return to the relationships between knowing and action that opened the previous chapter and elaborate how they differ for each type of process discussed thus far, and I use the captains' axiom, 'You never know until you tow' (which is discussed in greater detail in Chapter 3), to do so. This axiom contains, both explicitly and implicitly, three boundary-, property-, and meaning-making activities, two of which are cognitive—knowing and not knowing, one of which is physical—towing, all of which are mutually constitutive. The following differentiates the three types of processes discussed thus far based on the three parts of the axiom:

- Rational decision-making: You do not know, then you know, then you tow.
- Expectation-driven ecological sensemaking: You know, you tow, then you do not know.
- Indeterminacy-driven ecological sensemaking: You do not know, you tow, then you know.

In rational decision-making, people fill in all relevant gaps in information, move from not knowing to knowing, and then choose the instrumental action that will secure a pre-determined outcome; In expectation-driven ecological sensemaking, people think they know what is coming next based on expectations, they take action, after which they realize that in fact they did not know what was coming next, and then they recover by creating new expectations as to what will come next. Weick offers a similar formula: "Order, interruption, recovery. That is sensemaking in a nutshell" (Weick, 2006, p. 732). In indeterminacy-driven ecological sensemaking, however, people know that they do not know what is coming next, take instrumental action and enact the agential cut needed to bring 'next' into existence, after which they know what came next (after which they again do not know what is coming next).

Before we leave this section, I want to ward off any impression that the difference between 'expectation-driven ecological sensemaking' and 'indeterminacy-driven ecological sensemaking' is just about semantics. We can call it what we want, as long as we are talking about the same thing—the process through which one's actions are entangled with 'other' actions and, at the same time, both enact the 'otherness' of those actions and are co-constituted by those 'other' actions. Ecological sensemaking concerns how 'otherness,' primarily the otherness of the natural world, is enacted in order to create determinacy. Thus, there is no outside, there is only entanglement, which humans are not at the center of, for there is no center. There are only entangled boundary-, property-, and meaning-making relations, which engender indeterminacy as people move through their entangled practices, and therefore must engage in sensemaking to understand what their actions should be in terms of what they want to materialize through them. This is why ecological sensemaking is driven by, and the study of it should be focused on, indeterminacy.

Physical ambiguity and its operational indeterminacy

A particular fishing event that occurred in the GOA trawl fleet, as described by several captains, closes out this chapter by both illustrating the effects of indeterminacy[2] and helping to further clarify its role in ecological sensemaking.[2] The event demonstrates that the inherent ambiguity of the boundaries that we identify in entangled phenomena, and in turn the differentiated properties and meanings that are premised upon such ambiguity, results in indeterminacy as we use them to guide our organizing practices. Put simply, the superimposed nature of boundaries results in indeterminacy as to what will come next. As quantum mechanics has clarified, boundaries are inherently ambiguous when looked at with the expectation of seeing separate entities (Barad, 2007). This is because boundaries are always articulated by entangled activities; they are mutually constituted, and are never the clear dividing line, the signifier of inherent separation, that they purport to be. Thus, they do not, as Cartesian dualisms (e.g., mind–body, subject–object, society–nature, ontology–epistemology) would have us think, mark the separation of things that are constituted by their own rosters of non-relational properties. What purports to mark discrete individualities, and the boundaries that demarcate their self-contained properties and meanings, is actually constituted by entangled activities, which necessarily extend beyond the superposition of those boundaries. Although we perform agential cuts, our perceptions of clear-cut divisions, and in turn clear-cut entities and concepts, are built upon ambiguous foundations. The world articulates itself differently, but not separately (Barad, 2007).

While it was hinted at above, it becomes clear through the discussion below that ecological sensemaking functions to disambiguate the inherent physical ambiguity of boundaries, as well as the properties and meanings that those boundaries are helping to articulate. Sensemaking wrestles with the fact that "We can't know something definite about something for which there is nothing definite to know" (Barad, 2007, p. 118), and in doing so agentially cuts boundaries into physical phenomena, from which it performs differentiated properties and meanings. Sensemaking is not a tool for identifying clear, inherent distinctions, identities, and individualities, instead, it is a tool of 'agential separability' (Barad, 2007, 2014). Importantly, agential cuts, which perform "differentiation without individuation" (Barad, 2007, p. 378), run counter to 'Cartesian cuts,' which are born of presumed pre-existing and inherent individualities (from which we get Cartesian dualisms). Cartesian cuts elide the 'differentiation without' part of the phrase, 'differentiation without separation,' leaving us with only passive inherent separation. Sensemaking's agential cuts, in contrast, are always enacted into inseparable phenomena; they are actively performed in addition to the differentiations that are already there, which, as noted above, is why they are 'agential.'

While the distinctions and differentiations that are agentially enacted within the sensemaking apparatus are not pre-given, they are also not arbitrary. Quite the contrary, they are physically articulated, intra-related with the differentiations and superpositions of entangled physical phenomena. Sensemaking is not merely a conceptual practice, creating differentiation that is untethered to the physical world (Berthod & Müller-Seitz, 2018; Hultin & Mähring, 2017; Stigliani & Ravasi, 2012); rather, it is always, just as theories and concepts are according to agential realism, constitutively embedded in physical phenomena. Put simply, sensemaking is always entangled 'all the way down' (Slife, 2004). What sensemaking adds to the entangled differentiations and superpositions of physical phenomena are "specific intra-actions that enact cuts that make separations – not absolute separations, but only contingent separations – within phenomena" (Barad, 2014, p. 175); such contingent separations, or agential cuts, function to give sensemakers the 'workable levels of determinacy'[3] they need to conjecture what will happen next, take instrumental action, and then tell stories of what has happened, creating inclusions, superpositions, and constitutive exclusions all along the way. Those conjectures, instrumental actions, and stories are both physically articulated and further articulate the physical world in specific ways, performing certain actualities to the exclusion of others, and those actualities are embedded with certain potentialities (also to the exclusion of others). In short, ecological sensemaking is a boundary-, property-, and meaning-making apparatus which, in the interest of creating workable levels of determinacy, performs agential cuts that are enacted into, yet entangled with, the physical articulation of the world 'all the way down.'

On to the event: "A couple or three years ago," as stated in 2012, when fishing for rock sole, which is a bottom-dwelling flatfish, GOA trawl captains encountered a particular school of fish in a particular area, at a particular depth, during a particular time of the year. According to one captain, their sonars indicated that the fish were "plastered across the bottom, glued to the bottom" and "up in the shallows." Through the entanglement of their fishing practices with the differentiating activities that constituted (non-human) natural phenomena, the captains, prior to towing, found their world to be articulating itself much like it had in the past. From that initial articulation, the captains made sense of what they saw on their sonars, namely that it suggested that rock sole were aggregating on the ocean bottom. Then they conjectured that if they towed through what they saw on their sonar, they would catch rock sole.

The captains then enacted the instrumental actions involved in towing for rock sole (e.g., developing a tow route, setting the net, beginning to tow). Yet while towing, and using their instruments to monitor their catch rates,[4] the captains found their rate to be far too high, their nets filling far too quickly, to be catching rock sole. The captains sensed that their world was articulating itself differently, namely that the physical entanglement of their fishing activities and natural phenomena was articulating boundaries and properties that demanded a different sense of what was happening (a sort of entangled physical sensegiving). The captains found themselves constitutively embedded in a new extractive apparatus, one that was mutually exclusive of the one they thought they were embedded in. As Bohr teaches us in his key contribution to quantum physics, "concepts are not ideational but rather actual physical arrangements" (Barad, 2007, p. 147); I believe the same holds for our sense of what is happening. If we take a relational perspective seriously, as quantum physics requires, then concepts are relational 'all the way down,' all the way up, and all the way around; to support the notion that the relationality of concepts expands laterally across human minds, but neither expands 'below' human minds, nor beyond human relations (i.e., is segregated to the human realm), is to, at best, sneak dualism in the backdoor. The concept of which species captains are towing for and catching is *physically* articulated by the captains' fishing apparatus. This is the whole point of the axiom, 'you never know until you tow.' What the captains found while towing in this even was that the entangled world of ecological phenomena and their practices began articulating itself differently. It is not that their previous sensemaking, part of which was which their proposition of what to do next, namely to tow in a particular space for rock sole, was *wrong* so much as the world began articulating itself differently in relation to how it had been articulating when they were making their proposition. While towing, the captains began sensing that their proposition, that they had found a place to tow for rock sole, would turn out to not conform to how the world was physically articulating itself while they were towing. Not long after realizing that they were constitutively embedded in a different extractive apparatus, the captains decided that they needed to perform the agential cut of hauling up their nets, which would enact a boundary within their extractive apparatus between their 'objects of interest' (i.e., what the species composition of the catch in their nets was) and their 'agencies of observation/extraction' (i.e., the entanglement of their nets with the ecology beneath the vessel), from which they could gain determinacy regarding what was happening. Prior to enacting such a cut, all that captains have in terms of the various species they could catch is superposition. And, after towing, the captains discovered that they in fact were not catching rock sole while they were towing, but pollock instead. As one captain put it, "It was just minutes and it was 10,000 pounds of pollock in the net. It was gonna be way too much fucking pollock, and I was sole fishing ..."

Both before and during the process of towing, the species-based boundaries, properties, and meanings of the ecological phenomena that captains are entangled with are inherently ambiguous. Captains can only resolve this ambiguity by enacting the *additional* intra-actions, i.e., agential cuts, of hauling up their nets, examining their catch, and segregating it into species-based categories. In enacting these additional intra-actions, captains are enacting new differentiations, new boundaries, which open up the door to new properties and meanings (such as target fish vs. bycatch, and regular bycatch vs. prohibited species bycatch). Thus, it is only in towing that captains can turn the indeterminacy that is inherent in their practice before and during the process of towing into determinacy. As one captain described in this event, "somebody was towing for sole and then started seeing this stuff that just added up so fast, and then they hauled up a huge bag of pollock." Critically, captains cannot simply change what they are thinking while towing, or before towing, to resolve the indeterminacy inherent in their practice, and in turn create the determinacy of agential separability; they can create new propositions, but they still 'never know until they tow.' This is because indeterminacy is physically articulated, and therefore captains have to take action to physically perform the boundaries from which differentiated properties and meanings can be made (i.e., sense), which resolves the indeterminacy. As Barad puts it:

> meaning should not be understood as a property of individual words or groups of words. Meaning is neither intralinguistically conferred nor simply extra-linguistically referenced. Meaning is made possible through specific material practices. Semantic contentfulness is achieved not through the thoughts or performances of individual agents but through particular discursive practices.
>
> (Barad, 2007, p. 148)

The conceptual derives its meaningfulness from its differentiated embodiment in physical materiality. We get into trouble when we act as if the differentiations inherent in our concepts are physically embodied, when in fact they are not, i.e., when there is no matter of fact. Put differently, we get into trouble when the world is articulating itself differently, and we do not do so as well. It is not a question of the accuracy of one's sensemaking, for the sense one makes at the outset is also physically articulated; instead, it is a question of the ongoing coherence of one's entanglement 'all the way down.' Captains make propositions as to what they may catch at the outset, or more specifically, what stories they may be able to tell after towing, but the species-based meaning of their catch cannot be enacted until they after tow and haul up their catch, and in doing so physically enact the boundary-making relations that enable specific species-based properties and meanings to be physically articulated (either on the back decks of their vessels or in processing plants). Thus, it is only after they tow that captains are capable of segregating catch into mutually exclusive categories.

So what does all of this mean for real world practices and outcomes? Let's return to the quote above in which the captain stated, "It was just minutes and it was 10,000 pounds of pollock in the net. It was gonna be way too much fucking pollock, and I was sole fishing ..." What this captain means by 'way too much fucking pollock' is that federal fishery regulations allow up to 20% of catch on board, when one is fishing for rock sole, to be pollock (if pollock fisheries are closed, otherwise catching mostly pollock would mean that a captain has, intentionally or unintentionally, transitioned into the pollock fishery; similar percentages apply to combinations of various other target species). Under such conditions, captains have to discard any pollock they catch beyond 20% of the total catch they have on board (according to captains' real-time, *in situ* estimates, which tend to be pretty accurate). All of the discarded pollock in this event (as well as all discarded pollock in any fishing event) was wasted because all pollock are dead by the time they are hauled up from the depths and deposited on the back of a vessel. Captains know what they were catching after they intra-act the boundary-making activity of hauling up their nets and examining their contents, yet at that point the vast majority of the fish they caught is already dead (save 33% of the Pacific halibut and 20% of the crab; NPFMC 2007, 2014). Thus, an outcome of this event was hundreds of tons of wasted pollock that captains in turn had to, as one put it, "go out and catch again" (figuratively speaking of course) when the next pollock season opened a few months later. Another outcome of the event, however, was that captains learned that not only can rock sole be "up in the shallows" and "plastered across the bottom" at "35 fathoms deep in the fall," but pollock can as well. The captains gained a new sense of certain ecological phenomena, which was physically articulated by the entanglement of their fishing practice with ecological phenomena. Thus, from the actuality of this experience, the captains gained new potentiality for enacting certain desired material into, and excluding other undesired material from, future experiences. One captain alludes to their newfound boundary-, property-, and meaning-making potentiality in the following: "You got to know it's there. You can see it on both sonars, but if you didn't know what it was you would drive right over it ... you wouldn't think it was pollock at 35 fathoms in the fall."

But this sensemaking-based outcome does not resolve the problem of inde-terminacy. This is the problem in which boundaries are inherently mutually con-stituted, and therefore ambiguous in relation to clear-cut species-based categories of target catch and bycatch, and of retainable and prohibited species bycatch (which is, by regulation, not retainable). Captains are still faced with indeterminacy both before and during the process of towing, and the accompanying problem in which after towing it is too late—determinacy is gained, but the vast majority of the catch is dead. Which in turn means that the parts of the catch that cannot be retained and sold, such as prohibited species catch (see Chapters 2 and 3 for a discussion of prohibited species catch), is wasted. Until captains' ecological sensemaking apparatus can only remove fish from beneath the vessel that can be sold, the indeterminacy of commercial trawl fishing will lead to bycatch.

Yet, bycatch does not have to equal waste. The boundaries between retainable, usable, or sellable bycatch and bycatch that is wasted are not articulated by nature, nor by captains, alone, but also by markets and regulations. Boundary-, property-, and meaning-making relations enacted by markets and regulations within at-sea fishing practices co-articulate millions of tons of wasted natural resources worldwide each year (Kelleher, 2005), such that approximately 27% of catch is wasted between the time it is caught and would be consumed; the number raises to 35% of pre-catch waste is included (FAO, 2018, citing Gustavsson et al., 2011). In this book I theoretically and empirically demonstrate why it is not only unreasonable to expect captains to enact boundary-making relations that segregate ecological phenomena into discrete species-based categories both before and during the process of towing, but that such expectations run counter to physical science. The more reasonable approach, the one that is more scientifically grounded, would be to require any actors who enact boundaries into at-sea practices to take responsibility for the deleterious effects of their intra-actions with extractive apparatuses. At the very least those who enact boundaries that co-articulate the waste of natural resources should be required to demonstrate *why* they cannot alter or remove those boundaries, and why such boundaries are worth the wasted natural resources that they help articulate. Yet, thus far actors such as regulators and market managers, who enact such waste-articulating boundaries into at-sea fishing apparatuses, are largely excluded from sharing responsibility for the immense amount of waste they contribute to each year. Instead the onus is placed almost entirely on the shoulders of captains.

Captains make sense of what they may potentially find in particular fishing spots after steaming there, and what they may catch from particular spaces after towing there. Yet they also know that the physical articulation of their fishing practice and the material phenomena it is constitutively embedded in lacks specificity. Captains know that what they will find on the fishing grounds, and what they will haul up from the depths, will always be a superposition, and thus will be determined as much by the boundary-, property-, and meaning-making activities of natural phenomena as it is will be by the boundary-, property-, and meaning-making activities of their fishing practice, including regulatory and market-based relations. The accuracy-based view of ecological sensemaking elides entanglement, and in turn the agency that non-human natural phenomena, as well as such intra-acting phenomena as markets and regulations, have in the articulation of both fishing practices and their outcomes at sea. Savvy fishermen 'know how to make their gear work in any different situation to its utmost potential,' but they also know that what they catch with that gear is co-determined by the entangled market, regulatory, and non-human ecological and geophysical activities that they are entangled with.

To study and ultimately help manage and regulate ecological sensemaking is to recognize the articulating role that both human and natural phenomena play in the apparatus that is ecological sensemaking. Within ecological sensemaking, human social processes, which include the boundary-making effects of regulations and markets, and the material processes of nature are mutually constituted, as is the sense, the catch, and the waste that materializes through that entanglement. The ensuing chapters take a dive deep into the mutually constituted nature of captains' ecological sensemaking. In doing so they make the case that propositions of what will come next, locations and timings of agential cuts, and stories of what came next, are not exclusively performed by captains. Instead, they are co-created by the mutually constituted boundary-making activity of captains, natural phenomena, regulations, and markets.

Notes

1 'Abduction' is accompanied by what Peirce called "retroduction," in which the proposition is assessed in relation to concrete experience after instrumental action is taken. Thus, abduction is followed by retroduction, which subjects the proposition to empirical testing. While Peirce seems to have eventually called the entire process 'retroduction,' here I use the more familiar 'abduction' to describe the process of producing a proposition as to what will come next, i.e., what story will be able to be told after taking certain instrumental action.

2 From now on I will use 'ecological sensemaking' to encompass both 'indeterminacy-driven ecological sensemaking' and 'expectation-driven ecological sensemaking,' for the two are most likely complementary (though, as I argue, I believe indeterminacy-driven ecological sense-making is much more prevalent). I will differentiate them when it seems necessary to do so.

3 I use 'workable level of *determinacy*,' rather than the more common 'workable level of *certainty*' (in terms of the sensemaking literature) for two reasons. First, I do so to emphasize that, in the context of the book, managers do not presume to be able to gain complete determinacy, and thus are working to reduce indeterminacy. Second, I use 'indeterminacy' rather than 'certainty' due to the (over)emphasis on expectations in the sensemaking literature. When managers act with expectations for what will come next, they indeed may reach certainty. In the sensemaking elaborated in this book, however, managers are not so much expecting a particular thing to *come* next, but instead to learn what *came* next. Thus, they act in order to bring what they want to come next into existence, while knowing that, in being entangled with natural phenomena, what comes next is not just up to them.

4 Catch rates are produced through the use of magnetic instruments that are attached to different sections of a codend as it is being towed behind the vessel; those instruments produce a signal when the sections of the codend they are attached to are inflated with captured fish. Different sections produce different signals, which are perceived by a receptor in the wheelhouse. The meeting of signals and receptors enables captains to track the progression of their codend being filled with catch, section by section. When this progression is paired with time, a catch rate is created.

5

THE PROPOSITIONAL NATURE OF ECOLOGICAL SENSEMAKING

The previous chapters rejected rational decision-making as an appropriate framework to use to understand commercial trawl fishing operations in the Gulf of Alaska (GOA), and argued that a more suitable perspective is ecological sensemaking. Chapter 4 also argued, however, that ecological sensemaking must be adapted to account for the ongoing and pervasive situation in which managers are faced with indeterminacy stemming from the inherently ambiguous nature of their entangled relationship with ecological phenomena. Thus, Chapter 4 followed in the footsteps of Chapter 3 by continuing to elaborate ecological sensemaking through the lens of Karen Barad's agential realism (e.g., Barad, 1998, 2003, 2007, 2014). In this view, ecological sensemaking is an apparatus through which the boundaries, properties, and meanings that constitute fishing practices are mutually constituted by both human and (non-human) natural activities, which are themselves constitutively entangled (Chapter 6 dives deeper into the this entanglement, its role within and its effects on ecological sensemaking). This adaptation also involved incorporating Charles Sanders Peirce's concept of abduction into ecological sensemaking as a way to understand how it co-enacts its boundary-, property-, and meaning-making relations. In this updated version, ecological sensemaking involves the activities through which front-line managers, facing the indeterminacy of future actualities, engage in abduction to conjecture which instrumental action they need to take next so that in the future, after arriving at the next place or phase in their practice and enacting a particular agential cut that creates local and contingent separability between themselves and certain ecological materialities, they can potentially tell a certain desired story about what happened (e.g., a story of finding a large aggregation of fish, or catching a large amount of target species in a short amount of time). Ecological sensemaking is how frontline managers conjecture an answer to some version of the question 'What's next?', take instrumental action to bring what's next into actuality, after which they answer some version of the question, 'What's the story here?' In doing so managers move their practices forward, and ultimately turn the indeterminate into the determinate.

In an indeterminate world, it is through ecological sensemaking that determinate boundaries, properties, and meanings emerge. Yet from this determinacy *in*determinacy re-emerges as managers, needing to continue with their entangle practices, again find themselves faced with an indeterminate future. Ecological sensemaking is triggered not so much by an actual world that is found to be unlike the expected world (an understanding that has dualism and representationalism at its core), but instead by a world in flux, a world in the throes of creative emergence, a world that is articulating itself differently, which sensemaking processes are never apart from, but instead is always constitutively embedded in. Ecological sensemaking is, quite literally, sense-in-the-making, but in which what is doing the 'making' is both the human and the (entangled) physical world. For humans, sensemaking involves the need to determine what to do next as the world is articulating itself differently, in which what one does next is constitutively embedded in that articulation, as well as the need to determine what came next, recurrently. There is no break in entanglement, only local and contingent separabilities enacted through agential cuts; sensemaking, and its sensemakers, are always 'relational all the way down' (Slife, 2004). As Chapter 4 demonstrated, when captains sense that the world is articulating itself differently, sensemaking is not about representing and understanding an external world, instead it is about co-enacting boundaries, properties, and meanings that perform particular materializations, which articulate unambiguous meanings in the place where ambiguities had materialized. Making sense is an entangled continuation of, and an agentive participant in, the physical world articulating itself differently, but never separately, whether it is a physical world of people or fish (or both).

The entangled physical articulation of meaning at the heart of ecological sensemaking is why it, and perhaps 'physical sensemaking' more broadly, when properly construed, speak to something that is foundational to sensemaking, and that is largely missing from the current sensemaking literature. Meaning emerges by way of entangled human, technological, ecological, and geophysical actions that co-perform the boundaries, properties, and meanings necessary for the emergence of an unambiguous understanding of what has happened. If the world were, from a Cartesian perspective, constituted by separate minds and bodies, subjects and objects, ontologies and epistemologies, internal and external realities, sensemaking would look a lot like rational decision-making. A Cartesian view of practice at the frontline of natural resource extraction commits the fallacy of crafting determinacy by taking what has been differentiated through entangled actions (e.g., fish that are separated into discrete species categories after towing) and back-engineering those differentiations into actuality as inherent separations that were there all the time, prior to the act of differentiating, simply awaiting their proper representation (see Alfred North Whitehead's fallacy of misplaced concreteness; Whitehead, 1967b). From this Cartesian view of fishing practices the notion that if knowledge practices are just good enough, and often virtuous enough, then the people enacting them can know what the separate and internally separated world looks like in the present, and will look like in the future. This fallacy has unfortunately been cemented into the foundations of various scholarly domains (e.g., economics, political science, natural resource management), as well as into the structures of natural resource regulations and management practices. The institutionalization of this fallacy creates the problem in which we attempt to regulate, and in turn manage, resource extraction practices from an erroneous starting point.

What we need is a different framework for understanding, managing, and regulating resource extraction practices; the previous chapters, this chapter, and ensuing chapters constitute one attempt to offer one. The next step in this process is to transform what we have learned thus far into a visual framework, which will help us learn more. To create such a framework, this chapter dives deeper into the ecological sensemaking process elucidated in Chapter 4 in order to bring its core structure to the foreground, which forms the backbone of the framework. To produce this backbone I use Peirce's abduction as an entryway into Alfred North Whitehead's theory of propositions, and then I use Whitehead's theory of propositions as a window back onto Weick's sensemaking and Barad's agential realism. The structure that emerges is based on the transitional relationship between 'actuality' and 'potentiality,' which, as elaborated by Whitehead, are "natural starting points for understanding types of existence" (Whitehead, 1968, p. 70). According to organizational scholar Tor Hernes, the transition between actuality and potentiality is "a general principle of processes" (Hernes, 2008, p. 43). This chapter argues that, in the face of the indeterminacy of future actuality, ecological sensemaking is fundamentally concerned with managing the ongoing transition from actuality to potentiality and from potentiality to actuality, recurrently. Thus, this chapter elucidates the mechanics of how ecological sensemaking, in its entangled abductive and intra-active nature, moves practices forward in the face of indeterminacy. From these arguments I produce a framework for understanding and studying frontline practices in commercial fishing (which, I believe, is applicable to broader resource extraction contexts).

Whitehead's propositions

In the previous chapter, Charles Sanders Peirce's abduction contributed to our updated understanding of ecological sensemaking. Peirce's work has some overlap with the work of Alfred North Whitehead, which in turn allows us to use the former as a gateway into the latter. This move then allows use to learn more about how both are embedded in, and shape, ecological sensemaking.

Both Peirce and Whitehead were philosophers of science; both were concerned with the role of the conjectural, or as Whitehead preferred, the propositional, aspects of experience; and both worked to clarify the relationship between the abstract and the concrete in terms of the development of knowledge and science, and the creative advance of experience. But Whitehead goes much deeper in terms of understanding propositions (at least in my limited reading). Propositions were so important to Whitehead, in fact, that he categorized them as one of "four main types of entities in the universe" (Whitehead, 1978, p. 188). According to Whitehead, "a proposition is a notion about actualities, a suggestion, a theory, a supposition about things. Its entertainment in experience subserves many purposes" (Whitehead, 1967a, p. 244). By 'notion,' 'suggestion,' and 'theory,' Whitehead means "hypothetical futures" (Whitehead, 1978, p. 188) or "tales that perhaps might be told about particular actualities" (ibid., p. 256). A proposition is a "lure for feeling," (ibid., pp. 184–185), which acts as a vector for moving experience from potentialities of the present to particular actualities of the future.

Propositions are tales that, in terms of ensuing actuality, can be true or false. As Whitehead put it, propositions "may be conformal or non-conformal to the actual world" (Whitehead, 1978, p. 186). Conformal propositions align with the empirical outcomes of action, such that a sense of 'what's next' is congruent with the ensuing story of 'what has happened;' this congruence, according to Whitehead, functions in "procuring stability in the life-history" (ibid., p. 187). There is little novelty in the creation and enactment of conformal propositions, for new actualities align with past actualities: "There is a reign of acquiescence" (Whitehead, 1967a, p. 194). When conformal propositions predominate, activity is patterned and recurring, and how it plays out in the future is largely how it played out in the past. Thus, conformal propositions foster recurring, and therefore recognizable, patterns of activity, allowing onlookers to say, 'there it is again.' This type of proposition is commonplace in research concerned with the more recurring, structural, and abstract aspects of organizing, such as institutions (e.g., DiMaggio & Powell, 1983; Hoffman, 1999; Meyer & Rowan, 1977) and logics (e.g., Rao, Monin, & Durand, 2003; Thornton & Ocasio, 1999). Further, conformal propositions are at the heart of what Birnholtz, Cohen, and Hoch (2007) call "organizational character," which is "the ensemble of traits, habits, or even skills that generate the distinctive set of actions that onlookers associate with an organization." Conformal propositions provide feedstock for recognizing actuality that is 'in character,' which in turn lays the foundation for recognizing actuality that is 'out of character.'

While conformal propositions involve actuality that is 'in character,' *non*-conformal propositions involve actuality that is 'out of character.' These propositions inspire onlookers to say, 'that's new' or 'that's different.' Non-conformal propositions according to Whitehead are key to the creative advance of experience: "In their primary role, [non-conformal propositions] pave the way along which the world advances into novelty. Error is the price which we pay for progress" (1978, p. 187). By 'error' Whitehead means that non-conformal propositions are 'wrong' in terms of the relationship between the actuality that was propositioned to materialize , i.e., the story they thought that certain instrumental actions, including agential cuts, would enable them to tell, and the actuality that did materialize. In being untrue, non-conformal propositions are the source of variation of interest, unrealized possibilities, what could have been, and what else may be. Thus, when a non-conformal proposition is enacted, according to Whitehead, "A novelty has emerged into creation. The novelty may promote or destroy order; it may be good or bad. But it is new, a new type of individual, and not merely a new intensity of individual feeling" (1978, p. 187). Non-conformal propositions, therefore, align with one of the key attributes of abduction, namely its function in producing novelty (Rescher, 1978); As Peirce argued, "[Abduction] is the only kind of reasoning which supplies new ideas" (as cited in Rescher, 1978). Understood in terms of Whitehead's work, abduction supplies new ideas through the enactment of non-conformal propositions.

Determining if propositions are conformal or non-conformal, true or false, necessitates their empirical enactment. Such determinations require looking back from the actuality of the enactment of a proposition to the potentiality of its abductive creation. Thus, the conformal or non-conformal nature of a proposition is only known retrospectively after instrumental actions, including agential cuts, have enacted new actualities into experience, from which sensemakers solve the lingering puzzle of 'what's next?' Such a resolution materializes as sensemakers answer the other sensemaking question, 'what's the story here?' This means that the determination of a proposition as conformal or non-conformal occurs when the indeterminate becomes determinant, and thus when a sense of what is happening materializes. Both types involve a leap of faith into indeterminacy, even though they produce different types of ensuing determinacy.

Both conformal and non-conformal propositions are evident in the example that ended Chapter 4, in which captains enacted a non-conformal proposition regarding fishing for and catching rock sole, and instead catching pollock. The example illustrates how propositions determined to be non-conformal are a source of discovery, and in turn new potentiality. This new potentiality can be seen in one captain's statement, "You got to know it's there. You can see it on both sonars, but if you didn't know what it was you would drive right over it … you wouldn't think it was pollock at 35 fathoms in the fall." Thus, only through the non-conformal nature of their proposition that what they saw on their sonars, which had properties of being 'up in the shallows' and 'at 35 fathoms in the fall,' was intra-active with rock sole beneath the vessel, could captains in turn expand their potentiality to later propose that those same properties could also lead to catching pollock. The upshot is that the conformal or non-conformal nature of a proposition is *physically* articulated across entangled human and non-human phenomena; thus, not only is a proposition articulated by the human, natural, conceptual and physical boundary-making relations that constitute the apparatus through which it emerges, but so is its assessment as true or false, i.e., conformal or non-conformal.

It is clear that there are no conformal propositions without non-conformal propositions, and there are no non-conformal propositions without conformal propositions. Each type is dependent on the other, and each is enabler and constrainer of the other. As it is suggested from the sensemaking formula, 'How can I know until I see what I say?,' and testified to by the trawl captains' axiom, 'You never know until you tow,' quite often people know that their propositions may very well be non-conformal (i.e., they are aware of indeterminacy), and find such non-conformity an unsurprising, and perhaps even expected, materialization of their ongoing practice. Yet we understand very little about how they go about producing and enacting propositions, assessing them, and then doing so all over again.

The actuality-potentiality structure of ecological sensemaking

Whitehead's conformal and non-conformal propositions naturally lead to the actuality-potentiality dimension of experience. This is because propositions draw from what is actual to enact what is potential, and they take what is potential and help make it actual; they exist somewhere between the ideals of pure concrete actuality and pure abstract potentiality. If, as Whitehead defines, 'actuality' is "stubborn fact which cannot be evaded" (Whitehead, 1978, p. 43), then 'potentiality' is pliable fiction which can become stubborn fact, but which can also be evaded. Pure potentiality is the realm of mere possibility, of what may be, and pure actuality is the realm of empirical reality, of what already is. As Whitehead stated, "possibility is that in which there stands achievability [i.e., potentiality], abstracted from achievement [i.e., actuality]" (Whitehead, 1967b, p. 162). Together actuality and potentiality, as will be explained below, take the form of a dimension of experience in which potentiality bounds the more concrete side of life and actuality bounds the more abstract side of life. The importance of this dimension for understanding organizing processes cannot easily be overstated: According to Hernes (2008), the transition from actuality to potentiality, and potentiality to actuality is one of the "most important characteristics" of our "complex and living world" (p. 42). Whitehead describes these concepts, and their relationship, in more detail in the following:

> The notion of potentiality is fundamental for the understanding of existence, as soon as the notion of process is admitted. If the universe be interpreted in terms of static actuality, then potentiality vanishes. Everything is just what it is. Succession is mere appearance, rising from the limitation of perception. But if we start with the process as fundamental, then actualities of the present are deriving their characters from the process, and are bestowing their characters upon the future. Immediacy is the realization of the potentialities of the past, and is the storehouse of the potentialities of the future. Hope and fear, joy and disillusion, obtain their meaning from the potentialities essential in the nature of things. We are following a trail in hope, or are fleeing from the pursuit in fear. The potentialities in immediate fact constitute the driving force of process.
>
> *(Whitehead, 1968, pp. 99–100)*

Experience is assembled in the potentiality-actuality dimension, and vacillates within it, at times focusing more on potentiality, such as when asking the sensemaking question, 'What's next?,' while at other times focusing more on actuality, such as when asking 'What's the story here?' Yet, within this dimension neither side—actuality nor potentiality—ever escapes the other's influence; they are mutually constituted.

Considerations of actuality and potentiality have long been a key part of scholarly thinking about the processual nature of reality, going as far back as Aristotle, forward to Whitehead, further forward to Nobel laureate Ilya Prigogine, and forward still more to contemporary thinkers such as sociologist Piotr Sztompka and organizational scholar Tor Hernes. While most natural and social science research deals with actuality in some form or another, a large amount also deals, both implicitly and explicitly, with potentiality. For instance, potentiality has long been a topic of psychological, developmental, and neuroscience research involving recognition and learning in human and primate infants (e.g., de Haan, Johnson, & Halit, 2003; del Giudice, Manera, & Keysers, 2009). In terms of an example of research that deals with potentiality in natural science, the 'Lamb Shift' is, as explained by Barad (2007), is an explicit measure of the effects of unrealized possibilities in protons. Willis Lamb won the Nobel Prize in Physics for its discovery in 1955, which has since had a profound effect on the field of quantum electrodynamics (e.g., Pohl et al., 2010; Wilson et al., 2011). Further, it is not a stretch to argue that all research into genetics and evolution is, in one way or another, concerned with potentiality, some quite explicitly so (e.g., Hindorff et al., 2009; Rinke et al., 2013); the same holds for research into sustainability and climate change.

Beyond scientific research, the role of potentiality in human culture, particularly the development of potentiality and its transition into actuality, is a key concern of a vast array of social institutions. For instance, all criminal justice systems around the world, which tend to concern deterrence, prevention, and rehabilitation, focus on reducing or blocking the transformation from the potentiality to commit crime into its actuality. The same logic holds for systems of education—they concern the development of potentiality embedded in actuality, and fostering the transformation of that potential into something actual. It is not a stretch to say that the elaboration of potentiality into actuality, as well as the derivation of potentiality from actuality, is one of the key dimensions of all human and non-human forms of life.

One part of life where the actuality-potentiality dimension looms large is commercial trawl fishing in the GOA. For GOA trawl captains, whether they are at the docks determining where to steam to, are on the fishing grounds determining where to tow through, or are examining their catch on the backs of their vessels to determine where to tow through and/or steam to next, actualities of the present are the storehouses of potentialities from the past, and in turn are the feedstock for potentialities for the future; potential fishing spots or towing areas of the future in turn lure the abductive creation and enactment of certain propositions in the present. A key argument of this chapter is that, when future actuality is indeterminate, ecological sensemaking, in response to the question of 'what's next?,' cuts a pathway from the potentiality of the present to a desired future by articulating propositions (which is to say, carving boundaries, properties, and meanings into the vast superpositioned realm of potentiality embedded in any actuality), and then transforming those propositions, by way of instrumental actions (which include such activities as steaming, towing, and performing agential cuts), into particular actualities. Those particular actualities are materializations from a vast array of entangled phenomena, which is bounded, propertied, and giving meaning in experience through various intra-actions. And it is here where the sensemaker, facing a new articulation of actuality, can answer the sensemaking question, 'What's the story here?'

Propositions do their work between the relatively static and ideal structures of pure potentiality and the relatively dynamic flow of pure actuality. They operate as "a manner of germaneness of a certain set of [pure potentialities] to a certain set of [pure actualities] ...They are neither pure potentials, nor pure actualities ... Entities of this impure type presuppose the two pure types of entities" (Whitehead, 1978; p. 188). While there is always an indefinite number of potentialities that can lure and bound ensuing experience, most often we do not feel that way. The feeling of something less than infinite possibility is the propositional diminution of potentiality, and it is grounded in actuality. And while we may technically be able to act in any way possible, most often we do not feel that way either. The feeling of constrained activity is the propositional diminution of actuality, and it is grounded in potentiality. All phenomena are potentially explainable, for example, as being influenced by cartoon polka-dotted pink salamanders, yet such explanations are not advisable, for they are rarely believable. The actuality of experience bounds the potential explanations that will be entertained as realistic; actuality conditions potentiality. Yet moving into the future by exiting headlong through the closest window, for example, is also typically not advisable due the potential for harm that is embedded in it. Potential actualities (i.e., 'stubborn facts which cannot be evaded') such as shards of glass getting stuck in one's body, bound the actuality that will be enacted into experience; potentiality conditions actuality.

Sensemaking operates in the transition of actuality into potentiality, and potentiality into actuality, recurrently. This operation is akin to what Whitehead considered to be the function of reason:

> Reason is a factor in experience which directs and criticizes the urge towards the attainment of an end realized in imagination but not in fact ... Reason realizes the possibility of some complex form of definiteness, and concurrently understands the world as, in one of its factors, exemplifying that form of definiteness.
>
> (Whitehead, 1929, pp. 8–9)

For Whitehead, reason operates to produce potentialities for future experience, from the standpoint of actualities of the present. I argue that, in the face of the pervasive indeterminacy of future actualities that characterize commercial trawl fishing, ecological sensemaking uses abduction to create certain potentialities (i.e., propositions) for moving forward (by way of instrumental actions) into desired actualities (e.g., a certain spot on the fishing grounds, a particular space beneath the vessel, a certain amount and composition of catch on deck). The sensemaking-based transition from actuality to potentiality, and in turn from potentiality to actuality, is depicted in Figure 5.1. As the diagram indicates, actuality and potentiality are inseparable, but the relationship of future actuality to the present actuality (depicted in the dotted line in the center), is indeterminate. Sensemaking moves, by way of abduction, from (potentiality-conditioned) actuality (lower left corner) to (actuality-conditioned) potentiality (embodied by a proposition of what to do next) (upper left corner), and

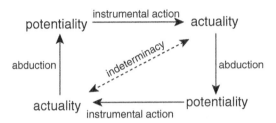

FIGURE 5.1 Ecological sensemaking framework based on Whitehead's 'actuality-potentiality formula.'

from (actuality-conditioned) potentiality, by way of instrumental action, to (potentiality-conditioned) actuality (upper right corner), which is a new place or phase in one's practice, such as a spot to fish in or a space to tow through, or catch on deck (embedded in which are the ultimate agential cuts that perform the local separations that enable such determinacies, or actualities, to take shape). The abductive and instrumental action-based activities are boundary-, property-, and meaning-making performances, which articulate something new, i.e., materiality, at each corner of the diagram. This is the skeletal structure of indeterminacy-based ecological sensemaking.

A key attribute of the actuality-potentiality framework is its relationality. By this I mean that 'actuality' and 'potentiality' are only epistemologically separable; ontologically, they are mutually constituted. This means that one does not exist without the other, that their boundaries and properties are not separately determinable, and each helps define what the other is and is not, can be and cannot. As Whitehead put it, actuality and potentially "require one another, namely actuality is the exemplification of potentiality, and potentiality is the characterization of actuality, either in concept or in fact" (Whitehead, 1968, p. 70). I take this statement to be the 'actuality-potentiality formula,' which is elaborated in terms of the framework in Figures 5.2 and 5.3. Figure 5.2 circumscribes the characterization of actuality, i.e., actuality-conditioned potentiality, as accomplished by the abductive-creation of particular potentialities (i.e., propositions); and Figure 5.3 circumscribes the exemplification of potentialities, i.e., potentiality-conditioned actualities, as accomplished by instrumental action. When the exemplification of potentiality coheres with the characterization of actuality, the process involves a conformal proposition, and when the two do not cohere, the process involves a non-conformal proposition. Both the characterization of actuality and the exemplification of potentiality constitute the 'making' of sensemaking, and 'sense' is the what materializes from the making. Sense, therefore, may be conformal or non-conformal.

Incorporating the sensemaking questions, 'What's next'? And 'What's the story here?' (Weick et al., 2005) into the framework helps further clarify how it works (see Figure 5.4 below). The sensemaking question, 'What's next?' concerns the abduction of a proposition from potentiality-conditioned actuality, namely a proposition as to what to do next in order to be able to tell a certain story in the future about what has happened (when what comes next is indeterminate); the

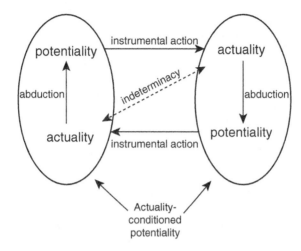

FIGURE 5.2 Ecological sensemaking framework emphasizing 'actuality-conditioned potentiality.'

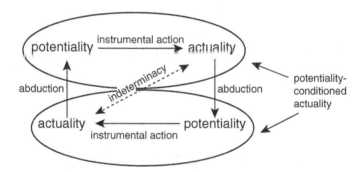

FIGURE 5.3 Ecological sensemaking framework emphasizing 'potentiality-conditioned actuality.'

sensemaking question, 'What's the story here?' concerns the elaboration of potentiality-conditioned actuality, which is the (retrospective) determination of what that next place or phase is after it was co-articulated into experience through instrumental action. Because future actuality is indeterminate in the commercial fishing context, and because captains expect propositions to be non-conformal, the exemplification of potentiality is a leap of faith, carried out by instrumental action.

Actionable propositions

For a proposition to function in the transition from (actuality-conditioned) potentiality to (potentiality-conditioned) actuality, and vice-versa, it must inspire instrumental action. Only then can new sense, which, as argued in Chapter 4, is

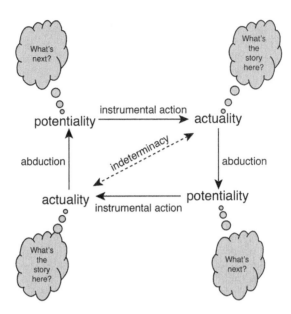

FIGURE 5.4 Ecological sensemaking framework highlighting the places where the sensemaking questions are answered.

physically articulated, materialize. Put differently, the proposition must be actionable. To study, regulate, and manage ecological sensemaking it is critical to understand what makes a proposition capable of being, or likely to be, acted upon (after which it can be judged to be conformal or non-conformal). Thus, if captains organize with natural systems by taking a leap of faith into the unknown, this begs the question, what is that faith made of? Based on the data, I argue that key attributes of actionable propositions are that they are efficient, plausible, and strategic. The following steps through each of these interdependent characteristics, and in doing so extends our understanding of the ecological sensemaking framework.

Efficient propositions

Efficiency is imperative to the within ecological sensemaking. While Peirce was a philosopher of science, he was also a scientific practitioner (he worked for the United States Coast and Geodetic Society, a precursor of the National Oceanic and Atmospheric Association), and much of his work on abduction was concerned with the missing role of practical concerns in our understanding of scientific inquiry (Rescher, 1978). Peirce argued that the idealistic understandings of science in his day, which still shape understandings of science in our day, ignored the practicalities of conducting inquiry in the real world. His elaboration of abduction encompassed the traditional lofty scientific goals of intrepidly diving into the unknown in order to emerge with new knowledge in tow, as well as practical impediments to doing so. According to Peirce, the leading consideration in abduction is "Economy of money, time, thought, and energy" (as cited in Rescher, 1978, p. 66). Scientists do not have the temporal, material, conceptual, or financial resources to engage in endless search or trial and error, and the same goes for trawl captains. For both, "Conjectural fancy is limitless, but resources are scarce and life is short" (ibid., p. 42). As business managers at sea, captains' propositions are governed by the need to efficiently progress from the (potentiality-conditioned) actuality that is the present to (actuality-conditioned) potentiality for a particular future, by way of propositions, and in turn from those propositions to particular new (potentiality-conditioned) actuality that is the determinate future, by way of instrumental action. The data indicate that concerns for efficiency pervade captains' fishing practice, especially the determination of which instrumental actions will efficiently give way to profitable actualities.

The role of efficiency in GOA trawl captains' abductive ecological sensemaking manifests as an imperative. The imperative nature of their need for efficiency stems from the fact that a necessary aspect of every commercial fishing process is the ability of the captain, crew, and owner to, as several interviewees put it, "make a living from it." Whether a fishing vessel is a small, owner-operated business or part of a corporation that owns multiple vessels and processing plants, captains have a common duty, as is the case with any business, of enacting profitable practices. More particularly, efficiency is an imperative in this context because the income of captains, crew, and owners lies in the margin between the overhead costs of catching fish and the value of caught fish. And as GOA trawl captains expressed, trawl fishing involves steep overhead costs, which they attempt to offset by catching lots of cheap fish. In the following a captain uses the framework of high volume/low margin to make this point:

> This is a high volume, low margin fishery. Unlike the crab fishery, we have high operating costs, the trawlers have the highest overhead. With towing you burn a lot of fuel. The other guys just drop their pots and pick them up. We have to tow a big net.

'High volume' indicates catching a relatively large amounts of fish, and 'low margin' indicates that the value of those fish is not far above the cost of catching them, as compared to other fishing fleets. GOA trawl captains face a heavy burden to enact profitable tows, and their job is to find a spot on the fishing grounds to steam to and an area beneath the vessel to tow through that together offer captains potentiality for catching enough fish, and doing so in a sufficiently efficient manner, to make a living.

Thus, when crafting propositions of where to steam to or where to tow through next, captains face the persistent need to enact an efficient process. One of the ways in which this persistent need manifests is the calculation that captains seem to be continually running in their heads as they enact a fishing trip. This is the calculation in which they compare the costs of fishing with the potential value of the fish they both have on board and may catch in subsequent tows. As one captain noted after completing a tow and examining the catch on the back of the vessel, "This tow only paid for itself. We had four hours invested in that tow, so we have to do better than that." Captains can make such a calculation because they know, to an approximate degree, what each trip is going to cost. Another captain demonstrated this knowledge in stating, "It's not cheap to take these things out fishing, it's not cheap. It's probably close to three thousand dollars a day just for fuel, plus [fisheries] observer costs and groceries and everything else." In fact, their calculation of comparing overheard costs with the value of caught fish starts even before leaving the docks, as a different captain exemplifies in the following:

> That's why I'm not fishing right now, the cannery wasn't going to pay enough money for the fish … They wanted me to go rock sole fishing, and I said, "I can't do it." The money isn't there because you are only getting 26 cents for those big rock sole; I mean we would get robbed. It's considered the best rock sole in the world right here, and we're getting the less price of any sole anywhere in the country … On an average trip this boat here will burn almost two thousand gallons of fuel, at $3.80 a gallon. So you are looking at seven thousand dollars off the top on just fuel costs.

The proposition of going fishing was a not actionable for this captain because he believed he would pay more for overhead costs, particularly fuel, than he would make from fishing for rock sole (a type of flatfish). As another captain put it, he would "go backwards," meaning that his future actuality would be worse than his current one, financially speaking. This captain, therefore, took the instrumental action of staying at the dock based on his conjecture of what his future actuality would be had he gone fishing. The following is an example of a captain making a similar calculation while steaming to the fishing grounds:

> We need to catch about 10 thousand pounds to make a living doing this. If you average out all the species, the sole, arrowtooth, skates, we are doing this for about 10 cents a pound. I figure if these guys can make $500 a day it's worth it, that $500 makes up for days when they don't make anything …

Potential efficiencies and inefficiencies shape which fishing grounds captains choose to steam to, the routes they take to fishing grounds, the areas beneath the vessel they choose to tow from, whether they change their fishing grounds or tow from a different area, as well as whether they fish at all. Efficiencies are a lures for experience, shaping the propositions, and ensuing instrumental actions, of captains' ecological sensemaking. Put differently, they influence the boundary-, property-, and meaning-making of captains' practices, and in turn what materializes through them.

Efficiency is one of the most important concepts in the disciplines of economics and political science, and in the rational decision-making theory they champion (Allison & Zelikow, 1999; Elster, 1989). Yet, in the trawl fishing context the persistent need for efficiency in the face of indeterminacy appears to lead fishing practice *away* from rational decision-making and *toward* ecological sensemaking. When practice is characterized by indeterminacy, rational decision-making processes are exceedingly impractical, if not impossible; in the face of indeterminacy ecological sensemaking moves practices forward, allowing sensemakers to swiftly leap into the unknown.

Plausible propositions

Even if a proposition is efficient, to be actionable it must be plausible. Management scholars argue that 'plausibility' is the standard for what is actionable in sensemaking (e.g., Maitlis & Christianson, 2014; Weick, 1995; Weick, et al., 2005), and for Peirce plausibility is essential to abduction (Rescher, 1978, p. 46). Peirce argued in fact that in scientific practice the need for efficiency makes plausibility, rather than accuracy, the standard for what is actionable. Yet this is not the case just for scientists, it is also the case for fishing captains—their pervasive need for efficiency, while also operating in the face of indeterminacy, means that their standard for what is actionable is plausibility as well. Note that this is about the plausibility of being able to tell certain desired stories after enacting future actualities into experience, such as what one will find at a certain fishing spot or will haul up from the depths after towing in a certain space. Just as it is the case for scientists, it is not about determining what the answers will be before acting, rather it is about being able to give answers of a certain nature to certain questions. This is not so much a 'representational accuracy' but a 'propositional plausibility.'

Mills (2003), in a study of sensemaking in a nuclear power plant, offers several characteristics of plausibility that highlight its role in the recurring transition from (actuality-conditioned) potentiality to (potentiality-conditioned) actuality, and from (potentiality-conditioned) actuality to (actuality-conditioned) potentiality. According to the author, a proposition of what to do next is plausible if it

> taps into an ongoing sense of current organizational climate, is consistent with other with other experiences through time and across the organization, facilitates, rather than disrupts, ongoing projects, reduces equivocality, provides an aura of accuracy (e.g., reflect the views of a consultant with a track record), and offers a potentially exciting way forward.
>
> *(Mills, 2003, p. 169, as discussed in Weick et al., 2005)*

We can see Mills's elements of plausibility at work in the following captain's story of why he choose to steam to a certain spot:

RESEARCHER: Why did you chose to fish up there [pointing to a location marked on a plotter]?

CAPTAIN: It's just been traditionally a really great spot and we don't have to compete with other groups when we go there. Like this time of year usually it's the cleanest, winter time is usually the time to fish in Portlock because the [Pacific] halibut aren't there.

The captain's answer is a proposition of what to do next based on what has materialized in past fishing practices (i.e., past actualities). What makes it plausible is that he thinks the spot will 'facilitate ongoing projects' by enabling him to catch his target fish and at the same time not catch an unacceptable amount of Pacific halibut bycatch. Catching too much Pacific halibut bycatch not only leads to an inefficient fishing trip (halibut both take up space in the nets that could be occupied by target catch and must be sorted out of the catch), but it can also impede the potential to enact future fishing trips by reducing the amount of Pacific halibut bycatch that other captains can use to catch their target quotas (see Chapters 2 and 3 for a more detailed explanation of this limiting function of prohibited species bycatch limits). To continue with Mills' elements, the issue of bycatch also 'taps into an ongoing sense of current climate' in that GOA trawl fisheries are highly scrutinized by fisheries stakeholders for their relatively high bycatch numbers as compared to other fishing groups (see Chapter 7 for examples of such scrutiny). The captain's proposition 'offers a potentially exciting future' in that he not only considered the spot to be 'traditionally a really great spot,' but that it also fostered the potential to fish while not having to 'compete with other groups.' Further, the proposition is 'consistent with other experiences through time and across the organization' in that the captain's current fishing activity, being in the winter, was aligned with his experience of fishing in past winters. The story has an 'aura of accuracy' in that it coheres with what has 'traditionally' and 'usually' occurred. In terms of Mills's appeal to expertise (i.e., 'reflecting the views of a consultant with a track record'), here the captain makes an appeal to recurring ecological phenomena of his target species. And finally, the captain's story serves to 'reduce equivocality' by organizing various sources and types of information into a coherent proposition regarding what story he and his crew may be able to tell about their profitability when they arrive to the chosen fishing spot (i.e., their ensuing actuality). In all, the proposition was abductively derived from actuality-conditioned potentiality, and it provided a plausible way forward, suggesting particular instrumental action that would give way to the potentiality-conditioned actuality that is his next fishing spot.

Strategic propositions

As the previous discussions imply, for a proposition to be actionable it must concern instrumental action that can co-articulate potentially fruitful future actualities. Captains are not disinterested, or merely marginally interested, in what their ensuing actuality, and its embedded potentialities, will be. A proposition might be both economical and plausible, but if it involves the potential for landing a person in the wrong place, such as in barren or dangerous actualities, then the proposition is generally not actionable. A proposition 'gestures' toward ensuing actuality, "vectorizing concrete experience" toward "something that matters" (Stengers, 2008, p. 96), and, as the data suggest, what matters is ensuing actuality that is embedded with desired potentiality.

Thus, while ecological sensemaking processes are like scientific processes in terms of their demand for efficiency and their reliance on plausibility, they are unlike scientific processes (or at least idealized scientific processes) in that they are aimed at enacting particular desired future actualities into experience, namely ones that have profitable potentialities embedded in them. Captains are not engaging in a mere quest for knowledge; rather, they engage in a quest for articulating profitable actualities (i.e., stages of their fishing practice that have certain boundaries, properties, and meanings), and their embedded potentialities for enacting ensuing profitable actualities, into experience. In other words, captains want to both enable themselves to tell certain stories of what happened after taking instrumental action and landing in a certain actuality, as well as to create certain propositions for what's next after they are there. Captains not only think about the story they might be able to tell when answering the question 'what's next?' and taking instrumental action, they also think about how they can answer the next question of 'what's next?' that will arise from that ensuing actuality (as they again face indeterminacy). Captains' propositions are always oriented toward enacting certain actualities in the future that enable, suggest, or even demand certain future propositions. Both future actualities *and* potentialities 'lure' captains' sensemaking, 'vectorizing' it towered something that matters.

Thus, if a captain proposes to steam to a certain fishing spot, he does so because it is plausible that after efficiently arriving there he will be able to propose to tow in a certain space in that spot. Likewise, if a captain proposes to tow from a certain space, he does so because it is plausible that afterward he will either be able to propose to efficiently tow again in that spot or, or if the vessel is full after that tow, head to port. This strategic nature of ecological sensemaking is exemplified below. In this example a captain presents a proposition of what to do next after finding too much Pacific halibut bycatch in his previous tow; his sensemaking is strategic in that he wants to enact a future actuality that will enable him to propose a place to tow that will result in catching less Pacific halibut bycatch. This conversation illustrates a current proposition acting as a tool for enacting future actuality that will foster the creation of a particular future proposition:

RESEARCHER: What's the plan now?
CAPTAIN: We are gonna run three or four miles and find a new spot, we had to move, there was just too much [Pacific] halibut in that spot.
RESEARCHER: A new spot just based on experience?
CAPTAIN: Based on one tow I made 11 years ago, but that was in May [this trip occurred in April]. Same thing, I couldn't catch anything here, the weather was blowing hard out of the Simidis, and we ran over there and loaded the boat up in three tows of straight arrowtooth. But they were schooled fish, so it's a whole different deal, it's a 'they are either there or they are not' sort of deal.

This captain was unsure if making a living would be possible in the next spot, yet he organized his operations to fish there anyway. He was able to do so because he had a plausible sense of what he would find once he arrived there, which would enable him to propose a place to tow there. It is by way of actionable propositions, and the instrumental actions that emerge from them, that captains attempt to enact actuality that will enable, promote, and perhaps even demand particular future propositions. Weick alludes to this strategic nature of (ecological) sensemaking in the following:

> The basic idea is that when people imagine reality, they start with some tangible clue and then discover or invent a world in which that clue is meaningful. This act of invention is an act of divination ... The essence of conjecture and divination lies in the faith that a fragment is a meaningful symptom which, if pursued vigorously, will enact a world where the meaning of the fragment becomes clearer.
>
> *(Weick, 2006, p. 1731)*

In the face of indeterminacy, captains must strategically invent and divine their way through their fishing practice. Yet, as we will see in the next chapter, captains are not the only creatures who are divining their way from actuality-conditioned potentiality to potentiality conditioned-actuality and back again, recurrently. In fact, captains are not even the only creatures who are doing it within their own sensemaking. The next chapter demonstrates how the ecological sensemaking process is co-enacted by both man and nature, and updates the framework accordingly.

6

THE ENTANGLED NATURE OF ECOLOGICAL SENSEMAKING

The previous chapters began developing an agential realist-oriented framework of ecological sensemaking at sea. Such a framework, they argued, is demanded by the role that indeterminacy plays in Gulf of Alaska (GOA) trawl captains' fishing practices, which the last chapter argued are enacted in the actuality–potentiality dimension of experience, and, according to Chapters 3 and 4, through ecological sensemaking. Chapter 5 in particular demonstrated that in the face of indeterminacy, ecological sensemaking uses abduction to derive (actuality-conditioned) potentiality for desired future experience from the (potentiality-conditioned) actuality that is current experience; that potentiality comes in the form of a proposition. If the proposition is economical, plausible, and strategic, ecological sensemaking enacts certain instrumental actions, including agential cuts, which transition the sensemaker from the (potentiality-conditioned) actuality of current experience to the (potentiality-conditioned) actuality that is future experience. And as potentiality becomes actuality, indeterminacy re-emerges due to the sensemaker's need to once again move from present actuality to indeterminate future actuality, by way of potentiality. Propositions are key to this process: they are conjectures as to what to do next in order to be able to tell desired tales after taking certain instrumental actions and landing in a new actuality. In the commercial trawl fishing context, key tales that captains may tell concern what they have found in a certain fishing spot after arriving there, or what they have caught from a particular space beneath the vessel after towing there.

So far the framework has been constructed almost exclusively out of the activities of captains. The discussion has only involved natural (i.e., non-human, non-technological) phenomena in terms of the indeterminacy that emerges from being constitutively embedded in a perpetually articulating entanglement of boundary-, property-, and meaning-making ecological and geophysical activities. The framework does not yet adequately account for the active role that natural phenomena play in GOA trawl captains' ecological sensemaking, and in turn what materializes through it. As the framework is currently constructed, nature is largely a passive player in captains' practices. Yet the data show that nature plays an active role in captains' practices, co-articulating their potentialities and actualities. In short, the current framework leaves out much of the story.

This chapter attempts to tell that broader story. This is a story of how nature is inherent to ecological sensemaking, such that the actuality and potentiality of captains' fishing practice is co-constituted by the actuality and potentiality of natural phenomena. Viewed in terms of Whitehead's actuality-potentiality formula (as elaborated in Chapter 5), which states that actuality and potentiality "require each other, namely actuality is the exemplification of potentiality, and potentiality is the characterization of actuality, either in fact or in concept" (Whitehead, 1968, p. 70), this chapter argues that natural phenomena mutually constitute captains' potentialities and actualities. Thus, this chapter updates the actuality-potentiality framework produced in Chapter 5 such that it traverses the Cartesian human–nature dualism that is integrated into, and which hinders, our current understanding of ecological sensemaking in particular, as well as the management and regulation of resource extraction industries in general. In traversing this dualism, this update moves us closer to studying and ultimately regulating and managing *actual* actuality, and its embedded potentiality, rather than the fictional version that depends on metaphysical individualism.

Thus, rather than studying, regulating, and managing commercial trawl fishing based on the false dichotomy of man and nature, this chapter makes the case that we should do so according to an entanglement-based understanding of human-natural organization, as it emerges through posthumanistic ecological sensemaking. In the entanglement-based understanding of ecological sensemaking that is articulated here, the boundary-, property-, and meaning-making *potentiality* of captains' fishing practice is co-constituted by the *actuality* of natural phenomena,[1] and the boundary-, property-, and meaning-making *actuality* of captains' fishing practice is co-constituted by the *potentiality* of natural phenomena; likewise, the boundary-, property-, and meaning-making *potentiality* of natural phenomena is co-constituted by the *actuality* of captains' fishing practices, and the boundary-, property-, and meaning-making *actuality* of natural phenomena is co-constituted by the *potentiality* of captains' fishing practices. In short, the materialization of potentially and actuality in captains' sensemaking is mutually constituted by the potentially and actuality of ecological phenomena.

This elaboration of the mutually constitutive nature of natural phenomena and ecological sensemaking is 'posthumanistic' (see Chapter 1 for more discussion of Barad's posthumanism). While there are several versions of 'posthumanism' out there, this book draws from the version articulated by Barad's agential realism (e.g., Barad, 1998, 2003, 2007, 2014). Barad's agential realism offers "a posthumanist understanding that does not fix the human (human concepts, human practices, human knowledge) at the foundations of the theory" (Barad, 2007, p. 334). As discussed in Chapter 1, agential realism draws heavily from Nobel laureate Niels Bohr's empirical and philosophical work on quantum physics in general, and his "central lesson of quantum mechanics" in particular, namely, "that we are part of the nature that we seek to understand" (Barad, 2007, p. 247). Implicit in this principle is its logical extension, that the nature we are part of and seek to understand is also part of us and our processes of understanding, as well as what materializes through such processes, whether it be physical or conceptual, human or nonhuman. It perhaps goes without saying that such a lesson has significant implications for our understanding of ecological sensemaking and the extractive practices, organizations, and industries that both emerge through and shape it.

From a posthumanistic perspective, nature has agency in human organizing in general, and in ecological sensemaking in particular. Thus, humans are not deified as the only creatures that engage in the ongoing transition from actuality-conditioned potentiality to potentiality-conditioned actuality, and vice-versa. Humans do not engage in ecological sensemaking because they exist apart from, gaze down upon, and *inter*-act with, nature; instead, ecological sensemaking, and in fact all sensemaking, is itself a natural phenomenon, which functions within broader phenomena to enact boundaries, properties, and meanings that enable human organization to continually and strategically form. In turn, posthumanism, according to Barad, "calls for a critical examination of the practices by which the differential boundaries of the human and the nonhuman, and the social and the natural, are drawn, for these very practices are always already implicated in particular materializations" (Barad, 2007, pp. 209–210). Ecological sensemaking is one such practice, and this book is one such examination.

Posthumanism recognizes the interpretive, social, and physical differentiation of humans and what humans call (i.e., differentiate as) 'nature,' but not their separability. It sees such boundary-making as something that is perpetually performed in the entanglements that constitute human and natural phenomena, not as something that exists apart from and prior to them. Posthumanism is particularly concerned with the difference between human and natural phenomena that tends to masquerade as separation and individuality. While humans and nature are regularly treated as different from one another, due in no small part to their differentiating ecological, biological, conceptual, physical, social, organizational, and institutional processes, humans and nature are not ecologically, biologically, conceptually, physically, socially, organizationally, or institutionally separable. Differentiating processes are never separable from whatever it is that they are differentiating; the best we can ever manage is the agential separability performed by agential cuts, which in turn create 'differentiation within' (Barad, 2014). Thus, differentiation is something that occurs within phenomena as a mode of entanglement; it cannot, by definition, be a characteristic of separate things. As Barad notes:

> What often appears as separate entities (and separate sets of concerns) with sharp edges does not actually entail a relation of absolute exteriority at all ... The relation of the cultural and the natural is a relation of 'exteriority within.' This not a static relationality but a doing—the enactment of boundaries—that always entails constitutive exclusions ...
>
> *(Barad, 2007, p. 93)*

Separation, even the psychologically, socially, and institutionally pervasive separation of mind and matter, organization and environment, and humans and nature, is always performed within, by, and through entangled phenomena. Cartesian dualisms, instead of being the signifier of inherently separate things that have their own rosters of non-relational properties, which occasionally come together to *act on* one another, are actually exemplars of the 'exteriority within' that is a key part of the boundary-making effects of mutual constitution. Thus, dualisms are exemplars of 'exteriority within'; they are not characteristic of a deeper, separated reality (as disciplines such as economics, political science, and natural resource management would have us think). In fact, there are no separate entities at all, only agential cuts, constitutive exclusions, and exteriorities within. From a posthumanistic perspective, the differentiation of humans and nature is not something to be taken for granted; instead, it is a key topic of inquiry.

But fisheries management scholars, deeply committed to rational decision-making assumptions and frameworks, see separate, rather than mutually constitutive, entities as the basic units of management. For example, eminent fisheries management scholar Ray Hilborn, in a laudable effort to correct for the pervasive and predominant role that natural science plays in current fisheries management, argues that, rather than fisheries management being hyper-focused on fish, instead should be focused on people, for 'managing fish is managing people' (Hilborn, 2007). Hilborn then goes on to elaborate the various ways in which "we have a long way to go" (p. 294).

This proposed shift in emphasis is a move in the right direction, but it goes too far. It suffers from the same assumption that supported the outdated notion that managing fisheries is primarily just managing fish. This is the assumption that we manage human and natural phenomena that, while they interact, are inherently separable. Hilborn overlooks perhaps the most important unit of analysis and management: the mutually constitutive relations, i.e., the entanglements, through which human and natural phenomena, including their differentiations, materialize.

The bio-ecological concept of speciation provides a useful lens through which to understand the difference between viewing entities as mutually constituted and viewing them as individually determined. Speciation is the process through which populations diverge into different species; it is a differentiating process. Yet an axiom of ecology is that no species develops and exists in a vacuum; rather, processes of speciation are constitutive of environments, and those environments are constitutive of those processes (Lewontin, 2000). Adherents to the notion of speciation as a species-differentiating process cannot also help themselves to the idea of pre-existing separate species (though ecological science and its regulatory practices regularly do so). Speciation is ongoing differentiation and assimilation, but never separation; it is exteriority within perpetually changing and evolving phenomena, through which innumerable species and their entangled environments continually and relationally emerge. When we lose sight of the basic fact of existence that is mutual constitution, inherent to which is 'differentiation within,' and when we ignore the inherent *in*separability of humans and nature, and in turn treat nature as if it is not human, and humans as if they are not natural, our ecological sensemaking (and in fact all sensemaking), and the organization that emerges through it, becomes less physically grounded. Thus, our sensemaking becomes more abstract and less concrete, and the abduction at the heart of it becomes more deductive and confirmatory and less inductive and exploratory. There is, in short, less wisdom, creativity, learning, and knowledge. The concrete fact is that what human ecological sensemaking is is constitutive of what nature is, and what nature is is constitutive of what human ecological sensemaking is; their ontological mutual constitution runs deeper than does our epistemological segregation of humans and nature into distinct categories. A posthumanistic perspective attempts to correct our tendency to get caught up in our epistemology and lose sight of our ontology. As Barad states:

> the acknowledgement that humans are part of nature entails the simultaneous recognition that our understanding of nature as that which is disclosed through scientific practices entails an appreciation of the fact that scientific practices are natural processes rather than external impositions on the natural world.
>
> *(Barad, 2007, p. 332)*

What goes for science goes for fishing—captains' fishing practices, and the ecological sensemaking through which they emerge, are both natural processes and part of the nature that captains are attempting to understand.

Thus, a posthumanistic perspective does not relegate nature to the background as a mere recipient of human activity. Instead, it sees nature as playing an active role in the emergence of human activity, materiality, ecological sensemaking, and organization. This chapter demonstrates how natural activities are integral to eco-logical sensemaking, and how together they mutually constitute the organization that is commercial trawl fishing in the GOA. The product is an amendment to the ecological sensemaking framework elaborated in the previous chapter in that it integrates natural phenomena into it as an active, constitutive participant.

Target species' propositional activity

As the last chapter demonstrated, ecological sensemaking involves telling proposi-tional tales about a spot on the fishing grounds to steam to or a space beneath the vessel to tow through next, then steaming to that spot or towing through that space, and then telling the story of having done so. These stories concern what materialized after taking that instrumental action, such as what one finds at that fishing spot or what one has hauled up from the depths, and whether the propositional tale was conformal or non-conformal. From there ecological sensemaking carries forth as current actuality, i.e., the stage in one's practice where critical materiality *has* emerged (e.g., an aggregation in a fishing spot, catch on deck), has an indeterminate relationship with the next actuality, i.e., the next stage in one's practice where cer-tain ensuing critical materiality *needs to* emerge next. That discussion, steeped in human propositional activity, drew heavily from the work of Alfred North

Whitehead. Yet Whitehead, in elaborating his theory of propositions, states, "in the realization of propositions, 'judgment' is a very rare component, and so is 'consciousness'" (Whitehead, 1978, p. 184). Whitehead argued across various works that his processual understanding of reality, including his theory of propositions, is both not specific to humans and should not be premised on human dualisms, such as those that serve to separate humans and nature (e.g., Whitehead, 1919, 1967a, 1967b, 1968, 1978). Stengers makes his arguments more explicit, stating that not only is human consciousness not necessary for the development and use of propositions, but neither are humans:

> the efficacy of propositions is not restricted to us ... propositions are needed in order to give irreducible reasons not only for the experience of words inducing disclosure, a world felt in a different manner, but also for the disruption, or variation of interest, that a rabbit or a dog may experience; and finally, for the possibility of the kind of disruption of social continuity that we may observe when even oysters or trees seem to forget about survival.
>
> *(Stengers, 2005, p. 51)*

To gain a richer and more appropriate understanding of ecological sensemaking, we must also appreciate how the propositional nature of (non-human) nature shapes how it unfolds and co-determines what materializes through it.

If we attempt to strip ecological sensemaking of its humanistic bias, and instead view it in a more posthumanistic light, then what we primarily see is the recurrent movement of entangled activities, that manifest in the transition from actuality-conditioned potentiality to new potentiality-conditioned actuality, by way of boundary-, property-, and meaning-making activity, and then from that potentiality-conditioned actuality to new actuality-conditioned potentiality, also by way of boundary-, property-, and meaning-making activity. To take such a view we have to focus, to the extent that our entity-oriented minds, language, and culture will allow us, more on entangled activities than on actors, for entangled activities always underlie and pervade actors, and actors emerge through, and in fact are, entanglements (Barad, 2007; Butler, 1990; Haraway, 1991; Latour, 2005). In doing so, what comes to the foreground are the entangled activities that accomplish the transition from the 'characterization of actuality' (i.e., potentiality) to the 'exemplification of potentiality' (i.e., actuality), and from the 'exemplification of potentiality' (i.e., actuality) to the 'the characterization of actuality' (i.e., potentiality), recurrently. These entangled activities create boundaries, such as those that manifest as differential densities and assemblages of activities, properties, such as morphological characteristics and recurring patterns of activities, and meanings, which are differential responses to differentiated densities, morphological characteristics, or patterns of activities.

If we understand 'meaningfulness' as a differential response (conceptual or physical) to something that is intelligible, and intelligibility as 'the world articulating itself differently,' as Barad's agential realism calls for, then we can get closer to a posthumanistic understanding of ecological sensemaking. Barad describes this posthumanistic view of meaning in the following:

In my posthumanist account, meaning is not a human-based notion; rather, meaning is an ongoing performance of the world in its differential intelligibility. Intelligibility is usually framed as a matter of intellection and therefore a specifically human capacity. But in my agential realist account, intelligibility is a matter of differential responsiveness, as performatively articulated and accountable, to what matters. Intelligibility is not an inherent characteristic of humans but a feature of the world in its differential becoming.

(Barad, 2007, p. 335)

The nature of meaning as the differential articulation and response of the world is why, according to Bohr, meaning is physically articulated by the broader apparatus it is embedded in, through which it is performed. This is why, for Bohr, whether light is a wave or a particle depends on how the apparatus that is measuring it is articulating itself. The upshot is that matter and meaning are always mutually entailed and physically articulated by an apparatus, regardless of whether humans are involved in the process, or if the deem it meaningful.

On the way to the articulation of meaning lies the articulation of ambiguity. If, from a posthumanistic view, meaning is a differential response to 'the world articulating itself differently,' i.e., to intelligibility, ambiguity is a differential response to 'the world *not* articulating itself differently *enough*,' i.e., to a lack of requisite intelligibility. Ambiguity is a lack of enough differentiation, in terms of what one needs, in terms of what one is doing, in how the world is articulating itself. We saw the articulation of ambiguity in the example of a pollock bycatch event that was elaborated at the end of Chapter 4. In that event certain *boundaries* and *properties* (e.g., the timing and location of particular sign on the sonar) were physically intelligible to captains before they towed, as they were searching for their target fish (rock sole), but differential *meaning* in terms of a particular species (e.g., pollock or rock sole) was not. Separability, whether it be the separation by species or in terms of any sort of grouping or category, is not inherent or absolute; it is a property of the particular measurement (or mere engagement) apparatus being enacted; the intelligibilities that are the subject of, and the meanings that are performed through, apparatuses are local and contingent phenomena. While the captains were towing their entangled worlds began physically articulating themselves differently, and in doing so enacting different intelligibilities. The problem was that the captains could attain unambiguous meaning at the species-level only *after* they ended their tows by enacting the additional differentiations, i.e., agential cuts, of hauling up their nets from the depths, dumping their contents on the backs of their vessels, and segregating the catch into species categories (or alternatively delivering unsorted catch to a processing plant where would be sorted). At that point in the process, however, the vast majority of the catch is dead. Meaning is the differential response to differential articulations, i.e., particular arrangements of boundary-, property-, and meaning-making intra-actions, of the world (i.e., intelligibilities), yet particular differential responses cannot be made where the necessary differential articulations (such as at the species-level) are not enacted. Thus, a response to the differential articulation of a particular species cannot be made where there is no species-based differentiation.

Meaning is the differential relational response to differential articulations of the world, whether that world involves humans or not. It is the enactment of activity in response to something that 'matters' (in both senses of the word), whether it is a fox, an idea, an emotion, a storm, a person, etc. (Barad, 2007). Meaning cannot be definitionally cloistered to humans, anthropomorphized by our own nascent and incomplete understanding of what meaning is. For doing so cements human modes of thought and communication, with their embedded biases and frailties, into the very foundations of what we purport to be a more universal understanding. As Barad clarifies:

> Knowing is a specific engagement of the world where part of the world becomes differentially intelligible to another part of the world in its differential accountability to and for that of which it is a part. In traditional humanist accounts, intelligibility requires an intellective agent (that to which something is intelligible), and intellection is framed as a specifically human capacity. But in my agential realist account, intelligibility is an ontological performance of the world in its ongoing articulation. It is not a human-dependent characteristic but a feature of the world in its differential becoming. The world articulates itself differently. And knowing does not require intellection in the humanist sense, either; knowing is a matter of differential responsiveness (as performatively articulated and accountable) to what matters.
>
> *(Barad, 2007, pp. 379–380)*

The version of meaning in which human language and thought mediates the relationship between an entity jn a separate external world depends on an individualistic and representational structure of knowledge and experience, which quantum mechanics has soundly rejected. Instead, meaning is the recognition of, or response to, materialization, it is actuality that is not only intelligible, but which has come to matter to some 'other' actuality. Like any materialization, meaning is articulated by entangled boundary-, property-, and meaning-making activities, which, due to the intelligibility of what materializes through those activities, shapes entangled boundary-, property-, and meaning-making activities. The things that materialize through such entangled activities may be as physically different as a rock is from an idea, but the mechanics of their materialization are much the same.

The chief argument here is that the actuality-potentiality structure maintains regardless of what sort of actor we assign to the phenomena it is structuring. The potentiality for boundary-, property-, and meaning-making relations, and their ensuing material actualizations, perform what matters to us, to other creatures, and to all of existence, continually. One of the more salient ways that the actuality-potentiality transition manifests in non-human phenomena is what is known in the natural sciences as 'life history traits.' Life history traits involve recurring patterns of instrumental activities, embedded in and emergent from the entangled evolution of genes, organisms, and environments (Lewontin, 2000), that promote growth, reproduction, and survival (Pruitt & Goodnight, 2014; Roff, 1992; Stearns, 1992).

Such recurring patterns of activities perform various materialities, from individual bodies to bodies of individuals. Just as it is with the materialization of a rock or an idea, what comes to matter through the entanglement of life history traits may be quite different depending on the particular apparatus through which they emerge, but the mechanics of the materialization are much the same. Put generally, life history traits are materializations that emerge through, and in turn perform, the entangled evolution of genes, organisms, and environments (Lewontin, 2000). These traits include such instrumental activities as migratory patterns, breeding routines, hunting strategies, rearing behaviors, among many others.

In what follows I argue that we can understand life history traits using the same potentiality–actuality framework through which we can understand ecological sensemaking (after which, in the next section, I combine the two). For example, a fish swimming in a certain direction based on the detection of a change in water temperature is acting according to the potentiality of feeding or breeding in some place, which is one of its desired future actualities ('desire' as used here refers to evolutionarily-developed and biophysically-defined tendencies rather than overt conscious deliberations). The inheritance of a trait for detecting water temperature change is potentiality-conditioned actuality, in which evolutionary processes have embedded the fish's biophysical systems with potentiality for detecting such a change. Thus, the fish's biophysical systems are embedded with the 'proposition' that some extent of change in water temperature matters in some particular way. The triggering of a change in swimming direction is the meeting of the actuality of changed water temperature and potentiality for its detection. The instrumental action of a change in swimming direction is the transition from the mere (actuality-conditioned) potentiality for detecting a change in water temperature, which is embedded in the fish's biophysical systems, to the (potentiality-conditioned) actuality of the fish swimming wherever its evolutionary 'proposition' tells it to go. This is a differential response to a differential articulation of the world; it is the entangled materialization of meaning. The change in water temperature, the detection of the change, and the response to it are materializations constituted by entangled phenomena (e.g., temperature, water, fish). The actuality and potentiality necessary for these materializations are entangled across differentiated phenomena; thus, the materialization of a change in swimming direction exists both in the fish and in the surrounding water, and cannot be isolated to one or the other.

To better understand the line of argument presented here, and in the rest of this chapter, let's look at the proverbial question, attributed to eighteenth-century philosopher George Berkeley, "If a tree falls in the forest and no one is around to hear it, does it make a sound?" According to the ecological sensemaking framework articulated here, a tree falling in a forest will be heard, and sense can be made of it, only if there is some apparatus within 'earshot' that has *already* proposed that the sort of disturbance created by the falling tree *matters*. The materialization of sound requires a 'belief' or 'conjecture' that it, or something like it, matters—ahead of the actuality of the tree falling. The ability to hear the falling tree is potentiality awaiting the actuality of a falling tree, in which the potentiality of hearing is conditioned by, and embedded in, previous, historically-contingent and evolved, actualities, and the actuality of falling is conditioned by, and embedded in, its historically-contingent and evolved potentiality. The (potentiality-conditioned) actuality of the falling tree creates aural disturbances, intelligibilities, that go in search of (actuality-conditioned) potentiality for perceiving and responding to them. For any thing to matter there must be potentiality awaiting actuality *and* actuality that alights upon that potentiality; both are required, and together they mutually constitute what materializes. A tree falling in a forest where there is no hearing apparatus nearby means that the actuality of the falling tree will not materialize as sound. Someone may subsequently find a felled tree, but it is the felled tree (rather than the falling tree) that has come to matter, for different potentiality has met with different actuality, from which different matter has materialized. Thus, the question, "If a tree falls in a forest and no one is around to hear it, does it make a sound?" is not the right question; in fact, it is nonsensical, for 'making a sound' is a relational activity—an entanglement—and therefore 'it,' i.e., the falling tree, cannot possibly do such a thing by itself. Making a sound, making sense, and all materialization require the meeting of (potentiality-conditioned) actuality and (actuality-conditioned) potentiality. A more meaningful question would be, 'If a tree falls in a forest and no one is around to hear it, does it matter?' To which the answer of course is, 'no,' for there is no potentiality there to enable sound to materialize. Subsequent actualities might come to matter (such as a felled tree), but the actuality of the falling tree has not mattered.

So where do life history traits fit into all of this? Life history traits involve: (1) the meeting of biophysical 'beliefs in' or 'propositions regarding' the phenomena that matter (i.e., potentiality) and the physical presence of that phenomena (i.e., actuality); (2) the boundary-making instrumental actions, including agential cuts between what does and does not matter, that materialize from that meeting; and (3) the evolutionary integration of the success or failure of those instrumental actions, in terms of the ongoing achievement of growth, reproduction, and survival, into biophysical systems (i.e., actuality) as potentiality, taking the process back to # 1. This is the entanglement that constitutes life history traits (as defined here), which they in turn perform.

The entangled relationality of the actuality-potentiality dimension of biophysical systems organizes nature, shaping phenomena into recurring boundary-, property-, and meaning-making activities. This organizational nature of nature, perhaps counter-intuitively, tends to take on a more structural, abstract nature in (what is differentiated as) non-human phenomena than it does in (what is differentiated as) human phenomena. Stengers discusses the relatively abstract nature of life history traits in the following:

> What we have forgotten is that if there are societies dominated by abstractions it is the ones we name trees and oysters, rather than ourselves. Sticking to their business of survival is sticking to abstractions, making a definite and rather stable difference between what this business defines as relevant and what does not matter.
> *(Stengers, 2005, p. 50)*

A definite and rather stable difference between what does and does not matter is a boundary-, property-, and meaning-making proposition as to what will lead to feeding, breeding, migrating, and often merely surviving, and what will not. It is the enactment of a constitutive exclusion, an agential cut that performs a differentiation between what does and what does not matter within phenomena. Salmon swim long distances to spawn in their natal rivers, not because they have rationally gathered all of the evidence that such a venture will work once they traverse hundreds of nautical miles, but because their biophysical systems direct them to enact certain instrumental actions in the face of certain triggers, which are evolutionarily-based on what worked in the past; there is no choice, only evolutionarily-derived differentiations between what does and does not matter. Life history traits are actuality-conditioned potentialities etched into biophysical actualities through the ongoing entangled materialization and evolution of genes, organisms, and environments. These biophysical materialities are embedded with the potentiality for playing out certain patterns of boundary-making activities that foster feeding, breeding, and migrating; the playing out of such patterns, if successful, in turn perpetuates those traits.

Natural science and ethnographic data both suggest that trawl target fish enact (and are enacted by) life history traits in the form of what I call 'migratory entanglements.' 'Migratory entanglements' are certain articulations of instrumental activities of fish that are intelligible to captains (and scientists); they are ways in which the ecological world has 'articulated itself differently' (which, as is argued below, are entangled with the way in which humans articulate 'their' world differently, and vice versa). In terms of natural science data, the National Oceanic and Atmospheric Administration's Stock Assessment and Fishery Evaluation (SAFE) reports[2] indicate that each trawl target species engages in both longitudinal and episodic migratory entanglements. Episodic migratory entanglements, or 'aggregations,' 'schools,' are spatio-temporal stopovers within broader migratory phenomena, while longitudinal migratory entanglements are the collective movements of fish from one episodic stopover to the next. The 'goal' of both types of activities is growth, reproduction, and survival. The following are examples of the migratory entanglements of each major trawl target species, taken from SAFE reports:

Flathead sole:

> Adults exhibit a benthic lifestyle and occupy separate winter spawning and summertime feeding distributions on the [Eastern Bering Sea] shelf and in the GOA. From over-winter grounds near the shelf margins, adults begin a migration onto the mid and outer continental shelf in April or May each year for feeding. The spawning period may range from as early as January but is known to occur in March and April, primarily in deeper waters near the margins of the continental shelf.
>
> (McGilliard, Palsson, Stockhausen, & Ianelli, 2013, p. 614)

Walleye pollock:

> Peak spawning at the two major spawning areas in the Gulf of Alaska occurs at
> different times. In the Shumagin Island area, peak spawning apparently occurs
> between February 15–March 1, while in Shelikof Strait peak spawning occurs
> later, typically between March 15 and April 1.
>
> *(Dorn et al., 2012, p. 56)*

Dusky rockfish:

> Adult dusky rockfish are concentrated on offshore banks and near gullies on
> the outer continental shelf at depths of 100 to 200 m ... Anecdotal evidence
> from fishermen and from biologists on trawl surveys suggests that dusky
> rockfish are often caught in association with a hard, rocky bottom on these
> banks or gullies.
>
> *(Lunsford, Hulson, Shotwell, & Hanselman, 2015, p. 1018)*

Pacific cod:

> Adults occur in depths from the shoreline to 500 m, although occurrence in
> depths greater than 300 m is fairly rare. Preferred substrate is soft sediment,
> from mud and clay to sand. Average depth of occurrence tends to vary directly
> with age for at least the first few years of life ... Pacific cod are known to
> undertake seasonal migrations, the timing and duration of which may be
> variable.
>
> *(A'mar, Thompson, Martin & Palsson, 2013, p. 174)*

Rock sole:

> Rock sole are most abundant in the Kodiak and Shumagin areas. The north-
> ern rock sole spawns in midwinter and spring, and the southern rock sole
> spawns in summer ... Northern rock sole spawning occurred in areas where
> bottom temperatures averaged 3°C in January, and Southern rock sole
> spawning began in areas where bottom temperatures averaged 6°C in June ...
>
> *(A'mar & Palsson, 2014, p. 454)*

Pacific Ocean perch:

> Adults are found primarily offshore on the outer continental shelf and the
> upper continental slope in depths of 150–420 m. Seasonal differences in depth
> distribution have been noted by many investigators. In the summer, adults
> inhabit shallower depths, especially those between 150 and 300 m. In the fall,
> the fish apparently migrate farther offshore to depths of ~300–420 m. They
> reside in these deeper depths until about May, when they return to their

shallower summer distribution (Love et al. 2002). This seasonal pattern is probably related to summer feeding and winter spawning.

(Hulson, Hanselman, Shotwel, Lunsford, & Ianelli, 2014, p. 556)

Each of these descriptions involves the patterned and recurring boundary-, property-, and meaning-making instrumental activities of particular species (in which 'meaning' is defined as the differential response to the world articulating itself differently - see previous discussions). These are particular instrumental activities that are intra-actively intelligible to scientists, which the scientists differentially respond to (i.e., make meaningful and put into their reports). Yet such meaning is distributed across 'human' and 'ecological' phenomena, found in the relationality of the intelligibility of one (in which the world is articulating itself differently) and the differential response of the other (which also articulates the world differently).

Further, while natural science research suggests that trawl target species engage in certain migratory entanglements, qualitative data from GOA trawl captains indicate much the same. For example, captains stated that dusky and Northern rockfish are known to form "little schools" on the ocean bottom, while Pacific Ocean perch tend to live "off the edge" in "mid-water" schools; at times and in certain places pollock recurrently assemble with other species into large, dense "feed bands," while at other times and in other places pollock can be found tightly grouped on the bottom, forming what captains call "carpet."

Life history traits encompass (actuality-conditioned) potentialities for enacting (potentiality-conditioned) actualities that promote feeding, breeding, and mere survival; their successes, as well as their failures, shape, and are shaped by, the mutually con-stituted, ongoing evolutionary assembling of genes, organisms, and environments (Lewontin, 2000). Such development etches particular potentialities into the biophysical systems that constitute individual fish, fish populations, and fish species, which are part and parcel of migratory entanglements. Figure 6.1 presents the actuality-potentiality framework previously developed as ecological sensemaking, modified to fit the concept of life history traits, as it is elaborated here. Where abductive processes that produce propositions lie in human-focused phenomena, 'propositions embedded biophysical systems' lie in the framework below. Migratory entanglements are lured into

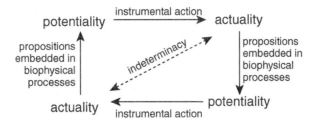

FIGURE 6.1 Ecological sensemaking framework posthumanistically applied to non-human ecological phenomena.

materialization by actualities of the past masquerading, by way of evolutionary processes, as potentialities for the future (actuality-conditioned potentiality). When those potentialities encounter certain actualities, which are made intelligible through certain boundary-, property-, and meaning-making activities, they give rise to certain instrumental actions; those instrument actions co-enact, along with innumerable other entangled activities, new actualities into existence (potentiality-conditioned actuality). While actuality-conditioned potentialities do not materialize as observable propositions, at least as we know them, their transitions to potentiality-conditioned actualities often produce intelligible patterns of instrumental actions, both to humans and to an array of other predators. As we will see next, these actualities and potentialities play an agentive role trawl captains' ecological sensemaking, mutually constituting what it looks like and the organization that materializes from it.

The already-entangled nature of human and ecological phenomena

In the actuality of ecological phenomena lies the potentiality of fishing practice, and in the potentiality of fishing practice lies the actuality of ecological phenomena; put differently, in the potentiality of ecological phenomena lies the actuality of fishing practice, and in the actuality of fishing practice lies the potentiality of ecological phenomena. Each of these statements is the entangled correlation of the other. The relationship they communicate, i.e., the constitutive embeddedness of the potentiality–actuality dimension across fishing practice and ecological systems, captures how the two *inter*-active phenomena of fishing practices and ecological phenomena are, in reality, *intra*-active, which is to say, mutually constitutive. This relationality of fishing practice and ecological phenomena, in which the potentiality–actuality dimension of each is anchored in both, is the crux of the posthumanistic ecological sensemaking (PES) framework articulated here.

The data suggest that ecological sensemaking in the GOA trawl context is an apparatus that is both constituted by and helps articulate the entanglement of fishing practice and ecological phenomena, including what comes to matter through that entanglement. Much like the materialization (i.e., the articulation of something that matters) of sound if a tree falls in the forest, key materiality (i.e., that which has the property of mattering) in captains' fishing practices can only materialize if those practices have certain potentiality already embedded in them. This is the potentiality that captains need to make sense of ecological phenomena and in turn co-articulate certain (physical and conceptual) matters into existence. This sensemaking bounds the actualities of ecological phenomena (life history traits) in certain ways and gives it certain properties and meanings (e.g., 'in the spring they spawn,' 'up in the shallows at 35 fathoms in the fall') which are inseparable from the assemblages of entanglements that we differentiate as fishing practices and those that we differentiate as ecological phenomena. Thus, the properties and meanings of ecological materialities are entangled 'all the way down.' Such properties and meanings in turn enable other materialities to be co-articulated. Key materialities include a fishing spot one has steamed to, a space beneath the vessel one can tow through, catch on deck one can sort through, and so on. From the meeting of particular potentialities embedded in particular fishing practices and particular actualities embedded in particular ecological phenomena, particular materialities are articulated; those articulations are mutually performed, and their materialities are mutually constituted, by human and natural phenomena. Put in terms of the current ecological sensemaking literature, captains' fishing practice must already be embedded with certain potentiality for 'noticing, bracketing, and making and selecting connections and acting on spatial and temporal cues arising from topography and ecological processes,' i.e., for making ecological sense as defined by Whiteman and Cooper (2011, p. 905), that potentiality must encounter the ecological actuality that it can notice, *prior to* the manifestation of certain ecological materiality. Ecological materiality does not exist separate from ecological sensemaking as something to be made sense *of*; instead, it materializes *through* ecological sensemaking, and is mutually constituted by human and natural phenomena. The data discussed below show that captains' potentiality for co-articulating the various ecological materialities of their fishing practice is embedded in technologies, such as trawl gear, plotters, and sonars, and in action dispositions, such as sharing information and fishing where one fished before.

The ecological materialities that emerge through fishing practices are mutually constituted by the potentiality of captains' practices and the actualities of natural phenomena. Yet the potentiality of captains' practices and the actualities of natural phenomena are *already* entangled, prior to their co-articulation of ecological materiality. Thus, the entangled articulation and constitution of the materiality that comes to matter through ecological sensemaking, including ecological materiality, is but one dimension of the entanglement of fishing practices and natural phenomena. The potentiality that captains' fishing practices have for engaging in the boundary-, property-, and meaning-making relations that, together with the boundary-, property-, and meaning-making relations of natural phenomena, co-articulate ecological materiality are *already* entangled with natural phenomena, prior to particular manifestations of materiality. This is because the technologies and action dispositions that embed captains' practices with potentiality for co-articulating certain materialities are also materializations that have been co-articulated through past entanglements, and continue to be co-articulated. This is another dimension of the entanglement of fishing practices and natural phenomena. As we will see below, technologies and action dispositions are tools of boundary-, property-, and meaning-making help accomplish the transformation of mere potentiality for catching fish into the actuality of caught fish (as well as other matters); these tools are themselves born of past manifestations of ecological materialities, such as fishing spots and fish on deck, and are continually performed (e.g., engineered, manufactured, sold, used, updated, replaced) in terms of those materialities. Thus, not only is the ecological materiality that is articulated in any trip, such as a fishing spot or catch on deck, mutually constituted by human and natural phenomena, so is the means of that mutual constitution (giving us two dimensions of entanglement). John Law, scholar of management and actor–network theory, eloquently makes a similar argument in the following:

> Look at it this way: the social is a set of processes, of transformations. These are moving, acting, interacting. They are generating themselves. Perhaps we can impute patterns in these movements. But here's the trick, the crucial and most difficult move that we need to make. We need to say that *the patterns, the channels down which they flow, are not different in kind from whatever it is that is channelled by them* ... [T]he social world is this remarkable emergent phenomenon: in its processes it shapes its own flows. Movement and the organization of movement are not different.
>
> *(Law, 1994, p. 15; emphasis original)*

If we take Law's 'social world' to be a posthumanistic 'human-natural world,' then we are discussing similar phenomena—the entangled human-natural articulation of material outcomes and the entangled human-natural articulation of the means by which such articulation is performed. In other words, 'we are part of the nature we seek to understand,' and that nature is part of us and our process of understanding.

Sense and the making of it are both mutually constituted by captains' fishing practices and ecological phenomena, which are already entangled. There is no stopping this regress (and progress) of entanglement. The potentiality of captains' fishing practices are co-constituted by natural phenomena, but the reverse is also true in that the potentialities of natural phenomena, particularly the biophysical actualities they are embedded in, are co-constituted by captains' fishing practices. Captains' fishing practices, including where, when, and how they tow, as well as how much they tow of particular species and populations, co-articulate the life history traits of ecological phenomena. Captains' fishing practices are boundary-, property-, and meaning-making activities that shape the migratory entanglements of various species and their populations, over both the short and long term. Such co-articulation, especially in which captains' fishing practices can limit the breeding potentiality of populations and species, is what sustainable fisheries science is all about.

What follows is a posthumanistic view of ecological sensemaking, which depicts how ecological phenomena exist within it and shape its processes and what materializes through them. While the concept of entanglement, as well as mutual constitution, emerges from experiments conceptualized and carried out in the relatively esoteric domain of quantum mechanics, such experiments and the lessons drawn from them are, according to Barad, "completely general, as far as we know" (Barad, 2007, p. 110). If we, as students of ecological sensemaking, mindfully heed Bohr's "central lesson of quantum mechanics" (ibid., p. 247), namely that 'we are part of the nature that we seek to understand,' it becomes clear that we cannot both adhere to natural science and understand nature as emerging through relational phenomena, such as the mutual constitution of genes, organisms, and environments (Lewontin, 2000), and maintain, or at times fall back on, a non-relational view of nature when it comes to its relationship with humans. Nature cannot be both distinct from humans, existing 'out there' with its roster of non-relational properties, and itself emerge through entangled, relational activities like feeding, breeding, and surviving. Thus, we cannot both recognize that nature involves entangled phenomena and assume that it is not entangled with us (Barad, 2007; Latour, 2005; Rouse, 2002). To do so would be to assume that there are two different versions of how reality articulates itself (i.e., ontologies), which change depending on whether humans are involved or not. Such an assumption not only depends on dualism, but it also smacks of deism, in which humans, made in God's image, are not only elevated above all other creatures, but are also endowed with a different ontology. Of course we distinguish entities, and compare and contrast their boundaries, properties, and meanings, but we have to be mindful of what we are doing (i.e., agentially imposing separations, or 'cuts,' into entangled phenomena) and what we are actually dealing with (i.e., entangled phenomena). This is especially the case when what we are doing can have significant detrimental impacts on what we are dealing with.

A posthumanistic framework of ecological sensemaking

The discussions below demonstrate several ways in which the actuality of captains' fishing practice is embedded with potentiality for articulating particular ecological materialities into existence; the discussions focus on how this potentiality is co-articulated by human and natural phenomena, making captains' practices entangled with ecological phenomena prior to their physical encounter in a particular fishing event. Thus, not only is the materiality performed in any particular fishing event co-articulated by human and natural phenomena, but so is that performative process. The discussions show how ecological phenomena, particularly the migratory entanglements and biophysical properties of particular species, 'vectorize' captains' fishing practices toward attempting to articulate particular materialities into existence, guiding them from within to use tools such as trawl gear, plotters, sonars, and to enact action dispositions such as fishing where you fished before and sharing fishing information, to make particular ecological sense of what to do next. Put simply, the discussions demonstrate how captains' ecological sensemaking processes, including what materializes through them, are co-articulated with natural phenomena. The discussions end by combining the two versions of the framework presented thus far, i.e., the ecological sensemaking and the life-history trait versions, into one posthumanistic framework.

The potentiality of trawl gear

One of the key ways that target species, and the ecological phenomena they are constitutively embedded in, vectorize captains' fishing practice is in terms of the type of gear that captains use. Captains use trawl gear due to the efficiencies it offers when targeting the ecological phenomena in which target species assemble into aggregations in the same general places at the same general time of the year, year after year. Thus, the recurring actualities of episodic migratory entanglements (i.e., aggregations, schools) offers potentiality, which captains make sense of and embed into their fishing practices in various ways, one of which is the use of trawl gear. In turn, embedded in the actuality of trawl gear is captains' potentiality for turning aggregations into the materiality of caught fish. Certain types of trawl gear are built to intercept aggregations on the ocean bottom ('bottom gear'), while other types are designed to intercept aggregations off the bottom and in the water column ('mid-water gear'). Yet, without the aggregations that target species both enact and emerge through, there would be no trawl gear; the very idea of trawl gear is physically articulated by the entanglement of fishing practices and ecological phenomena.

Through ecological sensemaking, captains transform the actualities of ecological phenomena, as encountered in past fishing practices, into the potentiality of their target species (e.g., aggregations), and that potentiality lures captains' practices toward the use of trawl gear. The use of trawl gear in turn shapes which propositions are efficient, strategic, and plausible, and therefore actionable (See Chapter 5). In the following a captain, while on a fishing trip, describes why certain instrumental activities of target fish dispose captains to use trawl gear:

> This area is huge, thousands of square miles of fishable ground. There's flathead, rex, dover, all the species of sole live in this area. All the species of midwater pelagic fish of Alaska live in this area too. But the problem with this area is it is vast, and we're only covering 500 feet of it, and the net is only actually covering 56 feet of it. Theoretically we are herding fish toward the net with our sweeps [see Figure 2.2 in Chapter 2], but how absolutely effective that is, we don't know. So the fish have to be aggregated to some degree to catch very much.

Or as another captain put it:

> When the fish are congregated together, when they are schooled up and are more interested in spawning or feeding or whatever, it's the easiest for us to catch them. When there's a million pounds between here and the jetty (pointing to a spot on a chart), it's easy for us to catch them, but when they are dispersed in the water column, it's difficult for us to catch them.

The instrumental activities of ecological phenomena that make themselves intelligible to captains agentially dispose captains to using trawl gear (in which 'agency' is understood as intelligibility that is part of a differential response, or a sense of meaning) . In turn, trawl gear disposes captains to target recurring episodic migratory entanglements, otherwise gear that more passively draws fish to it with bait would be a better approach. And in agentially cutting through aggregating fish, constitutively capturing some, constitutively excluding others, trawl gear co-articulates (along with ecological phenomena) materiality in the form of catch in the net and then catch on deck, which captains, through their sensemaking, integrate into their potentiality of where and when to fish next.

Yet ecological aggregations also agentially co-embed captains' practice with potentiality for danger. This is because the fleet fishes 'groundfish,' which means, just as it sounds, that most of their target species live on or close to the ocean bottom. For instance, two species of rockfish are typically found around rocky bottom, while another, Pacific Ocean perch, is found in the deeper water, "off the edge" or "up and down the bank." Certain species of flatfish are found on "sandy bottom"; others live on "rocky bottom"; while others are found "on the edge" between sandy and rocky bottom. Further, pollock, considered a "mid-water" or pelagic species, is often found tightly packed to the bottom, as well as "up in the shallows." For trawl vessels, the ecological activities of their target species are very often entangled with the geophysical activities of the ocean bottom. This in turn means that a common concern captains have is "hanging up" on rocky bottom, which often means tearing a trawl net (which are typically made of nylon). A captain exemplifies this danger in the following: "It's a kick in the ass! Plowing through the boulders, sometimes you bring a net back, sometimes you bring a rag." A torn net can reduce efficiency by detracting from fishing time, for crews usually repair torn nets at sea. Nets that sustain too much damage, however, have to be repaired on land, and a common sight in Kodiak is a trawl net laid out over a parking lot with three or four crewmen sewing it back together while multiple bald eagles scavenge from it.

The potentiality of plotters

The plotter is the primary technology that captains use to help them choose which spots out on the fishing grounds to steam to. Plotters belong to the family of geographical information systems that are now commonplace in academic, governmental, and technical industries. Tied to the vessel's navigational system, including satellite global positioning systems and the Automatic Identification System that both identify and track most commercial maritime vessels, the plotter is a computer program that integrates various types of information from various sources and plots them on a computer-based nautical chart. All vessels in the GOA trawl fleet tend to have a plotter on continual display on a computer monitor in their wheelhouses.

Plotters simultaneously depict captains' past fishing activities and characteristics of their current contexts. They do so by relating types of data with other types of data, what are called 'layers,' until a rich integrated picture is created, which is continually updated throughout a fishing trip. Such a display starts with the differentiation of sea and land, upon which plotters build in differentiated geophysical data (e.g., bottom depths), geo-political data (e.g., names of bodies of land and water), regulatory data (e. g., areas closed to fishing), socio-physical data (e.g., nearby vessels), and data from past fishing and navigational activities. Further, plotters allow captains to annotate those data with additional boundaries, properties, and meanings, in which they note such things as the size and composition of past catch, towing hazards, and places and times in which they previously spotted aggregations, even if they did not fish from them. As one captain stated while pointing to his plotter:

> We mark hangs where the boat's hung up, where other boats have hung up, fish marks, hard bottom marks ... these are all marks of all the stuff around here, this Christmas-tree stuff here is all of my personal marks ... I got thousands of marks from 20 years ago.

Like trawl gear, plotters are boundary-, property-, and meaning making devices. In integrating various sources of data, from both the past and present, plotters provide captains with information for producing propositions as to where on the fishing grounds they might find a sizable aggregation to fish from next. In other words, plotters embed captains' fishing practice with actuality-conditioned potentiality, which they use in their ecological sensemaking to help them articulate new potentiality-conditioned actuality into existence (i.e., a new spot to fish in).

Plotters are ecological sensemaking tools, helping captains articulate boundaries, properties, and meanings into experience, from which a sense of what to do next materializes. Figure 6.2 depicts the array of screens onboard a vessel during a fishing trip I observed, in which the captain used two plotters to aid his sensemaking of where to find his target species, namely Northern and dusky rockfish. Plotters are dynamic devices, for as the vessel moves, as vessels move around it, and as captains change and annotate layers of data, the plotter display also changes. The plotters and the vessels they are housed in are always embedded in, and are always contributing to, a perpetually evolving entanglement of human, technological, ecological, and

FIGURE 6.2 Typical array of screens captains use onboard a GOA trawl vessel to locate and catch fish, containing two plotters (the two monitors on the left).
Source: Photo taken by author

geophysical activities, from which ever-changing plots materialize. The following is an example of a captain using the plotters from Figure 6.2 to make sense of where to fish next:

> This set here I think is what I'm gonna try (pointing to a mark on his plotter). The last time I fished for dusky rockfish here, a couple of years ago, I did ok up in there. This is real tough towing up through here (pointing to a different area), and then this over here has always been fairly good (pointing to a different spot).

In materializing places and times that the captain fished before, and in embedding those materialities in the ecological, social, and geophysical activities that constitute the current context, the plotter performs a specific dynamic articulation of the world that captains are entangled in. This articulation in turn embeds captains' ecological sensemaking with potentiality for proposing where on the fishing grounds they might encounter aggregations of their target fish next.

The potentiality of sonar

Another key source of potentiality for making sense of what to do next, particularly where to tow next, is the sonar. While captains use plotters to help them propose a spot on the fishing grounds to steam to, they use sonars to help them propose a space beneath the vessel to tow through. 'Sonar,' which is called 'echo sounder' and 'downsounder' on fishing boats, is an acronym of Sound Navigation and Ranging.

Sonars work through echo. They emit waves of particular megahertz toward the ocean bottom at particular intervals, which are intercepted by material beneath the vessel, which echo those waves back to the sonar; echoes tend to be produced either by the sea floor or by material between the vessel and the sea floor, such as wrecks, lost fishing gear, and aggregations of fish. Large and dense materials have potential to produce larger and more sustained differences in echoed waves, and therefore are more likely to be detected by the sonar. Aggregations of fish involving species that have 'air bladders' are particularly visible, for an air bladder, which is an internal sack that helps fish move vertically through the water column, has properties that echo 85% of the sound waves it encounters back to the vessel (Bazigos, 1981). Thus, fish with air bladders tend to be embedded with higher potential for echoing sound waves than fish that do not have air bladders. 'Roundfish,' such as rockfish, pollock, cod, and salmon, typically have air bladders, while bottom-dwelling 'flatfish,' such as flounders, sole, and halibut, do not.

Sonars are boundary-making devices within the broader fishing apparatus. More particularly, sonars differentiate between the amplitude and frequency of sound waves they emit and the amplitude and frequency of the echoes they receive back. From those differences, sonars co-perform (along with the phenomena that do and do not echo sound waves back to it) a specific type of materiality, which involves estimations of the density, shape, and location of whatever it is that has echoed sound waves back; further, some sonars integrate historical catch data into their articulations to produce biomass estimates. Sonars present these co-articulations as a visual display on a computer monitor in the vessel wheelhouse, which captains tend to have continually running during a fishing trip. Like the plotter and trawl gear, the sonar is a boundary-, property-, and meaning-making tool of entanglement: through the ongoing transference of waves across differences in the densities of materialities (e.g., from the sonar to water to bodies of fish back to water and to the sonar), and the measurements of those differences, the sonar physically entangles fishing practices with phenomena beneath the vessel; as those phenomena change, as the vessel moves, and as the sonar continually transforms echoed differences into visual materialities, the sonar intra-acts with material beneath the vessel to perform a moving depiction of the water column and its inhabitants for the captains (see Figure 6.3 for an example of a sonar screen printout). The sonar is how fishing practices are embedded with the potentiality to produce (i.e., materialize) objects in the wheelhouse that are physically entangled with aggregations of fish and the ocean bottom beneath the vessel. Thus, the 'concepts' that sonars present are physically articulated by both human and non-human phenomena 'all the way down.'

As previously stated, captains rely on sonars to provide a visual depiction of the bottom and the water column beneath their vessels, including aggregations of fish both in the water column and on the bottom. While I say 'depiction *of*' the bottom and the water column, it is important to understand that sonars do not provide representations of something that is separate from it, and which does not have agency in terms of what those depictions look like. Sonar displays are materializations that are mutually constituted by various phenomena, including captains' activities, technologies, and natural activity. The display is not 'of' something that is separate from its own activities and entanglements; rather, what is depicted in the

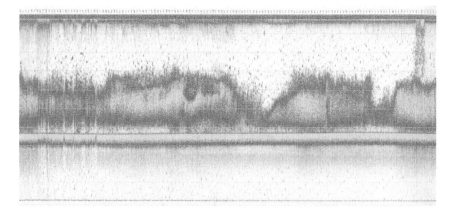

FIGURE 6.3 Printout of a sonar display; taken from a GOA trawl vessel fishing in a pollock fishery.

sonar display is something new that is co-articulated by various entangled activities. We can call it a 'depiction' or a 'representation,' but it is more accurate to say, following Barad (2007, 2014) and Haraway (1992) that the sonar display is a 'diffraction' (see Chapter 3 for more discussion of diffraction). By 'diffraction' I mean that the display involves various activities being superimposed and read through one another, in which each helps constitute the others, and together form an intelligible pattern. In terms of the tripartite representational arrangement described in Chapter 1, the sonar is not a device that mediates the gap between the sensemaker and that which is made sense of. Such a tripartite arrangement assumes that the depiction of the bottom and/or an aggregation of fish, or whatever is depicted by the sonar, is separate from the activities of the sensemaker. If, as argued above, neither that which is made sense of nor the sensemaker are separate, the sonar cannot be a device that mediates the relationship between two separate things. Instead, sonar displays are superpositions of various entangled activities, i.e., materializations, which serve an *articulating*, but not a *representing*, function.

Through their ongoing creation of materiality, sonars facilitate captains' ecological sensemaking of where to tow through next. While there are many "differences which make a difference" (Bateson, 1972, p. 459) to the sonar, the specific sonar 'differences which make a difference' to captains are materialities they call 'sign.' 'Sign' is a term for objects on a sonar display that suggest the presence of fish. Sign might be target species, or it might be some other object, such as krill or 'feed,' which has shown itself to be a recurring indicator of target species. As one captain described, "We look for what we call 'sign,' we are looking for feed. Guys will say, 'it looks like a bunch of feedy crap,' or 'it's a lot of something.' Nobody says, 'it's a lot of pollock.'" Yet, while sign is a key aspect of captains' sensemaking of where to tow next, it is always under-specified in relation to regulatory demands for an individualized, single species-based approach to fishing (and therefore an individualized, single-species based approach to making sense of where to steam to and tow from next) (see Chapter 2 for a description of the species-based regulatory structure of trawl fisheries). Sonars embed captains' fishing practices with potentiality for making sense of their ongoing and future entanglements with natural phenomena, but only in terms of the differentiations that matter to sonars, not in terms of the more specific differentiations that matter to regulators.

Due to regulations (and market demands), captains must target particular species, or in a couple of cases groups of two or three species, in particular areas at particular times of the year. Yet, the differentiations that sonars make are not all of the differentiations that captains need in order to make sense of where and when to catch their particular target species, and importantly to also not catch particular prohibited species (see Chapters 2 and 3 for descriptions of what prohibited species are, as well as discussions of their importance in terms of bycatch regulations). Fish are scientifically differentiated into species categories at the genetic level, yet many genetically *different* species have *similar* migratory entanglements and biophysical morphologies (i.e., life history traits). This means that, based on the differentiating potentiality that is embedded in sonars and the nature of the life history traits that are made intelligible by the ecological phenomena that captains encounter, different species can materialize in captains' practices as the same thing (i.e., as the same materiality). Thus, what materializes through the meeting of the actualities of ecological phenomena and the potentiality of sonar is, quite literally, underspecified in terms of regulatory demands (i.e., is it not differentiated at the species-level). In the following a captain describes this under-specification in more detail, particularly in terms of using the sonar to fish for sole, which is a type of flatfish:

> You can't see sole. The only thing an echo sounder will really truly show you is something that it can bounce sound off of, and to bounce sound off of something it has to have an air bladder in it, otherwise everything you see just looks like the bottom. A sole does not have an air bladder, but if you find a place where the sole is thick enough, if you get in a place where you are catching 100 thousand pounds of sole in an hour, the whole bottom looks a little bit different ... Feed, smelt, and stuff doesn't really have an air bladder, but sometimes there's just so much of it that it shows up like backscatter ... Like this stuff here (pointing to his sonar display), we don't really know what that is, I don't believe that we are actually seeing the sole so much as we are seeing what the sole is feeding on ... But it doesn't have to be feed, it could be a difference in water temperature, or a current rip could do the same thing. It picks up the difference.

While sonars differentiate mere water and relatively large solidities such as the bottom or aggregated fish, and aggregations of varying densities and spatio-temporal characteristics, they do not differentiate species that are enacting similar life history traits (in terms of those densities and spatio-temporal characteristics). Thus, the sonar will not measure differences between species that have air bladders and that swim in the same areas of the water column, such as pollock and Chinook salmon, or between species that do not have air bladders and occupy similar areas of the bottom, such as rock sole and Pacific halibut. Species, and the broader phenomena they are constitutively embedded in, that do not make themselves differentially intelligible in terms of the differences that sonars measure go undifferentiated, i.e., under-specified.

Multiple species can have similar (actuality-conditioned) potentialities, and therefore similar (potentiality-conditioned) actualities. When those similar actualities, such a aggregating behaviors and biophysical morphologies, meet the boundary-, property-, and meaning-making potentiality of the sonar, but are not differentiated in that meeting, multiple species will materialize as the same sign on the sonar. The result is that sonar displays tend to be under-specified in fisheries that are regulated and managed at the single species, or even the species-complex, level. The under-specified and ambiguous nature of sign is a prominent source of indeterminacy in captains' ecological sensemaking (see the end of Chapter 4 for a rich example of the under-specification of sign).

The potentiality of action dispositions

Another source of potentiality that captains take to sea with them as they attempt to organize with the migratory entanglements of their target species is action dispositions. By 'action disposition' I mean "a persistent collection of premises, response tendencies, and structural capabilities that produce action with recognizable character" (Birnholtz et al., 2007, p. 317). Like the plotters and sonars, action dispositions are ways in which target species' actualities co-constitute captains' potentialities, in turn vectorizing captains' instrumental actions, and therefore their actualities.

A particular action disposition that captains deploy is 'fishing where [they] fished before.' Thus, captains regularly, when determining where to fish next, fish where they fished before. The following are a few examples of captains either discussing or enacting this disposition:

> We tow in the same place year after year. For 40 motherfucking years we have been towing on the same edge of Chiniak Gulley [pointing to a place on a chart] or in any of our other spots, and we are still going there today … If you overlay the data for 40 years, trawlers will be here, here, and here [pointing to areas on a plotter], year after year after year. [...]
>
> There's only a few places we can fish, and we fish the same places year after year after year, and they are always productive … Like Chiniak Gulley, we've been fishing there for 30 years and you can still go out there at certain times of year and just load up in 24 hours on sole flatfish. [...]
>
> I know I've made this tow [points to a place on a chart] 250 different times in my life, and I know that I can go back there and make this tow in a given year in a given circumstances and I will catch the same amount of fish.
>
> RESEARCHER: Is this a tow you have done before?
> CAPTAIN: Yeah, you can see all the times I've been through here
> RESEARCHER: So what influenced you to fish here?
> CAPTAIN: Oh it's just where I've caught duskies before, I've done pretty
>   well out there.

The action disposition to fish where they fished before is entangled with the (actuality-conditioned) potentialities of their target species, and, through ecological sensemaking, it orients captains' propositions and instrumental actions to the (potentiality-conditioned) actualities of aggregations associated with their target species. Thus, this action disposition is constituted by the recurring nature of target species aggregations, and is a means by which captains' (actuality-conditioned) potentiality meets the (potentiality-conditioned) actuality of their target fish, by way of the boundary-, property-, and meaning-making activities involved in fishing where they fished before.

The second action disposition that stood out in the data was the tendency to for captains to share information with other captains about the potential timing and location of target species' actualities. Thus, captains' ecological sensemaking of where to steam to or tow through next is usually not an individual affair. The data show that captains often seek out information from one another (and in turn share information with one another) to enhance their potential to create plausible, efficient, and strategic (i.e., actionable) propositions as to where to steam to and tow through next. This action disposition is evident in one captain's response when asked how often he relied on other captains to determine where to fish: "Probably 50% or so. If there's a lot of fish around you don't need to ask a lot of questions, but if they're hard to find, then you get on the radio." Or as another put it, "There's lots of us out there, and if somebody finds something, we go to that spot; we're not going spend time driving around where there's nothing." Thus, the sense that captains' make is not only entangled with ecological phenomena, it is also entangled across captains, , and even time.

Captains recurrently share information with one another in patterned ways. These patterns include haphazard sharing, such as when captains pass one another when heading to and from the fishing grounds, less haphazard/more regular sharing, such as when captains gather in meetings before and after seasons, and more routine sharing, such as when captains operate in an established fishing group. The following radio conversation among two captains who are sitting at the dock preparing to go fishing and one who is already fishing exemplifies haphazard sharing:

> DOCKED CAPTAIN 1: It looks like you are traveling at tow speed, what are you doing?
> AT-SEA CAPTAIN: Towing my last tow then coming in.
> DOCKED CAPTAIN 1: Is this your first tow on the east side?
> AT-SEA CAPTAIN: Yeah, just made a three-hour pass.
> DOCKED CAPTAIN 2: You must have found some fish.
> AT-SEA CAPTAIN: Roger that.

The docked captains in this example were tracking the at-sea captain's movement on their plotters. From the nature of the at-sea captain's activity, they could tell he was fishing. Thus, the captains, while at the dock, located a fishing spot that another captain had evidently already proposed would be a profitable place to fish. Yet, they sought to further enhance their potential to propose a plausible place to fish by communicating with that captain and gaining more information about that spot.

A less haphazard situation of information sharing occurs at more regular, planned gatherings on land, such as at fleet meetings. Fleet meetings, as described in Chapter 2, are typically held so the fleet can structure how they collectively enact a particular fishery, and/or how they progress from one fishery to another, with the goal of giving each vessel a fair opportunity to maximize their potential. I often observed captains sharing experiences related to conditions at sea before, during, and after fleet meetings. The following exchange at a fleet meeting between two captains who are regular members of the Kodiak trawl fleet and one who is a regular member of the Western Gulf trawl fleet (but who attended a Kodiak trawl fleet meeting), all of which are members of the GOA trawl fleet, demonstrates a more regular situation in which one captain shares information with another related to determining where to fish next:

> KODIAK CAPTAIN 1: How much do we know about the boats from [the Western Gulf] that are coming out to harvest the pollock quota?
>
> KODIAK CAPTAIN 2: One of those guys is right here [points to another captain], why don't you ask him? [general laughs in the room]
>
> WESTERN GULF CAPTAIN: The reason we came out here is because there wasn't any fish around Sand Point. We're probably going to go back there and look again to see if there's any fish.
>
> KODIAK CAPTAIN 2: I saw plenty above Mountain Top.
>
> WESTERN GULF CAPTAIN: Pardon?
>
> KODIAK CAPTAIN 2: I saw plenty of fish above Mountain Top the other day.
>
> WESTERN GULF CAPTAIN: Did you?
>
> KODIAK CAPTAIN 2: Oh shit yeah, I would have loved to set on it!

This interaction involved one captain sharing information about a potential fishing spot with another. Like the example above, this conversation suggests that the actuality of sharing information enhances one another's potentiality. Although we cannot know the extent to which the Western Gulf captain integrated the Kodiak captain's information into his sensemaking of where to fish next, we can assume that his potential for creating an actionable proposition was improved.

Just as captains use experience from other captains to formulate actionable propositions regarding a spot to steam to, they also use experience from other captains to create propositions about where to tow through. Captains spend a lot of time at sea working with one another to make sense of the sign presented by their sonars as they determine which particular space beneath their vessel to tow through next. The following radio conversation between two captains fishing side-by-side for duskies, northerns, and perch, which are types of rockfish, exemplifies captains working work together to make sense of sign, and in doing so enhancing one another's potential to produce an actionable proposition of where to tow next:

> CAPTAIN 1: You saw a little bit of sign yesterday, right?
>
> CAPTAIN 2: Yeah, there was some decent sign early to mid-afternoon ...
>
> CAPTAIN 1: Roger ... I tried to set at 11:30, there was some fluffy stuff on the bottom, and then it all went up [into the water column], and then it came down [to the bottom] at around 3 p.m.
>
> CAPTAIN 2: In the afternoon it started doing that?
>
> CAPTAIN 1: Yeah, roger.
>
> CAPTAIN 2: Ok, well, I haven't figured out what they do in relation to the tides ... What depth was it when you got your duskies up north there?
>
> CAPTAIN 1: I was like 65 fathoms, yeah I think it was around 66, 65.

> CAPTAIN 2: Ok, same here. I fished here one trip last year and if I stayed at 66 and up I got duskies and northerns, but if I got much deeper I got into perch. Yesterday I got into 69 and 70 and there was still no real sign of perch.
>
> CAPTAIN 1: Yeah, up there a couple years ago, I think I was at 67, and boy I thought I was really in them, the sign looked the pretty much the same, just a lot better, and it was straight perch.

In addition to occasional information-sharing events, most captains have groups they regularly fish in. Fishing groups tend to range in size from three (e.g., "The Three Amigos") to five or six vessels, and the members of groups tend to share a common characteristic, such as delivering to the same fish processing plant (e.g., "The Trident Boats"), having the same general homeport (e.g., "The Oregon Boats"), perhaps even the same hometown (e.g., "The Newport Boats"), or they simply have common owners (e.g., "The Cochran Boats"). Groups share information across member vessels, enhancing each vessel's potential to create an actionable proposition as to where to steam to or tow from next. Here a captain, who is also an owner of three vessels, describes a group approach to finding a place to fish next at the beginning of a pollock fishery:

> I control three boats, it's a luxury. When we left town, most of the fleet was already out. I talked to them, asked how it was going. The three boats I control, we all went to the same spot we went to last year. That's what most people do. We went to three different areas. As for the fleet, half the fleet went to one area, half went to another area ... The other two boats would tell us what biomass they were seeing [on their sonar], and I would compare that to what I was seeing. Well, based on what I saw, the two other boats picked up and ran all night to get to where I was ... As an owner, I was looking at the bottom line of making money. Because I have three boats and work with the fleet, nine times out of ten I am on the fish.

A common strategy among GOA trawl captains is steaming to the fishing grounds a day or two before the regulatorily-prescribed start to the season in order to find potentially profitable fishing spots. Because the fishing season of interest in this quote was the first pollock season of the year, captains had time to go out to the grounds to look at natural conditions several days before the season started. In this ecological sensemaking process, there is the production of a group-wide proposition, but it is informed by differentiated actualities. Thus, by sharing and comparing information about natural conditions, the group collectively enhanced individual potential to enact a profitable fishing trip.

The posthumanistic ecological sensemaking framework

One cannot understand captains' ecological sensemaking without understanding the ecological potentiality that is a constitutive part of it. Likewise, one cannot understand the natural phenomena through which target species materialize in ecological sensemaking processes, without understanding ecological sensemaking. Just as we have to understand dynamics of fishing practices in order to understand dynamics of natural phenomena, we have to understand dynamics of natural phenomena in order to understand the dynamics of fishing practices; but perhaps more so, we have to understand their mutual constitution. If we slice captains' practices and natural phenomena apart and attempt to understand, regulate, and manage them separately, both become nonsensical; yet by understanding them together, through their entanglement, we can understand more about their mutual dependence, as well as their manifestations as individualities. A posthumanistic perspective of ecological sensemaking allows us to see that sense and the making of it are mutually constituted by the entangled actuality and potentiality of both captains' fishing practices and ecological phenomena. Such an understanding in turn gives us the potential to manage and regulate both more realistically, and thus more sustainably.

We can now use the ecological sensemaking and life history trait frameworks to construct a posthumanistic ecological sensemaking (PES) framework. I will first construct a general PES framework, then demonstrate its application in the GOA trawl context, using the material already provided. This more general indeterminacy-based, potentiality–actuality framework of entangled human-natural phenomena can be applied to various contexts. This a framework in which (actuality-conditioned) potentialities are articulated (i.e., agentially formed through boundary-, property-, and meaning-making relations) from (potentiality-conditioned) actualities, which manifest as some sort of propositional materiality (e.g., a captain's proposition of where to steam to, a biophysical proposition of which direction to swim in), and in which (potentiality-conditioned) actualities are articulated from (actuality-conditioned) potentialities, which manifest as some sort of physical materiality (e.g., biophysical structures, catch on deck). The mechanics of this general PES framework are depicted in Figure 6.4; they are apparent if you follow from the bottom arrow, with its potentiality and actuality anchors on either end of it, and which points to 'potentiality-conditioned

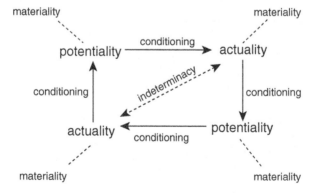

FIGURE 6.4 General posthumanistic ecological sensemaking framework (designed to be applied across various types of phenomena).

actuality' on the left hand corner, to the left side arrow, with its actuality and poten-tiality anchors, which points to 'actuality-conditioned potentiality,' and on around. At each corner there is materialization, whether it is a proposition that is articulated from potentiality (but which is conditioned by the actuality it is embedded in) or the phy-sical place of one's practice that is articulated out of broader actuality (but which is never separate from the potentiality that conditions its materialization). Importantly, what materializes at each corner is not all there is to experience; each corner involves what is included in the of materiality, as well as what is constitutively excluded from it (Barad, 2007; Whitehead, 1967b). And what is excluded in one part of experience often comes back to haunt ensuing experiences (Barad, 2014). This is the general indeterminacy-based, potentiality–actuality framework of entangled human-natural phenomena.

I should note that the frameworks presented in this book are meant to inspire new ways of seeing, thinking about, analyzing, understanding, and ultimately managing and regulating certain organizing practices. As analytical frameworks, they carve boundaries into inseparable phenomena, circumscribing them, and stretching them apart in the interest of starting and contributing to conversations that ultimately lead to new theoretical and practical pathways. This is not an argument that reality divides itself into distinct potentialities and actualities, but instead that it wavers between the edges of these ideals, in which relatively abstract potentialities and relatively concrete actualities constitute the materialization of phenomena, and in doing so constitute, constrain, and enable, i.e., condition, one another within the entangled progression of experience. It is also an argument that ecological sensemaking is how frontline managers in resource extraction industries manage such conditioning, shaping where experience goes, as they deal with issue of what experience means.

I currently see three ways in which the framework can be used. In the first two, the entanglement of human and natural phenomena is the overarching logic that pervades its construction, but the framework focuses on the processes through which either humans or natural phenomena 'manage' their progression through the actualities of some portion of their lives. Thus, one version focuses on humans, the other on nature. This natural phenomena-based version of the framework was demonstrated earlier in this chapter (focusing on natural phenomena), while the human-focused version is applied to an extreme case of bycatch in the GOA trawl fisheries in Chapter 7 (focusing on captains' fishing practices). In the third version of the framework, human and natural phenomena are separated within the frame-work, though their entanglement, both in terms of their actuality and their potentiality, is maintained. This version of the framework, in terms of how it plays out in the GOA commercial trawl context, is depicted below. Note that while the framework agentially separates actuality-conditioned potentialities in terms of cap-tains (on the left side) and ecological phenomena (on the right side), this is done for purposes of analysis; the framework is intended to help us understand and study entanglement and its effects (materializations), and therefore it speaks to our ten-dency to differentiate and divide, while also highlighting, and helping us understand, the entangled nature of that which we differentiate and divide. There is, in reality, no divided human and natural version of reality, only human-natural actualities that are formed by and embedded with varying potentialities with varying boundaries, properties, and meanings.

Depicted in Figure 6.5 is the third version of the framework, as applied to the ecological sensemaking practices of GOA trawl captains. In this framework, ecological activity stemming from the potentiality of life history traits (bottom arrow) meets the actuality of the sensemaking tools embedded in captains' fishing practices (e.g., trawl gear, plotters, sonars, action dispositions) (lower left-hand corner). In this corner we are concerned with captains' indeterminacy of what to do next in terms of what the next phase of their fishing practice will be. This meeting materializes as such things as plots on plotters, sign on the sonar, fishing where one fished before, and so on (lower left-hand corner). These materialities are embedded with potentiality for producing a proposition of what to do next. The human-natural actuality of the lower left-hand corner gives rise to, or conditions, through the use of sensemaking tools, the materiality that is a proposition of what to do next, which is actuality-conditioned potentiality (upper left-hand corner). The proposition of what to do next leads to instrumental actions (top arrow), which cut boundaries, properties, and meanings into the entanglement of captains' practices and natural phenomena (though here we are focusing on captains), and leads to the enactment of a new human-natural actuality (upper right-hand corner). For captains, new materialities emerge through this actuality, such as catch on deck or a spot on the fishing grounds. But this human-natural actuality, and what materializes in captains practices, is also constituted by the boundary-making instrumental actions and morphological properties of ecological phenomena; importantly, the manifestation of this actuality in captains' practices is

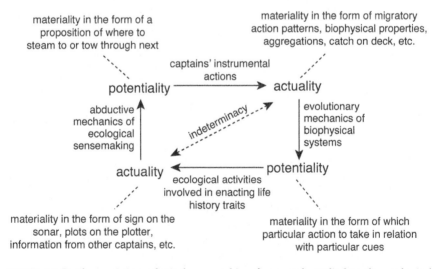

FIGURE 6.5 Posthumanistic ecological sensemaking framework applied to the ecological sensemaking apparatus as it has been elaborated thus far in the book.

conditioned by captains' preceding propositions and instrumental actions, particularly when, where, and how much captains tow, as well as by past propositions and instrumental actions of towing in certain places, at certain times, and towing certain amounts. Thus, both where and when captains propose to tow, and where and when they have proposed to tow, and how much they have towed, in the past co-articulates what materializes in their present.

In the upper-right hand corner our focus shifts to natural phenomena. The nature of captains' propositions and instrumental actions, namely where, when and how much they recurrently tow, co-constitutes the actuality that conditions, through evolutionary processes, ecological potentialities (right arrow). It is quite well established, for instance, that when, where, and how much fish captains remove from populations shapes their genetic processes, in turn their life history traits, and in turn their long-term viability (e.g., Enberg et al., 2012; Neubauer, Jensen, Hutchings, & Baum, 2013; Pauly et al., 2001). Overfishing is the fishing-based destruction of a species's potentiality for enacting life history traits such as feeding and breeding. Thus, certain ecological potentialities are 'propositions' for what comes next (lower right-hand arrow), which, when triggered, give rise to the recurring behavior patterns and morphologies that we call 'life history traits.' It is the enactment of certain life history traits (lower arrow) that captains encounter in their fishing practice. This is one example, albeit an abstract one, of how the posthumanistic ecological sensemaking (PES) framework can work in practice. A more concrete example, is provided in the next chapter.

Notes

1 Note that my individualized references to captains' fishing practices, phenomena, or processes, as well as to natural phenomena, processes, or systems—throughout the book—assumes differentiated, but not separated, phenomena (unless otherwise specified, such as in discussions of dualisms). Our language is constructed with entities. Such an abstraction-based language can offer clear, precise, succinct communication, which serves many purposes quite well. But we have to know what we are doing. Problems arise because we have unfortunately come to treat reality as if it were constituted by the distinct entities we use in the service of clear thought and communication. See Whitehead's (and other later scholars') elaboration of the Fallacy of Misplaced Concreteness, which he formally addressed in *Science and the Modern World* (Whitehead, 1967b), for more discussion of these problems. As Whitehead wrote, "You cannot think without abstractions; accordingly, it is of the utmost importance to be vigilant in critically revising your *modes* of abstraction" (ibid., pp. 58–59). My use of a language that is inherently entitative or abstractive does not presume that the things that the words and phrases refer to are inherently individual (again, unless otherwise indicated). Instead, the language assumes that the things referred to are differentiated entanglements that are constitutively embedded in entangled phenomena. My language therefore is an example of agential separability, or 'the world articulating itself differently' (Barad, 2007), but not separately.

2 SAFE reports are produced for each trawl target species by government scientists who are charged with the sustainable scientific management of the nation's fisheries resources, which are based on data are collected in partnership with trawl captains. They are the documents upon which various key fisheries management decisions, such as annual total allowable catch, are made.

7

WHEN LIGHTNING STRIKES

Making posthumanistic ecological sense of Chinook salmon bycatch

This chapter concludes this book's exercise in contributing to a new approach to thinking about, studying, regulating, and ultimately managing frontline organizing processes in natural resource extraction industries, as explored through the lens of the trawl fishing industry in the Gulf of Alaska (GOA). To do so, this chapter applies the posthumanistic ecological sensemaking (PES) framework constructed throughout the previous chapters to a real-world event that occurred in the GOA trawl fishery in 2010. After analyzing this event using the PES framework, I use that analysis to craft several recommendations as to how frontline human-natural organizing practices should be structured and regulated in the interest of reducing natural resource waste and improving business efficiency and effectiveness.

According to Chapter 6, fishing practices and ecological phenomena are entangled along two dimensions. The first dimension is the (posthumanistic) ecological sense-making apparatus. In this apparatus, the potentialities that captains have for making sense of where and when to fish next, to tow next, to haul up the catch, as well as for making sense of the composition of the catch, are entangled with the actualities of ecological phenomena. After captains turn those entangled potentialities into workable propositions, they perform the various key agential cuts that shape both what the apparatus is and what matters and meanings (i.e., materialities) emerge through it. Likewise, the actualities of captains' ecological sensemaking apparatus are entangled with the potentialities of ecological phenomena, particularly the plausible future locations and timings of episodic entanglements (i.e., aggregations, schools), which are embedded in the life history traits of ecological actualities.

The second dimension of the entanglement of fishing practices and ecological phenomena is, perhaps much more simply, the mutually-constituted nature of what the first dimension performs, i.e., what materializes through the (post-humanistic) ecological sensemaking apparatus. This is the meaning, or more broadly the sense, of what is happening and what to do next, as well as the matter that is target catch, bycatch, and other physical products of fishing. It is important to keep in mind that the meaning that manifests is relative to the physical configuration of the apparatus through which it is articulated. In other words, the apparatus determines what is meaningful and what is not, where there is actual 'matter of fact,' and where there is not (Barad, 2007). In turn, the material outcomes of this dimension of entanglement are actualities which are the feedstock of the potentialities that configure ensuing apparatuses. Thus, the two dimensions of entanglement are intra-active.

An important takeaway from Chapter 6 is that captains' practices are enacted in terms of the nature of the entangled human-natural materialities that constitute their sense of experience. Captains' sensemaking is not constituted by fish that are out there on the fishing grounds, or beneath the vessels, that come segregated into groups that align with the sharp boundaries of species-based categories. Segregated species groupings align with the clear-cut categories into which ecological science and rational management systems differentiate fish, yet those boundaries, properties, and meanings have a loose alignment with the boundaries, properties, and meanings that constitute at-sea practices. The clear-cut segregating (i.e., boundary-making) of wild fish swimming at sea into species-based categories is the stuff of laboratory, regulatory, and marketplace fantasy, not ecological actuality. Such categories are created by scientists and regulators in the interest of differentiating and individualizing ecological and industrial phenomena in ways that aid the ability to give clear conference presentations, craft publishable journal publications, and construct rational decision making-based regulations; yet these outcomes of boundary-making practices on land are different from the outcomes of the entangled human-natural boundary-making practices at sea. This difference in turn makes for messy management.

This messy management is the result of regulatory meanings being articulated through a different apparatus than meaning at sea is articulated through. The former is an apparatus that, being articulated according to the demands of metaphysical individualism, takes separation and inter-action as foundational, while the latter is an apparatus that, being articulated according to the demands of entanglement, takes inseparability and intra-action as foundational. As the latter is forced into the former within the same regulatory management system, byproducts and waste emerge as parts of the latter are cut away to fit the former. It is like re-assembling a metric system-based engine with a set of Imperial tools; while the end product might, if one is lucky, resemble an engine, the assembling process will involve a lot of byproducts (e.g., metal shavings, stripped bolts, unused parts) as well as wasted energy and frustration. The outcome may resemble what was desired, but it will not, either in the short or long term, function properly.

The chief purpose of the species categorization is to isolate phenomena based on certain life history traits, particularly traits involved in breeding. Yet other important, and often more prevalent life history traits traverse those categories. Such traits as feeding and migrating, for example, play a key role in the sense that captains and ecological phenomena co-create make at sea, yet in their particular manifestations, they are often common to more than one species. While discrete species-based categories can be used to identify similarities across species, such identifications start from the standpoint of separation; we can compare shared traits, but we still have separated species at the base of our understanding. Thus, doing so starts from an assumption of individualism, and takes an *inter*-active approach. Thus, it is a metaphysical approach. Starting from the standpoint of *inter*-action makes it difficult to organize and manage phenomena according to the *intra*-active realities of entanglement. Differentiated species emerge through boundary-making activities, such as feeding, breeding, and migrating—they do not precede them. Differentiation is always in-the-making; it is always being sedimented out of intra-active processes. Yet the species-based approach to regulating and managing fishing businesses puts the species first, and only afterward attempts to make some accommodations for entanglements that not only traverse species, but are the phenomena through which differentiated species emerge. One such accommodation that is built into regulatory structures and management practices is bycatch discard and waste.

More than one species can be part and parcel of (i.e., constitutively embedded in) ecological phenomena. Those species can in turn materialize in captains' fishing practices as the superimposed same (i.e., undifferentiated) phenomena. Different species can appear as the same because the ecological phenomena they are constitutively embedded in are undifferentiated by captains' ecological sensemaking tools (e.g., plotter, sonar, trawl gear, action dispositions). Thus, more than one species enacts the phenomena that captains' co-articulate, through their entangled (posthumanistic) ecological sensemaking, into the materiality of caught fish. For example, the same recurring intra-action patterns that captains find to involve rock sole on one occasion might involve pollock on another occasion (as we saw in Chapter 4), or the same phenomena might involve both rock sole and Pacific halibut, or pollock and Chinook salmon, or some other combination of species. What is individualized and isolated on land in scientific and regulatory boundary-making practices is often undifferentiated at sea in ecological sensemaking practices; the distinct species-based approach used in fisheries management is an ideal imposed from afar upon a context that only involves species-level differentiations in actuality *after* one has already towed, for every tow. This mismatch between regulation and management on-land and practice at-sea, as we will see in this chapter, has major implications for effective and efficient use of natural resources, and in turn for studying, regulating, and managing organizational practices in resource extraction contexts.

Bycatch discard

This chapter puts the analytical framework developed in the previous chapters into practice by focusing on the common occurrence in which more than one species mutually constitutes the ecological phenomena that captains co-articulate into the materiality of caught fish, by way of ecological sensemaking. The chapter does so by applying the PES framework to a real-world event involving one of today's most important sustainability issues—fisheries bycatch (Davies, Cripps, Nickson, & Porter, 2009; FAO, 2010; Lewison, et al., 2011; Patrick & Benaka, 2013; Phillips et al., 2016), and in particular, the discard and waste of bycatch. As discussed in Chapter 1, bycatch is "fish other than the primary target species that are caught incidental to the harvest of the primary species" (NOAA, 2006, p. 5), and bycatch discard is bycatch that is returned to the sea, dead or alive. While target fish can be discarded, and not all bycatch is discarded (as some may be retained for sale or personal consumption), the lion's share of what is discarded is bycatch.

Discarding is an important issue in the commercial fishing context due both to the large amount of fish that is discarded year after year and the tendency for the vast preponderance of that discard to be dead, and therefore wasted. Such waste occurs because most fish and other animals that are extracted from the depths are dead by the time they are deposited on the deck of a ship (and before they are then dumped back to sea). Thus, bycatch discard tends to result in high amounts of dead and unused fish, and therefore high amounts of wasted natural resources, as well as wasted time, effort, and other resources that are spent catching them. This is the reason that, as stated by Bellido et al., (2011, p. 318), "discarding is currently one of the most important topics in fisheries management, both from economic and environmental points of view."

Discarding tends to occur for one of three reasons. First, it can occur due to mechanical issues that prevent fish from being completely hauled on board or processed by a fish processing plant; second, there may not be a market for certain species; and third, regulations *require* that certain species be discarded. The focus in this chapter is primarily on the latter reason—bycatch that must be discarded due to regulation, in which the retention of certain species is prohibited by law. Such discarded bycatch is called 'regulatory discard,' and the species that must be discarded, that are prohibited from being retained, are known as 'prohibited species,' or 'prohibs,' in Alaskan federal fishery management.

Prohibs are certain bycatch species caught in Alaskan waters that trawl captains are required by regulation to discard, even though these species tend to be targets of other fisheries. These other fisheries are regulated by international or state agencies; thus, the requirement to discard valuable fish is grounded in the differentiation of management boundaries. The GOA groundfish fisheries management plan (FMP) offers more detail on prohibited species regulations:

> Prohibited species identified in this FMP are Pacific halibut, Pacific herring, Pacific salmon, steelhead trout, king crab, and Tanner crab. Species identified as prohibited must be avoided while fishing groundfish and must be immediately returned to the sea with a minimum of injury when caught and brought aboard
> …
>
> *(NPFMC, 2019, p. 40)*

An important aspect of the prohibited species discard requirement is that all herring, salmon, trout, 67% of the Pacific halibut (NPFMC, 2014), and 80% of the crab (NPFMC, 2007) die in the process of being caught groundfish fisheries (which include trawl fisheries).[1] This means that, for the most part, their discard is their wastage.

The particular event involving regulatory discards that is examined in this chapter was an extreme catch of Chinook salmon bycatch in a 2010 pollock trawl fishery in the Western Gulf regulatory area of the GOA (see Figure 2.1). An 'event,' as understood here, is a phenomenon that is limited to a particular location and time, here a particular fishing season in a particular fishing area. *Extreme* events are those that involve "significant interruptions, exaggerations of a type of stimulus that organizations routinely encounter on a smaller scale" (Christianson, Farkas, Sutcliffe, & Weick, 2009, p. 846). Such events are valuable as case studies because they allow us to see factors that may occur in daily practice, but which tend to go unnoticed or taken for granted (Eisenhardt, 1989; Yin, 2009). Thus, extreme events tend to be "abrupt and brutal audits," in which "every weakness comes rushing to the forefront" (Lagadec, 1993, p. 54). In examining this extreme event, this chapter presents a focused ethnography. Rather than examining commonalities across an array of events, a focused ethnography takes a particular event as its object of inquiry (Nicolini, Mengis, & Swan, 2012, p. 615, citing Alvesson, 1996).

Thus, this chapter is a focused ethnography that applies the PES framework to an extreme Chinook salmon bycatch event that occurred in a Western GOA pollock fishery in 2010 (see Figure 2.1). This was the single largest bycatch event on record in Alaskan fisheries, at least since the fleets were 'Americanized' in the 1990s (in which foreign fishing vessels became highly restricted). One goal of applying the analytical framework to this event is to gain a better understanding of the causes and solutions of bycatch in general, and bycatch discard in particular; such an understanding can in turn foster better research, theory, regulation, and management. Another goal is to demonstrate the PES framework's utility for understanding human-natural organizing practices in resource extraction businesses and industries. This chapter ultimately makes it clear that, in terms of the GOA, there is a mismatch between the rational systems approach to managing fisheries on land and entangled human-natural processes at sea, and that this mismatch in turn can lead to great amounts of natural resource waste. Through the lens of an extreme event, this chapter demonstrates how the effects of this mismatch can play out on a grand scale. It provides evidence that rational management systems, such as the one enacted by the North Pacific Fishery Management Council (NPFMC), in concert with the National Marine Fisheries Service (NMFS), which together govern fisheries in Federal Alaskan waters, co-articulate much of the bycatch discard they attempt to reduce.

An abrupt and brutal bycatch audit

In 11 days in October of 2010, approximately 21 vessels fishing for pollock accidentally caught over 28,000 Chinook, or 'king,' salmon. This was the pollock 'D' season in the Western area of the Gulf of Alaska (GOA); the D season is the last pollock season of the year in both the Central and Western Gulf regulatory areas, preceded by the A, B, and C seasons (A and B occur early in the year, C and D later in the year). The same group of vessels that fished in the Western Gulf 2010

D season also, for the most part, fished there in the 2009 D season, and caught a mere 178 Chinook salmon. Over the previous 10 years, GOA trawl captains caught an average of 1,500 Chinook salmon in the Western Gulf pollock D season. The total number of Chinook salmon that GOA trawl captains caught in all pollock seasons in the GOA in 2010 was 44,825, which was more than double the average of the previous 10 years (i.e., 20,319). Figure 7.1, which depicts bycatch rates (i.e., the number of Chinook caught for every ton of pollock caught) across pollock seasons in the Western Gulf, provides a stark visualization of the extreme nature of the Chinook salmon bycatch that was produced in the 2010 D season.

All Chinook salmon caught in Alaskan pollock fisheries is, by regulation, categorized as prohibited species bycatch, and therefore all must be tossed overboard (or delivered to a food bank). All the Chinook that was caught in the 2010 Western Gulf D season was discarded at sea (after being delivered to a processing plant where it was sorted from the catch and then placed back on the vessel that caught it to be discarded at sea when the vessel went back out). Like most fish, all Chinook salmon die in the process of being caught by a trawl net. Thus, all of the Chinook that was caught in this event, and most that were caught in previous and subsequent years, has been wasted. I say *most* because there has been, off and on, donations of bycaught salmon to food banks. While the Kodiak trawl fleet made some donations to local schools prior to 2010, in 2011 the Kodiak trawl fleet and the local Kodiak processing plants worked with SeaShare, an Alaskan food bank, to set up a donation system. Yet donation amounts remain relatively low in terms of the amount of bycaught fish.

The amount of waste produced in the 2010 Chinook bycatch event was staggering. Using a conservative estimate of the weight of the Chinook caught in the focal event - 7.5 lbs/fish (based on NPFMC analyses, NPFMC, 2011, p. 117) - approximately 95 metric tons of Chinook was discarded in the 2010 Western Gulf D season pollock fishery. The approximate tonnage bycaught and discarded in all GOA pollock fisheries in 2010 was 153 metric tons. The amount caught since 2010 (2011–2018) is 126,051 fish,[2] or approximately 430 metric tons. One way to understand this much waste is to look at it in terms of the number of salmon fillets it could have provided. A conservative estimate of the amount of meat that one salmon yields is about 40% of its total weight (based on various internet searches). Let's subtract another 10% to account for the damage that trawl nets cause to salmon flesh; 30% of 95 metric tons is about 28 tons; 28 tons is about 61,700 pounds, which is about 987,200 ounces. At about 5 ounces per meal (i.e., a salmon steak), the Chinook salmon wasted in the 2010 Western Gulf bycatch event was roughly equivalent to over 197,000 meals. In 2009 The Justice Center at the University of Alaska estimated Alaska to have about 4,583 homeless people,[3] and therefore the amount of Chinook salmon wasted in the event would have provided over 40 meals for every 1 homeless person in the state. Discussions such as this become even more profound when we remind ourselves that all of the fish in US waters are public resources, large amounts of which are prescribed by regulation to be

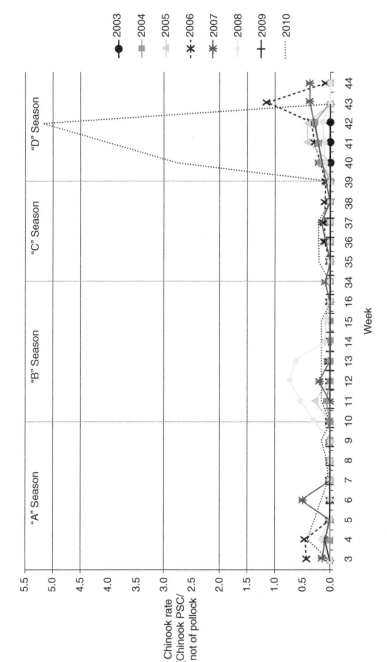

FIGURE 7.1 Seasonal (A, B, C, D) and annual Chinook salmon bycatch rates in the Western Gulf pollock fisheries. A and B seasons are, by regulation, scheduled to start on January 20 and end by May 31, and the C and D seasons are scheduled to begin on August 25 and end by November 1. The 2010 spike in the D season is the at-sea portion of the Western Gulf bycatch event.

Source: NPFMC (2011, p. 57)

wasted. The upshot is that the amount of waste that is *regulated* to occur in federal Alaskan fisheries, especially when we include Chinook salmon that are wasted in the Bering Sea (as well as the GOA), and the Pacific Halibut that are wasted in both the GOA and the Bering Sea, is immense.

But the extreme event of interest did not end with a mass catch and discard of Chinook salmon. The NPFMC, which is the body charged with regulating all federal fisheries in Alaskan waters (as explained in Chapter 2), had for several years been analyzing and discussing how to manage Chinook salmon bycatch in the GOA trawl fisheries. This is because National Standard 9 (see Chapter 2 for a description) requires all Regional Fishery Management Councils (of which there are eight spanning the coastal regions of the US) to create "Conservation and management measures" that, "to the extent practicable, (a) minimize bycatch and (b) to the extent bycatch cannot be avoided, minimize the mortality of such bycatch." Prior to this extreme event there were no conservation and management measures for Chinook salmon bycatch in the GOA groundfish fisheries, beyond the prohibited species rules that prevent trawl vessels from retaining (and therefore selling) it. But the amount of Chinook salmon caught in the GOA in 2010 violated the Endangered Species Act (ESA), which in turn elevated the NPFMC's ongoing analysis and discussion of Chinook salmon bycatch in the GOA to emergency status. In particular, the amount of catch in the event exceeded the 'incidental take statement' that accompanied the 2000 ESA listing of nine 'evolutionarily significant units' of Chinook salmon in Washington, Oregon, and California. An 'evolutionarily significant unit' is a population that is considered vital to a species' genetic wellbeing. The ESA statement involved trawl fisheries in the GOA because Chinook salmon from the listed 'evolutionary significant units' had previously been found in GOA trawl catch (which were identified through genetic analysis). The incidental take statement set the amount of Chinook that could be 'taken,' or killed, in the GOA trawl fisheries at 40,000 per year. Thus, the amount of Chinook caught in all the 2010 GOA trawl fisheries (but primarily because of the Western Gulf pollock D season) exceeded the allowable incidental take; once that occurred, the ESA required 'Section 7 formal consultation' between federal agency administrators. In this case the agencies were the Alaska and Washington regions of the National Marine Fisheries Service. Consultation processes typically mean that some sort of action has to be taken to ensure that similar violations will not recur. The body that had the burden of action in this case was the NPFMC.

The ESA consultation process, however, was not the only source of pressure to act that the NPFMC faced as a result of the extreme amount of Chinook salmon bycatch in the 2010 event. The NPFMC also faced pressure from various Chinook salmon stakeholders to do something about Chinook salmon bycatch in the GOA. This pressure is related to the fact that Chinook is the largest, least abundant, and most expensive of the five species of salmon that swim in Alaskan waters. It is also the Alaska State fish, and is arguably the most culturally significant of the Alaskan salmonids. Thus, the fish has a large amount and a broad range of stakeholders.

Such stakeholders include people who fish in fisheries that target Chinook salmon, from commercial, including subsistence, sport/charter, and personal-use fishermen, as well as people who simply consider themselves to be affected by the sustainability and traditional use of Alaska's Chinook salmon.

Yet, the public outcry was not just due to the high amount of bycatch in the event. The extreme amount of bycatch and waste occurred in the midst of a trend of poor 'runs' of Chinook salmon, which has not abated through 2019. 'Runs' are the return of salmon *en masse* from the ocean to spawn in the rivers they were born in (thus, they are longitudinal migratory entanglements); all directed salmon fisheries, from commercial, to subsistence, to sport, to personal use, depend on healthy runs, as do the broader ecosystems that the runs are part of. Runs are monitored by state fisheries managers, with the size of a run determining how big a particular Chinook fishery can be (how many fish can be caught), if there can be one at all. To better understand the health of various Chinook salmon fisheries in Alaska during the time of the extreme bycatch event, the following is a list compiled by Mike Campbell of the Anchorage Daily News in 2010:

- The early Kenai River run is down 43% since 2006
- The Deshka River return, while on the rebound, is still down 51% from a robust 2005 run.
- Both the Karluk (down 61%) and Ayakulik (down 80%) rivers on Kodiak Island have dropped precipitously and were shuttered to anglers last summer [2010] in an effort to rebuild them
- Alaska's biggest king run, to the Nushagak River in southwest Alaska, cratered last year, down 80% in just five years. (Campbell, 2010 November 9)

The coupling of poor runs of Chinook salmon with the wastage of tons of Chinook salmon in non-Chinook salmon fisheries meant a lot of unhappy Chinook salmon stakeholders.

To give a sense of the stakeholder pressure that the NPFMC faced after the event, the following are headlines and excerpts from a few of the newspaper articles on the event that were published in 2010 or 2011:

- **Bycatch kings irk sport fishermen—CONTROVERSY: 59,000 were caught unintentionally by pollock trawlers**

  Some sport fishermen are seething after a report last month showed more than 59,000 king salmon in the Gulf of Alaska were taken by pollock boats and other commercial fishermen this year. 'There's a feeling of frustration among most recreational anglers,' said Chris Fiala, owner of Kodiak Island Charters and a Kodiak resident since 1985. 'The king salmon is huge because it's our wonder fish. It's our, marlin; it's the fish that really signifies Alaska.' ... How many kings is 59,000? Nearly as many kings as returned all last year to the Kenai River, the biggest return in Southcentral Alaska ... Perhaps it's no wonder that concern about kings is growing. Even though king salmon population numbers pale beside pollock, each fish is worth far more. 'I made $1,000 for every king salmon I caught last year,' Fiala said. 'It's a big lure to visitors, so if I lose that lure, I'm in trouble. I live here, and that money stays in Kodiak.'

(Campbell, 2010 November 9)

- **Coastal Alaskans ask federal council to cap gulf bycatch**

More than 500 residents of Alaska's coastal communities have signed a letter urging the NPFMC to put a cap on the number of king salmon that may be caught incidentally in Gulf of Alaska Pollock trawl fishery ... The signers said that significant and unrestricted Chinook salmon bycatch has occurred in the Gulf of Alaska for decades and that the level of bycatch is unacceptable, particularly in a time in which many Gulf of Alaska salmon stocks are struggling, and this puts undue hardship on Alaska's commercial, sport, recreational, personal use and subsistence salmon harvesters.

(Alaska Newspaper Staff, 2011, June 3)

- **Federal council moves to stem Chinook bycatch in Gulf**

Federal fishery managers are taking steps to limit the incidental harvest of Chinook salmon in the Gulf of Alaska trawl fishery, in the wake of a 2010 season that saw the numbers of king salmon caught by trawlers soar ... Over 600 coastal Alaskans signed a letter saying this level of king salmon waste is unacceptable and called for a bycatch cap. Duncan Fields, a council member and commercial fisherman, cited the letter as a powerful show of public interest from those who rely on the king salmon for their commercial, sport and subsistence use.

(Bauman, 2011, April 3)

- **Fishery council to take bite out of bycatch in Nome**

The council is scheduled meet June 8 through June 14 with the bulk of its time—four days—to take final action on a hard cap for Chinook salmon bycatch in the Gulf of Alaska and select a preliminary preferred alternative to control chum salmon bycatch in the Bering Sea ... The Federal Subsistence Board has recommended a cap of 15,000 Chinooks in the Gulf and 70,000 chum in the Bering Sea. It once appeared the council was heading toward the 15,000 cap, but uncertainty over the composition of Gulf Chinook bycatch and retrospective analysis that showed pollock fishery closures in all but three years since 2004 under that cap led to the selection of 22,500 Chinooks ... During 2010, an estimated 51,000 Chinooks were taken in the Gulf by trawlers, about 41,000 of those by the pollock fleet. The spike in bycatch rate—which exceeded the threshold of 40,000 set under the Endangered Species Act—combined with struggling returns of Chinooks around Alaska put tremendous pressure on the council to move a regulatory package forward as quickly as possible.

(Jensen, 2011, June 3)

The ESA Section 7 consultation process, along with the intense media interest and outcry from Chinook salmon stakeholders, meant the NPFMC *had* to act—they had to produce some sort of new rule regarding Chinook salmon bycatch in the GOA pollock fisheries.

The ensuing NPFMC's Chinook salmon bycatch rule-making process occurred in NPFMC meetings in 2010 and 2011. The NPFMC normally holds five meetings per year, at the same times each year but in different locations in Alaska, Washington, and Oregon, and the rule-making process spanned four of these meetings. More specifically, the meetings of interest were held in December of 2010, February of 2011, April of 2011, with the final one in Nome, Alaska in June of 2011. Like all NPFMC rule-making processes, this one was guided by a 'Problem Statement,' which shapes the content of an accompanying 'discussion paper,' which in turn guides NPFMC deliberations. The Problem Statement that guided the NPFMC process after the extreme event, beginning with the December 2010 meeting, was the following:

> Magnuson-Stevens Act National Standards require balancing optimum yield with minimizing bycatch and minimizing adverse impacts to fishery dependent communities. Chinook salmon bycatch taken incidentally in GOA pollock fisheries is a concern, historically accounting for the greatest proportion of Chinook salmon taken in GOA groundfish fisheries. Salmon bycatch control measures have not yet been implemented in the GOA, and 2010 Chinook salmon bycatch levels in the area were unacceptably high. Limited information on the origin of Chinook salmon in the GOA indicates that stocks of Asian, Alaska, British Columbia, and lower-48 origin are present, including Endangered Species Act-listed stocks. The Council is considering several management tools for the GOA pollock fishery, including a hard cap and cooperative approaches with improved monitoring and sampling opportunities to achieve Chinook salmon PSC reductions. Management measures are necessary to provide immediate incentive for the GOA pollock fleet to be responsive to the Council's objective to reduce Chinook salmon PSC.
>
> *(NPFMC, 2011, p. i)*

The problem statement guided the process through its culmination at the June 2011 meeting. Using what we learned in Chapter 3, this problem statement clearly takes a rational decision-making approach to addressing Chinook salmon bycatch in the GOA pollock fisheries, signaled by the goal of imposing "control measures," the top-down need for captains to be "responsive" to the NPFMC objectives, and finally the more particular approach of creating and imposing incentives to shape fishing practices, all with the aim of enacting boundaries into outcomes at sea (i.e., amounts of Chinook salmon bycatch).

In the NPFMC rule-making process, once an issue is given a problem statement and a discussion paper, if it is deemed worthy and ripe enough to be advanced, discussion papers turn into Initial Review Drafts. Initial Review Drafts then become Public Review Drafts as they further guide the NPFMC toward the production of a new rule. The Chinook salmon issue advanced to the Public Review Draft stage in April 2011, and two months later in June the NPFMC's rule-making process culminated in a 25,000 "hard cap" on the number of Chinook salmon that GOA trawl captains can annually catch when fishing for pollock. This means that each year the GOA trawl fleet, including both Central and Western boats, can catch 25,000 Chinook salmon as bycatch in order to catch their pollock quotas. If the fleet surpasses the cap, all fishing for pollock ceases (making it a "hard," as opposed to a "soft," cap, which would trigger measures other than a closure of all pollock fisheries). Such a closure would remain in place until another annual limit becomes available the following year. But this also means that 25,000, or, using the estimates made above, approximately 85 tons of Chinook salmon, are allowed by regulation to be bycaught and wasted each year. This limit became active in the fall of 2012, and since then (through the end of 2017) approximately 105,040 Chinook have been bycaught in GOA pollock trawl fisheries. This amounts to approximately 357 tons, all of which is federally authorized to be wasted, the vast majority of which was wasted.

Mutually articulating potentiality: Natural, regulatory, and economic boundary-making

So how does this event look through the PES framework? At the start of the 2010 pollock D season in the Western Gulf, captains made sense of a particular actual spot to fish in, from the various spots they had the potential to fish in. Thus, the function of captains' ecological sensemaking at this point in their fishing process was to abductively articulate a proposition of a particular fishing spot to steam to next.

Propositions of where to fish next are focused on the spatio-temporal location of a potentially profitable aggregation of target fish. An 'aggregation of fish,' as discussed in Chapter 6, is an episodic migratory entanglement in which fish, preferably belonging to one's target species, are articulating themselves, making themselves intelligible, in a particular way, in a particular place, at a particular time. Most species engage in recurring spatio-temporally located aggregations as part of their life history traits; those traits in turn constitute part of captains' potentiality, luring their practices to produce and deploy the action disposition to fish where they fished before.

Captains fishing in the Western Gulf engaged in ecological sensemaking at the start of the 2010 pollock D season to conjecture which spots out on the fishing grounds will potentially have aggregations of pollock constitutively embedded in them. As Bohr instructs us, concepts, rather than being mere conceptual entities, are always physically articulated (Barad, 2007). The physical articulation of captains' potential fishing spots is an important part of this focused ethnography. The data show that various physical properties of natural phenomena in the Western Gulf around the timing of the D season relate boundaries into captains' sensemaking, limiting the actionable propositions as to where to fish next. These are physical actualities that condition and constitute captains' potentiality, and thus play a constitutive role in their ecological sensemaking.

According to captains who took part in the event, there are only two or three potential spots where they can find aggregations of pollock in the Western Gulf in the fall of the year. As one captain testified to the NPFMC, "There's not a vast amount of square miles where we fish, there's three predominant areas, so if you are not here, you are there." From the meeting of the (potentiality-conditioned) actuality of captains' fishing practices and the (actuality-conditioned) potentiality of recurring aggregations of target fish in certain areas at certain times of the year, boundaries materialize into captains' abductive propositioning of which fishing spot to steam to next. In terms of this event, the boundary that manifested in captains' sensemaking of what to do next was the fact that they typically only find a suitable aggregation of target fish in one of three fishing spots at a time in the Western Gulf in the D season.

While captains' determinations of where to fish next are bounded by the life history traits of their target species, those traits are further entangled with geo-physical phenomena in the form of the ocean bottom. Thus, because captains' ecological sensemaking is entangled with natural phenomena 'all the way down,' the geophysical phenomena that their target species is entangled with intra-act, or agentially cut (see Chapter 4), boundaries into captains' determination of where to fish next. One captain describes such boundary-making entanglements in the following: "A trawl net can only fish in specific areas, and they are very limited areas. They can't fish in rocky bottom, they can't fish on too muddy of a bottom." During my fieldwork, a common concern captains had in fishing trips was "hanging up" on rocky bottom, which often meant tearing a net (see Chapter 6 for additional elaboration of the boundaries that the ocean bottom relate into captains' ecological sensemaking). The dangers associated with certain types of ocean bottom materialize in and configure captains' sensemaking; these dangers involve potential meetings of the relatively fragile actuality of the trawl net and the destructive potentiality of hard or rocky bottom, which captains know through past experiences (their own or others'). A torn net can reduce efficiency by detracting from fishing time, for crews have to spend hours to days repairing torn nets; a hung-up net can also pose a danger to life and limb, for they can strain and damage gear on board. Captains tell stories of boats actually sinking after getting hung up. The potentially perilous outcomes of the entanglement of ocean bottom and trawl net is one of the reasons that captains employ the action disposition of fishing where they fished before (as elaborated in Chapter 6), as one explains in the following:

We fish the same spots; for one reason, some of the bottom isn't conducive to fishing. There's fish there, but the bottom's not good and after you have had to repair enough nets, you find out that it's not beneficial to go into these places, so you don't go in there. I mean, you got to have pretty good reward to take a big risk. So you've learned that you fish these other areas—fish come in there different times a year, and you fish them.

The upshot is that when determining which spot to fish in, captains do not just make sense of where to fish based on the boundaries enacted by the ecological potentiality of recurring aggregations of target fish, they also make sense within the boundaries that other natural phenomena, such as the ocean bottom (and the weather as Chapter 4 indicated), agentially cut into their practice. A captain who fished in the extreme bycatch event describes the boundaries that their entanglement with the bottom in the Western Gulf cut into their practice in the following: "A pollock net is extremely fragile, and we have two areas that have soft bottom where you can fish … And typically there is not fish in both areas – if the fish are in one, they are not in the other – they are not in both areas at the same time."

In addition to boundaries involving natural phenomena, captains' propositions of where to fish next are also bounded due to their entanglement with economic and regulatory phenomena (and their entanglement with economic and regulatory phenomena is inseparable from their entanglement with natural phenomena). In particular, these are boundaries in which captains cannot fish past certain spatio-temporal limits, and cannot tow in areas that are, by regulation, closed to trawl fishing (see Chapter 2 for a discussion of such regulatory areas; here I will focus primarily on economic spatio-temporal boundaries). In terms of economic spatio-temporal boundaries, the further out to sea a vessel travels the more the trip will cost due to spent fuel, which tends to lower their profit margins, which in turn means that the captain and crew's take-home pay will be less than what it otherwise could have been. This in turn limits where captains can propose to fish next (see Chapter 5 for more elaboration of this boundary). In addition to spatio-economic boundaries, captains also cannot spend too much time at sea (either steaming around or fishing) because beyond a certain period of time the catch that captains have on board deteriorates past the point at which it can fetch an economically viable price (fresher fish are more valuable than fish that are not as fresh; fish that have decomposed beyond a certain point may be worth close to nothing). Potential fishing spots that are inside areas that are closed to fishing by regulation, or that are outside of economic spatio-temporal boundaries, are not actionable as propositions of what to do next. Such regulatory and economic boundaries are another key reason captains are disposed to fish where they fished before, which shapes how fisheries, fishing seasons, and years of fishing materialize.

Taken together, natural, economic, and regulatory phenomena are entangled with captains' ecological sensemaking, co-articulating boundaries, properties, and meanings into their propositioning of where to fish next. The following excerpts from testimonies made by GOA trawl captains to the NPFMC after the extreme event evidence this natural, economic, and regulatory boundary-making:

I'm gonna be a bit loose with guesstimates here, but there's basically two trenches, one north of Sand Point, one south of Sand Point, and 80% of the pollock is taken out of those two trenches. And sometimes the only place there will be fish is in one of those two trenches. And we will take the C and D quota or the A and B quota out of that one area. [..]

We're limited in areas that we can fish … I've fished [in the Central Gulf], and we've towed over 50 miles in one direction. The longest tow we have in the Western Gulf, where our fish is traditionally caught in C and D seasons, is about eight miles long. And a lot of times there will only be fish on half the tow, so it will work an area of maybe six miles long. We just don't have a lot of options.

In the Western Gulf, pollock tend to recurrently form aggregations that are sufficient to fish from in only two or three areas. Further, as captains argued, pollock tend to be in only one of those areas at a time. The data suggest that, in the 2010 pollock D season in the Western Gulf, captains initially conjectured to fish primarily in one spot. This aspect of the event is integrated into the PES framework in Figure 7.2. According to this figure, captains used their sensemaking tools to perform the proposition, as articulated through ecological, geophysical, regulatory, and economic boundary-making intra-actions, that one potential fishing spot would be workable. Captains then took the instrumental action of steaming to that spot.

Mutually articulating actuality: Fishing practices and feed bands

After enacting the instrumental action of steaming to their chosen fishing spot, the captains found an aggregation of fish there. The data indicate that the particular type of aggregation that captains encountered in the 2010 D season pollock fishery in the Western Gulf was what they call a 'feed band.' Feed bands are large, dense aggregations of multiple species physically intra-acting in the same place at the same time to feed on a mass of eupheusiids, or perhaps some other type of krill

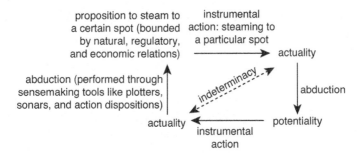

FIGURE 7.2 Analysis of the 2010 extreme bycatch event using the posthumanistic ecological sensemaking framework, focusing on how the natural phenomena shaped captains' determination of where to fish next.

(which is itself aggregating according to its own life history traits). The following are examples of captains discussing the feed band that occurred in the Western Gulf during the fall of 2010. These excerpts are taken from testimonies to the NPFMC; the first three excerpts are from trawl captains, and the last is an unspecified non-trawl captain:

> We have really thick feed bands ... Guys will say, "It looks like a bunch of feedy crap" or "It's a lot of something." Nobody says, "It's a lot of pollock." Or as one guy said, "If 1% of this is pollock, we're doing good." You just can't tell using your electronics. [...}
>
> This area is usually just alive with fish and feed, and last fall it was just a dead zone. Usually we have a lot of whales, I know when we got that hit [of Chinook salmon] I counted 60 to 70 whale spouts on the horizon. [...]
>
> I think what we all noticed was a change in the whole area we call Woolly Head where we fish, it was alive with krill, or we don't know what it was, we saw it on the [sonar], but it was alive. There were hundreds of whales there, more than we've ever seen. Something definitely changed in the whole ecosystem just in that little space that for some reason there was more Chinook. And you would see fish jumping, this was late August, middle of September, you would see fish jumping, and we were wondering what they were; we thought they might be silvers (coho salmon), but I think they were smaller Chinook, and we've never seen that before. I don't know what changed but something changed to bring them in like they were, there was definitely more of them around. [...]
>
> This year with my boat I went back and forth across the north end of the Shumigans [which are islands in the Western Gulf] quite a bit and the ecosystem has changed. There are a lot of fin-backed whales that I've never seen before except the last couple of years with a huge biomass of feed, and that's where some of the pollock boats fish. I think they are capelin myself and we did catch some in the harbor in Sand Point when the whales were around ...

The takeaway is that in the event, pollock and Chinook (as well as eupheusiids, whales, and other species) were entangled in the same space at the same time, in relation with the same bottom, same currents, and the same weather. These entangled activities articulated a broader superimposed phenomenon, which materialized through captains' ecological sensemaking, and through the particular sensemaking tool that is the sonar, as a feed band.

Feed bands, in their densely entangled multi-species nature, are sources of ambiguity. More specifically, feedbands are actualities of ecological phenomena that, when read through captains' sensemaking tools, emerge as undifferentiated materiality (in terms of specific species). They are, in other words, ambiguous in terms of specific species-based boundaries (i.e., they are under-specified) (see Chapter 6 for further elaboration of this type of ambiguity). The feed band materialized as ambiguous in terms of specific species-based boundaries because captains' ecological sensemaking tools did not (and do not) have the potentiality that is necessary for differentiating ecological phenomena at the species-level—until after they perform the agential cut of extracting their nets and examining the catch. The relationship between feed bands and the ambiguity of species boundaries can be seen in the following conversation with a veteran trawl captain:

RESEARCHER: Do you still see things out there that you are not sure what they are?
TRAWL CAPTAIN: The big question is fishing what you can't see on the sonar. Those are all the flatfish, sablefish are hard to see, halibut, salmon, things that are in the feed bands.

RESEARCHER: Do you fish the feed bands?
TRAWL CAPTAIN: Lots of times, most of the time that's where the fish is. Your net only pulls out the big stuff ... That's how it is fishing in the Shelikoff, it has a big feed band with salmon, sharks, everything

What captains often refer to in their ecological sensemaking as feed bands are under-specified superpositions, which have been articulated in their sensemaking through its entanglement with the densely intra-active ecological phenomena.

The actuality of the feed band that captains encountered in the event is integrated into the PES framework in Figure 7.3 below. It is important to recall, as elaborated in Chapter 6, that this actuality is always a human-natural actuality in that it is mutually constituted by entangled human and natural phenomena. As depicted in the upper right-hand corner of the framework, the feed band was the particular materiality that a particularly configured ecological sensemaking apparatus, entangled with particularly articulating ecological phenomena, articulated into experience. The materialization of the feed band was 'relational all the way down' (Slife, 2004) in that it was articulated by the way in which ecological and geophysical phenomena were articulating their world, and in doing to making

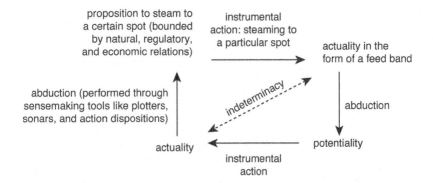

FIGURE 7.3 Analysis of the 2010 extreme bycatch event using the posthumanistic ecological sensemaking framework, focusing on the articulation of the feed band that captains encountered at their chosen spot.

themselves intelligible (i.e., performing certain boundary-, property-, and mean-ing-making intra-activities), which captains' practices already had the potentiality embedded in them (in such sensemaking tools as plotters, sonars, trawl gear, and action dispositions) to appreciate. We can say that the materialization of the feed band was 'relational all the way down' because, while the boundary-, property-, and meaning-making activities of natural phenomena were entangled with the boundary-, property-, and meaning-making relations of captains' sensemaking tools in the particular fishing spot that captains steamed to in the event, captains' sense-making tools, even as they were sitting on their vessels at the dock, were *already* entangled human-natural materialities in that they were crafted in terms of the potentiality (e.g., morphologies, breeding patterns, and other life history traits) that is embedded in natural phenomena. Thus, the materialization of the feed band in captains' practices was mutually constituted by ecological sensemaking and natural phenomena, yet ecological sensemaking and natural phenomena are already entangled. The practice of fishing is all relational 'all the way down.'

Mutually articulating towing potentiality

As discussed in Chapters 4 and 6, there is a common phenomenon at sea, and presumably in many resource extraction contexts, in which the observing, mea-suring, or extracting apparatus at the frontline lacks the differentiating potentiality that regulators and markets demand. In lacking such differentiating potentiality, the frontline apparatus does not articulate differences to the level, or of the nature, that is demanded. Thus, these are situations in which the world of resource extraction is articulating itself differently, but not *differently enough.*

The data demonstrate that captains' ecological sensemaking apparatuses in the 2010 D season pollock fishery in the Western Gulf were not endowed with the necessary differentiating ability when they encountered ecological phenomena that consisted of multiple species, as is always the case with a feed band. Other research has found similar results (though crafted using dualistic thinking). Heery and Cope (2014), for example, when studying different species of rockfish living off the United States Pacific coast, found what they call 'co-occurrence,' in which more than one species engages in similar behavioral patterns, through which they con-stitute the same assemblages and appear as the same on sonar displays; Pulver, Liu, and Scott-Denton (2016) also encountered such co-occurrence in reef fisheries in the Gulf of Mexico. These studies suggest, in the terms of the analytical framework being constructed here, that more than one species can have similar potential evolutionarily embedded in their biophysical systems; this similar potentiality in turn gives rise to similar 'propositions' (see Chapter 6 for an explanation of this sort of proposition), which give rise to the 'same' life history traits, such as morpholo-gical characteristics and breeding patterns, that are intelligible to captains' ecological sensemaking. When captains' ecological sensemaking apparatuses do not have the potential to further differentiate those life history traits (and when the traits are not further differentiating themselves), the ecological phenomena that involves two or more species will materialize in captains' ecological sensemaking as superpositioned materiality. Until, that is, after captains perform the agential cuts of hauling up their nets, dumping their contents on the backs of their vessels (or dumping it directly into the fish hold and delivering the unsorted catch to a processing plant) where the subsequent agential cuts of separating the catch by species are performed. But by then the vast majority of the extracted ecological phenomena, which has materialized through the ecological sensemaking apparatus as catch, is dead. What fishing captains tend to find is that the materialities that emerge in their fishing practice, such as a spot to steam to, sign on the sonar, and a space to tow through, are ambiguous in terms of species-specific boundaries; the materialities are under-specified. The effect that such under-specification has in captains' fishing practices is pre-tow and during-tow indeterminacy, for each tow. This indeterminacy is why GOA captains repeat the axiom, 'you never know until you tow.'

What this comes to is that materiality tends to be underspecified in relation to regulatory and market demands for species-based specificity, both prior to and during the process of towing. Such regulatory and market demands require certain species to be extracted and other others to be avoided. In terms of the 2010 Western Gulf bycatch event, at least two of the species that were constitutively embedded in the same ecological phenomena as it materialized in captains' practice (i.e., as a feed band) were Chinook salmon and pollock. This means that the materiality in the form of the feed band was ambiguous in terms of the species-based differentiation of the Chinook salmon and pollock that were constitutively embedded in it. The problem is that pollock is a target species for GOA trawl captains, and Chinook salmon is a prohibited bycatch species (which means it must be discarded or delivered to a food bank).

Chinook salmon bycatch materializes in GOA trawl captains' fishing practice through the meeting of ecological actuality and fishing potentiality, and fishing actuality and ecological potentiality. More specifically, the materialization of bycatch involves the meeting of the ecological actuality-conditioned potentiality of captains' fishing practice (as embedded in such sensemaking tools as trawl gear, plotters, sonars, and action dispositions) and the fishing potentiality-conditioned actuality of ecological phenomena (in which how, when, where, and how much captains fish shapes the ecological phenomena captains encounter, both in the short and long term); yet the converse is also true: bycatch materializes through the meeting of the ecological potentiality-conditioned actuality of captains' fishing practice (which plays out in the boundary-, property-, and meaning-making activities of captains' sensemaking tools and instrumental actions) and the fishing actuality-conditioned potentiality of ecological phenomena (which is embedded in the biophysical systems of various species, shaping the actualities they enact). When both Chinook salmon and pollock are constitutively embedded in the same eco-logical phenomena, yet captains' fishing practices do not have the potential to dif-ferentiate those species, including the potential to exclude one (Chinook salmon) and not the other (pollock) from the extractive parts of their fishing practice, both species will tend to materialize through the same fishing practices as catch.

The underspecification of Chinook salmon and pollock is born in part by their overlapping migratory and morphological life history traits. Yet little is known about Chinook's life history traits outside of its capture either in 'directed' Chinook salmon fisheries (fisheries in which Chinook salmon are the target species) and as bycatch in other fisheries (NPFMC, 2011). As a member of the Kodiak Fisheries Advisory Committee, who was also a salmon sports fishing captain, commented, "They're highly migratory, they wander all around the ocean and nobody really knows what their life is like out there." What we do know, however, is that after spending their first three months to two years of life in freshwater river systems, Chinook spend up to five years in the ocean, after which they return to the same river in which they were born in order to spawn (which means they are anadromous species) and then die. These 'runs' of Chinook salmon recur annually May through July (NPFMC, 2011). Directed Chinook salmon fisheries, including commercial, sport, personal use, and subsistence, form each year in relation to this instrumental activity, primarily at the mouths of various river systems in Alaska. This recurring instrumental behavior of Chinook salmon contributes to the (ecological actuality-conditioned) potentiality of these various fishing groups, from which they enact the instrumental activity of engaging with and catching Chinook salmon at the mouths of rivers each year.

Aside from the freshwater bookends of the lives of Chinook salmon, most of what is known about the marine portion of their lives is due to their capture as bycatch in pollock fisheries. This bycatch follows "a predictable pattern," occurring January through April and in October and November (NPFMC, 2011, p. 116; Witherell, Ackley, & Coon 2002, p. 59). From such intra-actions we know that, while at sea, Chinook primarily feed on eupheusiids (i.e., krill), though they have also been found to prey on immature pollock (Davis, Armstrong, & Myers, 2003).

The at-sea entangled activities through which Chinook salmon continually materialize in fishing practices mirror, in certain ways, at certain times, and at certain places, the activity through which pollock continually materialize. Pollock spend their entire lives at sea constitutively embedded in what appear to scientists and captains to be annual migrations between summer foraging locations and winter spawning grounds (NPFMC, 2011, p. 110). Thus, pollock engage in longitudinal entanglements, which are spotted with episodic entanglements in which they aggregate in a certain area at the same time. One of the purposes of this behavior is spawning, as a SAFE report describes in the following:

> Peak spawning at the two major spawning areas in the Gulf of Alaska occurs at different times. In the Shumagin Island area, peak spawning apparently occurs between February 15–March 1, while in Shelikof Strait peak spawning occurs later, typically between March 15 and April 1.
>
> *(Dorn et al., 2012, p. 56)*

In addition to spawning, pollock also form recurring annual migratory entanglements for the purposes of feeding. In these entanglements their primary feed source is, like Chinook salmon, eupheusiids, ibid.). These migratory entanglements are intelligible to captains, and in turn recurrently materialize in captains' practices; thus how pollock articulate their world enables themselves, when coupled with captains' ecological sensemaking potentiality, to be a target of fishing activity. Put differently, their annual recurrence in similar places at similar times inspires captains' fishing practices, 'vectorizing' it by offering it potentiality. Yet, just as Chinook salmon bycatch follows a 'a predictable pattern' in pollock fisheries, pollock, according to NPFMC testimony by Chinook captains, are recurrently bycaught in Chinook salmon fisheries, which seems to also follow a 'a predictable pattern.' The following testimony a Chinook salmon captain made to the NPFMC evidences the tendency for pollock to be bycaught in Chinook fisheries:

COUNCIL MEMBER: Do you do salmon charters in [Katchemak] bay there?"

SALMON CAPTAIN: Salmon and halibut.

COUNCIL MEMBER: Because I know I do a lot of sport trolling there and a last couple of months I noticed a really high incidence of pollock and really high incidence of king salmon in Katchemak Bay, and I don't know if that's just me getting lucky or is everybody noticing the same thing.

SALMON CAPTAIN: It has been a good fall, and there is a high incidence of pollock, you are right.

COUNCIL MEMBER: It just seems like, that's, I don't know what you make of that. I'm not trying to be scientific about it but I noticed it, they seem to hang together. There's a lot of bait in the water and they all showed up at the same place, same time.

SALMON CAPTAIN: It's good for the people who sell bait [laughs].

It is clear that (1) Chinook salmon are commonly bycaught in pollock fisheries, (2) this bycatch follows 'a predictable pattern,' (3) pollock are commonly bycaught in Chinook fisheries, and (4) pollock and Chinook feed on the same species. Further, we also know that pollock and Chinook tend to have similar morphological characteristics, such as both being roundfish, being of similar size in the early portion of the lifespan of Chinook (and the later portion of the lifespan of pollock), and both having air bladders. From these understandings we can plausibly conjecture that: (1) Chinook salmon and pollock are often constitutively embedded in the same ecological phenomena; (2) those phenomena materialize in captains' fishing practices as aggregations through such ecological sensemaking tools as trawl gear, plotters, sonar, and action dispositions; and (3) when such materiality is not differentially measured in terms of life history traits that are *not* common to Chinook salmon and pollock, the two species will appear as the same materiality. Thus, in the process of fishing, Chinook salmon and pollock are scientifically and economically, but not practically, differentiated— until after captains enact the additional boundary-making agential cuts of towing and examining the catch for its species composition on the back deck (or delivering it to a processing plant and being informed of the composition afterward).

Matter, meaning, measurements, sense, and the like, are materiality, or what has come to matter. What comes to matter is born of differentiating agential cuts, i.e., boundary-, property-, and meaning-making, intra-actions within in phenomena (Barad, 2003, 2007, 2014). Particular materialities, whether meanings or matter, require particular apparatuses, which involve particular arrangements of entangled boundary-, property-, and meaning-making activities, to materialize. Thus, it is through certain apparatuses that "matter is iteratively and differentially articulated" (Barad, 2007, p. 170). If the entanglements that Chinook salmon and pollock are constitutively embedded in are 'measured' by the same boundary-, property-, and meaning-making tools (i.e., apparatuses), which do not differentiate them in terms of materialities that are not common to Chinook salmon and pollock, then Chinook salmon and pollock will materialize as the same matter. In short, they will not be differentially articulated through captains' ecological sensemaking.

Captains' ecological sensemaking tools—their plotters, sonars, trawl nets, and action dispositions—have the potential to co-articulate certain senses of what is happening at sea, and lack the potential to co-articulate other senses. And they can only co-articulate a certain sense if certain ecological phenomena is there to co-articulate it with them. Like the tree falling in the forest and the materialization of sound, there must be actuality available for potentiality and potentiality awaiting actuality for certain sense (or meaning, matter) to materialize. Meaning, matter, and sense are always mutually constituted by actuality and potentiality, and in terms of ecological sensemaking, it is always in terms of actuality and potentiality that span entangled human and natural phenomena. There is no sign, for example, for captains to read on the sonar screen prior to the sonar bouncing sound waves off phenomena beneath the vessel and then measuring differences as waves are echoed back to it. The sonar does not retrieve sign that is floating about in the water and then bring it inside the wheelhouse for the captain's viewing pleasure. Sign is mutually constituted by the potentially inherent in the sonar and the actuality of ecological phenomena beneath the vessel; sign is a materialization of entangled phenomena that matter to the sonar and to captains. Yet what matters to the sonar is not all of what matters to captains. Differentiations at the genetic level that bound one species off from another, which matter to regulators and markets, and in turn to captains, do not matter to sonars. Nor do they matter, for the most part, to trawl nets. If were recall discussions across previous chapters of Bohr's key contribution to quantum mechanics, that "concepts are meaningful, that is, semantically determinate, not in the abstract but by virtue of their embodiment in the physical arrangement of the apparatus" (Barad, 2007, p. 117), it becomes clear that the concept of how much Chinook salmon one will catch does not become semantically determinate, or meaningful, i.e., unambiguous, until after captains enact the agential cuts of towing, hauling up the catch, and examining it. The paradox is that, for most fish of most species, extracted fish are already dead at the point at which they can be 'measured' at the species-level, i.e., physically segregated into mutually-exclusive species categories.

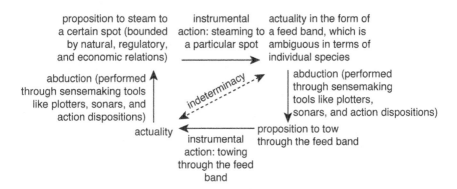

proposition to steam to   instrumental   actuality in the form of
a certain spot (bounded   action: steaming to   a feed band, which is
by natural, regulatory,   a particular spot   ambiguous in terms of
and economic relations)   ──────────▶   individual species

abduction (performed ▲   │ abduction (performed
through sensemaking tools   │ through sensemaking
like plotters, sonars, and   │ tools like plotters,
action dispositions) │   ▼ sonars, and action dispositions)

indeterminacy

actuality ◀────────── proposition to tow
            instrumental   through the feed band
            action: towing
            through the feed
            band

FIGURE 7.4 Analysis of the 2010 extreme bycatch event using the posthumanistic ecological sensemaking framework, focusing on the articulation of captains'
proposition to tow through the feed band.

All ecological sensemaking can do prior to towing is produce species-level propositions as to what will come next. Such propositions, however, are always
guesses based on under-specified materiality (the only materiality that can be specified to the species-level is catch that has been hauled up from the depths). In the
2010 extreme bycatch event, captains propositioned that towing through the feed
band would allow them to tell a story afterward about catching pollock. Figure 7.4
adds the mutually constitutive nature of captains' propositions of where to tow in
the event to the PES framework.

The mutual constitution of catch: Lightning strikes of Chinook bycatch

In the 2010 D season pollock fishery, captains located the spot in which the feed
band was located, and then they proposed to tow there. They did so either by
employing their action disposition of fishing where they fished before, or by
looking on their plotters to see where other captains were located on the fishing
grounds, or by talking with other captains on the radio, or by searching one or
more spots, or by some combination of these tools. The point is that captains
located the spot because their practice was embedded with potentiality to do so
(potentiality which was derived from recurring materialities in past fishing practices). Then, because of the materiality that captains found there (as bounded,
propertied, and given meaning through entangled ecological phenomena and
ecological sensemaking), captains decided to tow there. From there captains towed
using the tool of a trawl net, whose actuality, in the form of mesh sizes, is constructed based on the biophysical characteristics of pollock. This actuality met the
potentiality that certain ecological phenomena have for being overtaken and captured in the trawl net, which in turn materialized catch. The converse is also true:
trawl nets have certain potentiality for capturing certain ecological phenomena, and
when that potentiality meets that actuality, catch materializes. NMFS data indicate

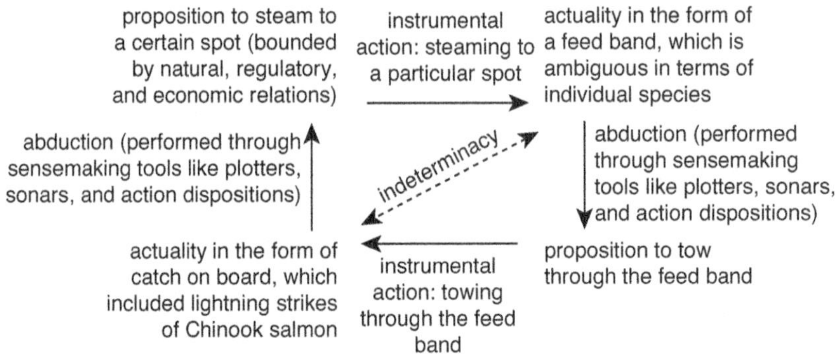

proposition to steam to
a certain spot (bounded
by natural, regulatory,
and economic relations)

instrumental
action: steaming to
a particular spot

actuality in the form of
a feed band, which is
ambiguous in terms of
individual species

abduction (performed through
sensemaking tools like plotters,
sonars, and action dispositions)

indeterminacy

abduction (performed
through sensemaking
tools like plotters, sonars,
and action dispositions)

actuality in the form of
catch on board, which
included lightning strikes
of Chinook salmon

instrumental
action: towing
through the feed
band

proposition to tow
through the feed band

FIGURE 7.5 Analysis of the 2010 extreme bycatch event using the posthumanistic ecological sensemaking framework, focusing on the articulation of lightning
strikes of Chinook salmon.

that each of the 21 or so vessels that fished in the event completed one to two
fishing trips before exhausting the pollock quota (i.e., the specific amount that
could be caught in the 610 D pollock season in 2010). This means that after the
first tow, captains continued to conduct tows, and ultimately completed the pollock fishery. Ultimately, the vessels that fished in the event extracted over 8,000
tons of pollock, but also over 28,000 Chinook salmon.

This Chinook salmon bycatch came in the form of what captains' call 'lightning
strikes.' Lightning strikes are relatively large catches of prohibited species, usually
limited to one fishing trip or even one tow. Incurring a lightning strike is one of
the primary sources of the axiom, 'You never know until you tow.' In terms of the
current case, lightning strikes are short-term yet relatively high-volume meetings
of the actuality of Chinook salmon in the ecological phenomena captains were
towing through and the captains' unchecked potentiality for catching it. Put
conversely, lightning strikes are short-term yet relatively high-volume meetings
of the potentiality Chinook salmon have for being overtaken and trapped in a
trawl net, and the actuality of that trawl net overtaking and trapping the salmon.
In Figure 7.5 below, lightning strikes are incorporated into the PES framework as
the actuality of catch that materialized through captains' ecological sensemaking
apparatuses. The factors that fostered this materialization in the event of interest
are elaborated next.

The materialization of lightning strikes: Unchecked potentiality within the ecological sensemaking apparatus

When catch is pulled from the water it is undifferentiated actuality in terms of the
boundaries between target and bycatch species. Thus, the process of extraction, in
materializing new catch, is merely the feedstock of potentiality for enacting the
agential cuts of differentiating it into categories. Yet the need for such agential cuts,
for the differentiation of catch into fish that will be kept and caught fish that must be

discarded (in this case between pollock and Chinook salmon) is intra-acted into at-sea phenomena by on-land regulatory practices. But to enact such boundaries into their catch captains must have the potentiality to do so already embedded in their fishing practice. Making sense of Chinook salmon bycatch, like hearing the sound of a falling tree, is an entangled materialization in that it requires the meeting of potentiality and actuality across human and natural phenomena for it to occur, i.e., for such sense to be articulated. Without both, or if one or the other—natural actuality or human potentiality—is missing, sense of Chinook salmon does not materialize. Captains may catch Chinook salmon while fishing for pollock, but they only become aware of it if they are constitutively embedded in (i.e., are part and parcel of) the ecological sensemaking apparatus that can articulate that awareness.

Data in the form of interviews and NPFMC testimony indicate that during the event captains were either unaware, or only vaguely aware, that they were catching Chinook salmon. The data suggest that captains lacked potentiality for conducting the boundary-making that was necessary for Chinook salmon to materialize in their ecological sensemaking. There were four factors that limited the captains' potentiality making sense of Chinook salmon bycatch—the mechanics of towing, a systemic lag in feedback, the absence of observers, and the lack of communication.

Mechanical limitations to ecological sensemaking

The first factor that limited the captains' potentiality for making sense of Chinook salmon bycatch is related to the mechanics of towing. The data indicate that in the event captains had a tough time seeing which species were in their catch after they hauled up their nets and dumped their codends (which are the ends of their nets where fish is collected while towing; see Chapter 2) into the fish holds of their vessels (which are located below the back deck of the vessel). Note that in the Alaskan pollock fisheries, catch is typically not sorted at sea (unless the vessels have fish processing facilities on board); instead, catch is delivered to a shoreside plant for sorting and processing. After hauling up a net full of pollock from the depths, codends regularly weigh upwards of 80 tons in the GOA trawl fleet, creating dangerous conditions when hauling them on board. Due to their size, vessel crews typically haul one 20 to 30 ton section of codend on board at a time, dumping it directly into their fish holds. This means that, especially when the crew is working through the process of dumping the first few sections of codend, anywhere from 30 to 60 tons of catch can be hanging off the back of the vessel in heaving seas. This process creates stability issues, and therefore crews attempt to finish dumping each section of the codend into the fish hold as fast as they can. It is at this transition point, as the catch leaves the codend and enters the fish hold, that captains and crew technically have an opportunity to see what sort of bycatch is in the flow of fish. Yet, often all one can see is a blur as the fish rapidly flow from the codend into the fish hold. The following are examples of trawl captains who fished in the event discussing this issue with the NPFMC:

We have no idea what's going in our hauls. We fill that bag up, pull the zipper, drop it in the well, and it all goes there. We thought that we would see a few salmon or something like that but … the talk on the grounds has been a real struggle in that sense.

I think that's what I was trying to explain how it kind of works when we go out fishing. A lot of times half of our delivery is still in the codend when we get to the dock. We fill the boat up, and then we go towing again, and we fill the codend up, so we have got 150 thousand pounds in the boat and we have got 150 thousand pounds in the codend to make our trip limit. So that still hasn't been touched. I was looking through videos to try and find what I could bring to show what actually happens when we dump a bag … It's literally, there's a zipper in the bottom of the net, its right over an 18 by 24 Freeman hatch … it's virtually impossible for us to try to sort anything out …

Due to the mechanics of hauling up and emptying a codend full of pollock, captains often have limited potentiality for enacting agential cuts that differentiate pollock and Chinook salmon, or other bycatch, within their catch. There might be a tree falling in the forest (Chinook moving from the net to the fish hold), but the hearing apparatus nearby (captains and crew) is not configured such that the differential intelligibility of different species flowing from the net to the fish hold can be differentiated by captains and crew, and then responded to. If the necessary differential responses are not performed, Chinook salmon bycatch does not materialize into captains' ecological sensemaking, through which it can inform their propositions and shape their instrumental actions regarding where to tow next. Thus, despite the axiom, 'You never know until you tow,' it is not always the case that captains know after they tow.

Systemic lags in ecological sensemaking

The second reason captains were not fully aware that they were incurring lightning strikes appears to be a systemic lag in feedback from processing plants. This feedback, or lack thereof, concerned the measurement of the catch that captains delivered to them, particularly in terms of its species composition. Due to the nature of emptying codends of pollock into fish holds, in pollock fisheries captains tend to deliver differentiated, rather than sorted (as is the case in Pacific cod and flatfish fisheries), catch to a processing plant. Because they deliver unsorted catch, captains typically do not perform the agential cut (see Chapter 4) of segregating the catch into mutually-exclusive species, and in turn catch/bycatch, categories. Instead, these cuts are performed at the plants. This means that captains must rely on what they call 'fish tickets' to find out which species, and the amounts of each species, they caught and then delivered. A fish ticket is like a receipt in that it itemizes what was delivered. Often captains get fish tickets right after they deliver their catch and before they head back out to sea; Yet often they do not, and instead have to wait until after the *next* trip to get their ticket for the previous trip.

Several factors shape when captains get their fish tickets from the plant. These factors include how fast the plant works in terms of sorting the catch and then communicating the data to the plant office, whether or not someone is in the office of the plant to process the data into a ticket (perhaps the delivery is at night), how long captains can wait for fish ticket before heading back out to sea (which is related to factors such as weather, how competitive the fishery is, and whether or not captains need to complete trips in one area in order to take advantage of a fishery opening up in another area), and generally how busy the plant is.[4]

In the case of the 2010 event, captains seemed to not receive their fish ticket for their first trip until after their second trip. Thus, there appeared to have been at least a one-trip lag in receiving their fish tickets, and therefore itemizations of the composition of the catch they delivered. The following testimonies by captains to the NPFMC discuss this lag in feedback:

> We've all been talking about this—better information. We literally didn't know how many Chinook we caught until a week or two after the D season was over. If we get better daily information from the plants we can absolutely address the issue.

> We didn't have the data in a timely fashion, we didn't even know there was a problem until after the D season closed.

> In the Gulf, we get after the fact bycatch accounting at the processing plant, and a vessel could be well into the next trip before we know what's going on in the grounds.

> We need data sharing and catch accounting between the processors and vessels. Even during the A and B seasons we were not getting the hard data, i.e., fish tickets, in a reasonable time frame … we are very dependent on this information.

Viewed through the lens of the captains' axiom, 'You never know until you tow,' captains not only often do not know what they caught until after a trip, sometimes they do not know until after *two* trips.

Observer-based limitations to ecological sensemaking

The third factor that could have helped captains make sense of Chinook salmon bycatch was the presence of National Marine Fisheries Service (NMFS) fisheries observers on board the vessels. As described in Chapter 2, NMFS fisheries observers are government-contracted biologists who work onboard fishing vessels and within processing plants; their primary duty is to scientifically collect data on vessels' catch, which includes statistically measuring the species-based composition of the catch (performing, in other words, one of the key agential cuts of fishing practice).. These data are the foundation of how NMFS managers manage fisheries in season, and how NPFMC regulators understand and regulate fisheries out-of-season.

Observer data are also, however, used by captains to understand what they have caught after they have towed (typically vessel-based observers sample catch at sea). Captains usually get these data directly from the observer onboard their vessel. Thus, observers are one of the key ways that captains 'know *immediately* after they have towed.' Yet, there were no observers assigned to GOA trawl vessels in the 2010 pollock D season in the Western Gulf. The vessels were lacking that potentiality for differentiating Chinook salmon in their catch, and in turn articulating a sense of what they were bycatching.

Communicational limitations to ecological sensemaking

Communication tends to enhance ecological sensemaking. In particular, communication among captains tends to add to the potentiality that captains have for enacting boundaries between species in their catch, for materializing certain properties and meanings related to the amount of bycatch they are catching, or that they might catch, and in turn for changing practices to reduce the bycatch they might catch in later tows (see Chapter 6 for more discussion of communication among captains and ecological sensemaking). Yet the captains who fished in this event cited a lack of communication among them as a key reason that they either did not realize they were incurring lightning strikes of Chinook salmon bycatch, or that they did not realize the need to alter their fishing practice in order to avoid incurring such lightning strikes. Thus, even as some captains began to realize that they were catching Chinook salmon, the data suggest that they did not share that information to the extent needed to stem the transition from a few lightning strikes to a large-scale bycatch event. The following data, which are excerpts from captains' testimony to the NPFMC, either speak directly, or allude, to the role of communication in materializing, as well as in potentially avoiding, lightning strikes of Chinook salmon:

> Bycatch is a concern. It has always been a concern of mine, and I have noticed it to be a concern in the fleet. I think [another captain] spoke to it, we sort of got blindsided by this ... I guarantee you that next D season there's gonna be a lot of talk on the channel that we share and with our processors about king salmon.

> The fishermen, we all talk amongst ourselves, there is one general channel we are all on. We don't necessarily share all of our fishing information, but when it comes to the possibility of losing fishing time because somebody has gotten into some Chinook, we are gonna be sharing that [in the future].

> We talk a lot [at sea] and we don't want to be shut down [in the future due to too much Chinook salmon bycatch]. The biggest problem for us has been C and D season; and in the C and D seasons in the last three, four, five years abundance [of pollock aggregations] really hasn't been an issue. We could move [where we fish] a little bit. In the A and B seasons abundance is kind of

an issue sometimes, and you get stuck fishing somewhere because that's the only place there's any fish, but we haven't had a Chinook problem in the winter. In the fall when we have a couple more places where we can actually fish, it's easier. We are definitely willing to talk with each other to move around to different places.

It's hard, I mean, communication is everything. We only fish in a couple of different spots. We have to fish very close to each other most of the time. I mean, this winter [after the extreme bycatch event] the first question everybody asked, was, "Did you catch any salmon?" "Did you catch any salmon?" "Did you catch any salmon?"

Captains have potentiality embedded in the actuality of their practice for sharing information regarding what they are catching; when they share such information, they give one another greater potential to constitutively exclude unwanted species from their catch. Yet that potentiality went largely untapped in this event; this untapped potential for constitutively excluding certain species from the catch helped a few lightning strikes accumulate into a large-scale bycatch event.

Altering potentiality to change actuality

The collective effect of the mechanical, systemic, observer-based, and communicational impediments to ecological sensemaking was to decrease captains' potentiality for making sense of lightning strikes of Chinook salmon bycatch. This impeded potentiality in turn meant that captains were less likely to see the need to alter their fishing practices in relation with how the world beneath their vessels was articulating itself, how it was making itself intelligible, and therefore knowable. 'Intelligibility,' in terms of Barad's agential realism, is "an ontological performance of the world in its ongoing articulation" (Barad, 2007, p. 379); 'knowing,' in turn, is the differential responsiveness to intelligibility. Embedded in the intra-active actuality of natural phenomena and captains' fishing practices is the relational potentiality for knowing lightning strikes of Chinook salmon bycatch—unless that potentiality is impeded. Like sound that materializes in the forest, lightning strikes only materialize in captains' sensemaking (as opposed to merely on their vessels) if the actuality of how the world is articulating itself, how it is making itself intelligible, meets with a certain articulation of potentiality, namely potentiality for knowing it—for accounting for and responding to that intelligibility. What the analysis above suggests is that captains' potentialities for accounting for and responding to lightning strikes of Chinook salmon bycatch were hindered by mechanical, systemic, observer-based, and communicational entanglements.

Put differently, mechanical, systemic, observer-based, and communicational factors were agential relations within captains' ecological sensemaking, which intra-acted cuts, or boundaries, between lightning strikes of Chinook salmon and captains' knowledge of them. Only with potentiality for making sense of lightning strikes of Chinook salmon can captains in turn alter their propositions of what to do next, and thereby change their fishing practices in order to avoid incurring more lightning strikes. One of the captains, in fact, did just that:

RESEARCHER: So you said you had a trip with a lot of salmon, and then you went back out and made a tow. What happened?

TRAWL CAPTAIN: There was a lot of salmon in it. I got right on the radio, there were two other boats there, and [one captain] told me, "I was over on that other edge further to the southwest and I didn't have that salmon problem." Well he was fishing during the day, and I went over there but I didn't get there until night. And low and behold I had another bad salmon tow. So I said "OK that's it, I can't do this anymore." So I moved over to the other side of the islands and found some fish and whacked 'em and it was clean as a whistle. There wasn't one salmon in it. Full boatload, not one. So you know, with a little communication amongst the fishermen …

This captain apparently had more potential to perceive the actuality of Chinook salmon than other captains had. After seeing that salmon, he proposed that by moving to another spot to fish, thereby altering the actuality of his fishing practices, his potentiality for catching Chinook salmon would decrease. Which was the case. Thus, the captain, after perceiving Chinook salmon in his catch, abducted a proposition for catching less Chinook salmon, took the instrumental action of towing in a different spot, and then found the proposition to be conformal (See Chapter 5's discussion of 'conformal' and 'nonconformal' propositions).

In closing, there were several ways in which captains' potentiality for materializing Chinook bycatch lightning strikes into their fishing practice, and then acting to stem the accumulation of those strikes, was impaired. Some captains seemed to be aware of Chinook salmon bycatch, others seemed to not be aware, some were more aware of high amounts of bycatch than others, and there seems to have been some variation as to when those who were aware became aware. The tree falling in the forest made a sound in that some heard it and others did not, some heard it more loudly than others, and some heard it later than others.

The perverse rational management of bycatch, and what to do about it

I have argued throughout the past few chapters that ecological sensemaking is a posthumanistic boundary-, property-, and meaning-making apparatus. In other words, it is an intra-active articulation of entangled human and natural phenomena through which differential materializations, differential intelligibilities, and differential responses emerge in commercial trawl fishing in particular, and, we can assume, in other resource extraction contexts more generally. Preceding chapters also argued that the articulation of such materializations, intelligibilities, and responses depends on the potentiality embedded in the actuality of ecological sensemaking, and that this potentiality is embodied by such sensemaking tools as trawl gear, plotters, sonars, and action dispositions. Yet Chapter 6 further argued that this potentiality is conditioned by differential articulations of natural phenomena, which emerge through ecological sensemaking as such materialities as episodic migratory entanglements and morphological properties of fish species, weather conditions, and configurations of the ocean bottom. Thus, for particular articulations of natural phenomena to materialize as particular materialities in captains' practices, captains' practices must already be embedded with potentiality for accounting for, and in turn making sense of, those actualities. Yet those potentialities are already entangled with ecological phenomena in that they have been derived from past ecological sensemaking processes (particularly the materialities they articulated). The converse is also necessarily true, and it is an equally important part of the ecological sensemaking apparatus: Ecological sensemaking depends on the potentiality that ecological phenomena have for enacting differential materialities (i.e., their life history traits), which is conditioned by the actuality of captains' fishing practices (such as where, when, and how much they tow). This means that current potentialities for articulating particular materialities, whether those potentialities are embedded in phenomena we consider to be human or non-human, are derived from the articulations and materializations in past ecological sensemaking.

Bycatch is a materialization of entangled agencies. Entanglement is the lack of separately-determinable boundaries and properties among actions, actors, systems, etc. More specifically, bycatch materializes through the entanglement of a multiplicity of boundary-, property-, and meaning-making activities, including those enacted by captains, (ecological and geophysical) natural phenomena, the NPFMC, markets, and others. Bycatch is not solely the outcome of inadequate institutions or inaccurate fishing practices; it is not the outcome of faulty, thoughtlessly, and negligently enacted representational practices at sea; this is because such practices would impossibly depend, as Barad elaborates, on "a geometrical optics model that positions language or representation as the lens that mediates between the object world and the mind of the knowing subject, a geometry of absolute exteriority between ontologically and epistemologically distinct kinds" (Barad, 2007, p. 374). There is no tripartite arrangement of mediated relationships between distinct humans and natural phenomena at sea (or anywhere), through which humans actively make sense *of* and *inter*act with a separate nature. Captains' relationships with natural phenomena, and in turn with bycatch, are not mediated by ecological sensemaking. There is no ontological gap between captains and natural phenomena, which is bridged by ecological embeddedness, out of which concerns for the accuracy of ecological sensemaking, conceptualized as a practice that mediates the tripartite relationship between ontologically separate entities legitimately arise.

In fact, there is no absolute separation between human and natural phenomena at all (Barad, 2007; Haraway, 1991; Latour, 2005; Rouse, 2002). There is only 'agential separability,' which results in 'differentiation without separation,' 'differentiation within,' 'exteriority within,' and 'constitutive exclusions' (Barad, 2007, 2014). The world articulates itself differently, but not separately. The practice of commercial trawl fishing, therefore, cannot be a representational system; rather, catch and bycatch emerge through the apparatus of ecological sensemaking at sea, within which natural phenomena, captains, markets, and the NPFMC, among others, agentially intra-act boundaries (e.g., between densely aggregating fish and non-densely aggregating fish, between open and closed fishing areas, between catch that can be sold and catch that must be wasted), properties (e.g., characteristics of sign on the sonar, a change in water current), and meanings (e.g., the contrasting definition of 'target catch' and 'prohibited species catch,' the effect of a change in water temperature on swimming behavior). Such boundary-, property-, and meaning-making actions are 'agential' in that they are performed by entangled and differentiating activities, rather than existing prior to such activities.. Captains' decisions and actions are merely one of multiple agentive elements within the apparatus of ecological sensemaking; yet they are the one that is most aligned with both *our* spatio-temporal notion of causality (i.e., the closer in time and space, the greater the causality) and *our* notion of nature as an opaque canvas passively awaiting the etchings of cultural, business, and scientific practices for its boundaries, properties, and meanings (Barad, 2007).

Through the apparatus of ecological sensemaking, natural phenomena, captains, markets, and the NPFMC each perform boundary-, property-, and meaning-making agential cuts that shape the articulation of fishing phenomena at sea, including what does and does not emerge through them. Without the boundary-making relations enacted by the ocean bottom, for example, trawl captains would be able to fish anywhere that aggregations of fish are located (within legal boundaries of course); or, without the captains' meaning-making in terms of which sign on their sonars indicate particular target species, fishing practices would exhibit only random variation in terms of which species are caught and which are not; or, without the NPFMC's boundary-making agential cuts that impose differentiations between bycatch that can be retained and sold and bycatch that must be discarded, thousands of tons of salable, edible fish would not be wasted each year. Each actor that enacts agential cuts into ecological sensemaking apparatuses has a measure of responsibility for what materializes through them. As Barad states, "Accountability and responsibility must be thought of in terms of what matters and what is excluded from mattering" (Barad, 2007, p. 220). If we can identify who imposes particular agential cuts into particular ecological sensemaking apparatuses, or any other form of measuring, observing, or knowledge-making, we can identify who is responsible for their effects.

Only together do the entangled agencies of natural phenomena, captains, markets, the NPFMC, and others articulate certain configurations of the world at sea. Each element that constitutes the ecological sensemaking apparatus of that world plays an agentive role in the articulation of its outcomes. Unfortunately such articulations can, as we have seen, produce high amounts of natural resource waste. Having agency in the articulation of deleterious outcomes means, in a fair and just system, also being accountable and in turn having responsibility to act to change those outcomes. And such responsibility is not reduced just because (non-human) nature also plays an active role in what materializes. Quite the contrary, in fact, as Barad argues: The acknowledgment of "nonhuman agency" does not lessen human accountability; on the contrary, it means that accountability requires that much more attentiveness to existing power asymmetries" (Barad, 2007, p. 220). 'Responsibility' is the ability to respond. With boundary-, property-, and meaning-making agency in an apparatus comes responsibility for its outcomes; and with more ability to respond comes more responsibility.

Mechanical, systemic, observer-based, and communicational impediments to the ecological sensemaking of Chinook salmon bycatch lightning strikes are boundaries within at-sea fishing practices, which are enacted by various actors who are entangled with those practices. These boundaries are constitutive exclusions between Chinook salmon bycatch and captains' practices, partitioning off actuality, negating its potentiality. This 'exteriority within' is the boundary between Chinook salmon that has materialized on the back deck of a vessel, or in catch that was delivered to a processing plant, or in information shared between a captain who has accounted for Chinook salmon and others who have not, and its materialization into the ecological sensemaking of captains' who have not accounted for it. Due to such exteriority within at-sea fishing practices, potentiality for adjusting to materialized bycatch, such as moving to a different fishing area, is impeded. In keeping with the metaphor of a tree falling in the forest, actuality goes unheard due to a dearth of potentiality for hearing it. Only if lightning strikes can materialize within captains' ecological sensemaking can captains in turn use their sensemaking tools to craft different actionable propositions, take different instrumental actions, and in turn change their actualities in order to include certain desired entanglements in, and to constitutively exclude unwanted entanglements from, their practice. The following proposes several ways in which actors that have agency in the articulation of ecological sensemaking apparatuses at sea , and therefore also have responsibility for them, can change the boundary-making in those apparatuses, and in doing so change the amount of natural resource waste that materializes through them.

Removing institutional boundaries: From races to catch shares

All GOA pollock, Pacific cod, and flatfish fisheries, are institutionally structured to be 'races.' Only the comparatively small rockfish fishery is structured differently. In race, 'Olympic-style,' or 'derby' fisheries (see Chapter 2 for a discussion of different fisheries structures), captains compete with one another to catch a collective, fleet-level quota. The faster an individual vessel fishes the more fish he or she will likely catch before the quota is exhausted. Due to the nature of these fisheries, in which captains compete to have access to a limited resource, captains do not have the financial freedom to fish more slowly and carefully, to examine their catch more critically, and to communicate with one another more openly (Birkenbach, Kaczan, & Smith, 2017; Rosenberg, 2017). In terms of the boundaries that a race structure cuts into ecological sensemaking apparatuses, one captain stated, "If you give away your secrets you lower your opportunity to catch more." In the following another captain explains the effect that a race structure has on communication in more detail:

> These guys are my friend friends, but I don't fish with them … It's just that the fishing spots aren't very big … If you call them up and tell them, "Hey, there's some really hot fishing over here, you should come over here," then they call another guy and go, "Hey, what's his face just said there's some hot fishing over here," and then he says it to somebody else, and then fuck it's over with.

What this captain means by "it's over with" is that the greater the number of vessels that fish from the same aggregation, and the more they are racing to fish, the faster that one aggregation will become depleted. The depletion of an aggregation reduces efficiency in terms of the amount of time and fuel it takes to fill a trawl net, as other captains explain:

> If there's nobody else messing with them it's a lot easier to catch them; if you are the only boat in an area and if you find some fish it's certainly a lot easier to catch them. And that just means less bottom contact, less time towing, less fuel, less everything, more productive fishing.

> You can imagine, ok each boat, 25 boats … the gear is about a quarter mile wide roughly, so quarter mile, quarter mile, quarter mile [indicates with hands multiple quarter mile lengths side by side], a mile wide … and we are there at the back [of the line of boats]. It doesn't take a rocket scientist to know what's gonna happen with your [catch efficiency], it's gonna go to hell. And that really affects us, you know, our income.

> Usually it is 30 guys running over the top of each other, saying, "Get out of my way asshole!" and "I was there first!" and "My boat is bigger than yours, so if you don't move I'm going to mow your ass over."

> I'm one of those guys that, if there are 25 boats in one spot I'm the guy that drives 20 miles away, me and one or two other guys. Which doesn't always work out so well—there is a reason those 25 guys are there usually. It's just a hassle to fight with them sometimes.

> So here's where you are gonna run into the economics of fishing. I've got fuel to pay for, and say I'm at Portlock Bank, where am I gonna run to? Fuck it, I'm just gonna catch these fucking cod and let the [bycatch] numbers be what they may … In a race fishery, which sometimes only goes a few days, you can't fuck

around. You are gonna go fishing, and if the fish are there you are going to stick your net in it.

We are all are free spirits; it's the spirit of competition. Most would favor a race, but now there are too many race car drivers, and there's not enough room on the track.

While race structures are commonly recognized to have various negative impacts, one of the biggest, yet-to-be identified impact is their tendency to enact boundaries into at-sea ecological sensemaking apparatuses. Chapter 5 argued that propositions must involve an efficient way forward for them to be actionable, while Chapter 6 made the case that a key ecological sensemaking tool is the action disposition to communicate with other captains. From the data elaborated in this chapter, coupled with what we already know about how race structures speed up fishing practices, we can deduce that one of the effects of race structures, beyond enacting boundaries to communicating and 'giving away secrets,' is that they amplify the efficiency imperative. This amplification makes the efficiency imperative act as a boundary to taking the time to communicate with other captains about a different spot to fish in after one has discovered he or she is catching too much bycatch, as well as to taking the time and expending the fuel to steam to such a spot.

The response regulators had to the extreme bycatch event was not oriented toward enhancing captains' potentiality for making sense of, and in turn actuality for avoiding, lightning strikes of Chinook salmon bycatch. Rather than asking something like, 'How can we help assemble a system that both incentivizes and enables captains to engage in practices that are necessary to reduce Chinook salmon (and other types of) bycatch?,' the NPFMC instead asked, 'How can we create incentives that force captains to engage in the sort of rational decision-making that results in less bycatch?' Such an approach is in keeping with the NPFMC's nature as a rational management system, in which they continually strive to close their system by pre-determining their own inputs (Scott & Davis, 2006), and in turn reducing their uncertainty. Their rational management approach can be seen in the problem statement that guided the NPFMC's deliberative processes after the at-sea portion of the event (provided above), as well as in the following examples of questions that NPFMC members asked GOA trawl captains during their deliberations:

If there isn't a [hard cap bycatch limit], what's the incentive to change your behavior? If the council was to take no action, or delay action into some time in the future, what's the incentive to change your behavior?

How do we as a council make sure that everybody out there is sort of similarly motivated and operating on a level playing field relative to bycatch reduction expectations?

If there were an incentive or a disincentive economically in the Gulf, don't you think your fleet will respond and work within a bycatch cap and figure out how to catch the pollock?

If there's a cap or some type of closure or some type of action that limits bycatch, wouldn't that create an incentive within the fleet to look at all different ways of reducing bycatch including gear modification versus having to mandate that? Because there could be many ways of reducing bycatch.

These quotes exemplify (1) the NPFMC's emphasis on incentives as a means to 'change behavior' by determining how decision-making will unfold at sea, and (2) the NPFMC's assumption that the structures and activities required to reduce Chinook salmon bycatch can be installed and enacted by the fleet alone. This latter point not only takes the rational perspective that human decision-makers, through their omniscience and supreme powers of rationality, are capable of making just about any outcome happen, but it also demonstrates the NPFMC constitutively excluding themselves from taking responsibility for reducing bycatch. This 'exteriority within' is the NPFMC, rather than removing boundaries to ecological sensemaking within at-sea fishing practices, instead strengthening them. Thus, the NPFMC excluded themselves from responsibility—beyond merely strengthening existing limits that others face (i.e., changing the ESA's 40,000 to their own 25,000 limit of Chinook salmon per year)—and instead puts the responsibility for changing practices almost entirely on the captains.

Thus, rather than creating structures that would foster, or remove boundaries that hinder, the ecological sensemaking of bycatch, the NPFMC instead enacted rules that were intended to foster more accurate rational decision-making. This approach is indicated in their focus on incentives, which is the chief tool of economic theory, and rational decision-making (Elster, 1989). Yet, as Chapter 3 argued, there is no such rational decision-making process that occurs at sea as captains make sense of where to steam to, and what to tow through, next.

Although incentives are almost always associated with rational decision-making frameworks and processes, perhaps they can operate within ecological sensemaking as well. It is not a stretch to imagine that incentives can shape the creation and enactment of particular propositions, and in turn which instrumental actions are enacted. Thus, though little to no research has been done on the relationship between sensemaking and incentives, perhaps captains can be incentivized to articulate ecological sensemaking processes that tend to materialize smaller amounts of Chinook salmon bycatch. In other words, maybe it is not fair to criticize the NPFMC's hyper-focus on incentives, for perhaps either the NPFMC was actually intending to use incentives to shape the articulation of what I have identified as 'ecological sensemaking apparatuses,' in turn influencing what materialized within them (i.e., less Chinook salmon bycatch), or their intent does not matter (whether they intended to affect rational decision-making or something else); instead what is important is only the effects of their incentive-based approach, namely enhancing the ecological sensemaking that can lead to acceptable levels Chinook salmon bycatch. The problem with this objection to my analysis of the NPFMC's incentive-oriented rational management approach (in which they use incentives to shape rational decision-making such that the NPFMC predetermines their own inputs, thereby closing their system) is that such an incentive-based approach to managing ecological sensemaking makes little sense if the structure in which it would operate, i.e., the rational management-based race structure, blocks any improvements in ecological sensemaking that would result from those incentives. In race structures, captains cannot readily communicate where they should or should not fish in order to avoid catching Chinook salmon bycatch (which would enhance their potentiality for avoiding Chinook bycatch), for doing so 'gives away one's secrets'; captains also cannot readily change where they are going to fish next after seeing Chinook salmon bycatch in their catch (or hearing about Chinook salmon bycatch from a nearby captain), for changing where one is fishing runs into ecological barriers (in terms of where fish are, and are not, aggregating), geophysical barriers (in terms of where captains can safely tow a trawl net), regulatory barriers (in terms of when fisheries close, i.e., how much time captains have to steam to a new area, and which areas are open to fishing), and economic barriers (will the fuel costs involved in moving lower one's profit margin too much? Will moving reduce one's potential to catch as much as they can of a shared quota?), as well as more generalized issues related to pervasive indeterminacy (will moving actually result in catching less bycatch?).

What the NPFMC needs to do, regardless of whether their approach is rational management or ecological sensemaking management, or something else, is remove the boundaries it enacts to making sense of, and altering their relations with, bycatch. The first type of boundary the NPFMC can remove is embedded in the 'race' structures they have constructed and continually enact (all but one of the GOA trawl fisheries are structured as 'race' fisheries). As elaborated above, race fisheries impose boundaries to taking time to make sense of the catch, to waiting for fish tickets from processing plants, and to sharing information with other captains.

To remove the boundaries within captains' ecological sensemaking apparatuses that are enacted by race structures, the NPFMC needs to transform them into cooperative catch share structures. In catch-share fisheries, captains are given their own share of a larger quota, which they can catch when it is most effective for them to do so. Thus, they can fish when it is best to enact extractive apparatuses with desired, and without undesired, ecological phenomena, and in such a way that, when doing so, they can enact their agential cuts in times and in places that result in low amounts of bycatch. Captains know that at certain times of the year pollock and Chinook salmon, and as various flatfish and Pacific halibut, are more likely, while at other times less likely, to be entangled in the same aggregations. With the freedom given by a catch share program, captains can adjust when and where they fish according to when and where certain migratory life history traits of their target species are more naturally differentiated in time and space from certain migratory life history traits of particular bycatch species. A captain, testifying to the NPFMC after the event, speaks to the need for such freedom:

> We have a problem with the time of year we are mandated to fish pollock in the GOA in the fall, which in turn creates a high bycatch rate of Chinook salmon, a federally mandated non-retainable species on board a trawler. My employer and his partner pioneered the pollock industry in Alaska, along with others of his generation. They chose not to fish pollock in the month of

October while fishing shoreside, if at all possible … we are mandated to fish pollock in October, and from October to February it is well known there is a lot of Chinook salmon as well as other salmon swimming around. If we could move the season up into September, we wouldn't be sitting here today, I don't think it would be an issue … Just let us fish earlier and we won't be here, we won't have this problem.

In addition to offering a better ability to make sense of, and organize with, naturally differentiating entanglements of target and bycatch activities, competition is also greatly reduced in catch share systems. This is because captains have their own mini-quotas, or shares, to catch, and cannot catch any more than their shares (unless they can trade other captains for more shares). Thus, the amount that captains can catch is largely predetermined. This means that their potentiality cannot be reduced by the actuality of how much fish other captains catch, and therefore how much of a collective quota they exhaust. A reduction in competition helps remove boundaries to sharing information. As one captain stated, "I think guys are more secretive in the race, the derbies, because you are trying to get as much as you can. But the catch share you know, guys are pretty open, you are given a set amount so you are not gonna get any more than that."

This recommendation—to change from race to share-based fisheries—is nothing new. Scholars have long been calling for a shift from race to cooperative structures, albeit often in the name of better decision-making. None have examined the case from the view of sensemaking. Further, while the NPFMC has, on at least two occasions, started a process aimed at exploring the possibility of transforming some, or all, GOA trawl fisheries into catch-share structures, both occasions were halted by political maneuvers. Such stoppages were largely done on ideological grounds— many in Alaska see catch shares and other cooperative fisheries as privatizations of public goods. The problem with such an argument is that much of the fisheries resources in Alaska are already largely privatized in one way or another. Boundaries related to access have been enacted for decades, often for the sustainability of the resources and the communities who rely on them. From the Exclusive Economic Zone to sea lion protection zones, from fleet-wide quotas to individual shares, each boundary creates inclusions and exclusions, winners and losers; some reap great financial rewards, others do not. Catch share and other cooperative-based fisheries impose boundaries, but they do so in the name of removing others, specifically those that hinder efficient and effective fishing practice and usage of natural resources. What this book does is provide a much deeper and extended empirical- and theory-based argument for the transformation of the GOA trawl fisheries, and in reality most fisheries, from race- to cooperative- and share-based structures.

Mutual constitution and full retention

While boundaries within ecological sensemaking apparatuses can be removed through structural changes, regulators must still account for the fact that ecological sensemaking, and what materializes through it, is mutually constituted. Bycatch, and other materializations within the phenomena of fishing, must be managed according to their own entangled nature, and the entangled phenomena through which they are articulated, not according to how rational decision-making fantasies assume bycatch occurs. Current approaches to managing waste in the form of bycatch discard impose temporal and spatial boundaries into our appreciation of the emergence, and causes, of such waste. The only actions that matter seem to be those that can be given meaning in terms of classical notions of cause-and-effect. Thus, the actions that matter in terms of bycatch are only those that occur at sea, within the bounds of a fishing trip, and that can be given the label 'human.' The effect of such predeterminations, however, is to set an explanation in motion prior to undertaking an analysis; such an approach greatly undermines management systems that claim to be 'based on the best available science.' Predetermining types of analyses, and in turn their answers, limits the NPFMC's own potentiality for finding solutions. Physical science has long taught us that causes and effects do not follow one another 'like beads on a string': "Effect does not follow cause hand over fist, transferring the momentum of our actions from one individual to the next like the balls on a billiards table" (Barad, 2007, p. 394). Why should social science, as well as a science that seeks to capture both (human) social and (non-human) physical phenomena, adhere to a different version of reality? Certainly the nature of how matter materializes, part of which is the nature of cause and effect, is not different depending on whether we are talking about humans or non-humans, micro or macro, culture or nature, and so on. The notion that there are different types of reality, and that the differences depend (implicitly or explicitly) on whether humans are present, or even on some fantastical size-based threshold, is a Cartesian legacy. Such dualistic and humanistic notions say more about human self-centeredness than they say about reality. The alternative to a dualistic ontology is entanglement; entanglements, as Barad argues,

> bring us face to face with the fact that what seems far off in space and time may be as close or closer than the pulse of here and now that appears to beat from a center that lies beneath the skin. The past is never finished once and for all and out of sight may be out of touch but not necessarily out of reach … Causality is an entangled affair.
>
> *(Barad, 2007, p. 394)*

Responsibility and causality are mutually entailed, which is to say, they are entangled. To understand who has responsibility for an effect, i.e., for what has materialized, we have to understand the nature of materialization. And to understand the nature of materialization, we have to understand the nature of entanglement. An entanglement is a perpetually roiling sea of boundary-, property-, and meaning-making activities, through which individualities and 'things' continually materialize and change, are re-worked, and materialized again. To understand responsibility we have to understand who and/or what is enacting particular boundaries, properties, and meanings within the entanglement of interest, what boundaries, properties, and meanings constitute those actors, what is included and excluded by their entangled activities, and what materializes through them. Cutting certain boundaries, properties, and meanings out of an examination of a particular entanglement of interest, such as one that produces bycatch, simply in adherence to Cartesian notions causation, as well as to humanistic notions of blame, is to retrospectively, and prejudicially, enact *new* boundaries, properties, and meanings into the entanglement of interest. This is what the NPFMC did when they examined the 2010 extreme bycatch event. Rather than examining the specific entanglements that were involved in the articulation of bycatch in any given event, i.e., conducting a genealogical analysis of the activities that enacted the boundaries, properties, and meanings through which the bycatch was articulated, the NPFMC conducted a very different, very classical, very Cartesian, and a very familiar analysis.

In examining the 2010 extreme bycatch event, the NPFMC agentially enacted additional relations, i.e., additional boundaries, properties, and meanings, into the analysis. These additional relations involved temporal and spatial boundaries of causation, culturally biased properties in terms of who gets blamed (e.g., captains who fished in the event) and who does not (e.g., regulators who create differentiations of catch and bycatch, and who require that certain bycaught fish be discarded and wasted), as well as rational actor-based meanings as to what to do about causation and blame (e.g., impose incentives to pre-determine outputs at sea and therefore the inputs to the NPFMC). Certain actions are not simply 'the cause' of an effect, or more responsible for an effect, because they appear to match our human ways of thinking, our biases, our frameworks for efficient sensemaking—such as the nearness in time and space of certain actors being the boundary conditions for the causes of certain effects. Responsibility is not diminished due to the passage of time or the span of space. Such enacted spatial and temporal boundaries are arbitrary at worst, and at best are based on metaphysical and humanistic notions of individuality and cause and effect. As Barad simply put it, "accountability and responsibility must be thought in terms of what matters and what is excluded from mattering" (2007, p. 394). To understand who has responsibility, we need to look to the constitutive inclusions and exclusions of their boundary-making intra-actions. To limit our understanding of causality, and in turn responsibility, to certain actions that occurred just prior to the emergence of a certain outcome, or that occurred within some spatial vicinity of the outcome, or that were merely enacted by humans, is to unscientifically set an explanation and a response in motion prior to conducting an analysis.

Approaching causality and responsibility based on retrospectively imposed biases, biases which have been scientifically rejected, should fly in the face of sound science and management. The isolation of responsibility solely, or even primarily, to particular men who are nearby the effect in time and space rests on deeply ingrained assumptions related to the super rational actor who is not only capable of engaging in the decision-making that is *the* cause of a particular effect, but who conversely can, if only properly incentivized, make the decisions that avoid the particular effect. Because this hero can leap tall informational hurdles in a single bound, and defeat indeterminacy with a single blow, *he* is responsible for a given effect, and therefore *he* is *the* medium through which the effect can be avoided. Thus, because *he* alone is responsible for untoward outcomes, such as lightning strikes of Chinook salmon bycatch, 'he' alone should be manipulated to avoid those outcomes. Limiting our understanding and management of deleterious materializations within entanglements of humans and nature to the super rational actor not only ignores the nature of humans as a perpetually materializing entanglements of a multiplicity of contemporary and historical human-natural relations, it also prejudicially rejects other causes and responsibilities, and in turn other means of avoiding unwanted materializations.

Whole swathes of entangled relations that are entailed in the materialization of bycatch tend to be excluded in analyses guided by rational decision-making frameworks. In excluding certain entangled relations, an array of potentialities for addressing unwanted outcomes are removed. Entangled relations that are constitutive of bycatch, but which are excluded when analyses and deliberations are guided by rational decision-making frameworks, include relationalities of ecological and geophysical phenomena that create boundaries as to where captains can fish, two or more species being constitutively embedded in the same ecological phenomena, but which are undifferentiated in captains' ecological sensemaking (as discussed in Chapters 4 and 6), among various others elaborated throughout the book. To understand bycatch, and to in turn properly manage and regulate it, we have to understand its entangled emergence, which is accomplished through the mutually constituted and constitutive apparatus of ecological sensemaking. Thus, we have to account for, regulate, and manage the ongoing articulation of ecological sensemaking, while also knowing that such management, and its regulatory structures, are always constitutively embedded in, part and parcel of, that ongoing articulation of ecological sensemaking, as well as its materializations, such as bycatch.

Thus, we need to shift our presumptions of responsibility for bycatch and its discarded waste from one of the isolated super rational actor to the mutually constituted, human-natural organizing apparatus that is ecological sensemaking. Responsibility means being responsive to more than just our prejudicial, individualistic, and artificially narrow notions of how processes unfold, as well as embedded prejudicial presumptions of causality. Accounting for, managing, and regulating the organizing apparatus of ecological sensemaking means attending to specific boundary-, property-, and meaning-making practices that articulate it, and which it in turn entails and engenders. A key lesson of this book is that captains' potentialities and actualities are mutually constituted by natural phenomena, and that, due to this mutual constitution, captains find their future actualities to be indeterminate, from the standpoint of their current actualities. Ecological sensemaking in turn is the mutually constituted boundary-, property-, and meaning-making means by which captains, facing indeterminacy, transition from (ecological potentiality-conditioned) actuality to (ecological actuality-conditioned) potentiality, and from (ecological actuality-conditioned) potentiality to (ecological potentiality-conditioned) actuality, recurrently. In these transitions various things that matter materialize, such as fishing spots on the fishing grounds, towing spaces beneath the vessel, plots on the plotters, sign on the sonars, target catch and bycatch on trawl decks, among others. Thus, ecological sensemaking is the apparatus through which what matters in commercial fishing materializes, and what matters is mutually constituted by all the boundary-, property-, and meaning-making relations that articulate that sensemaking. To manage and regulate what matters in commercial fishing requires managing and regulating the intra-actions that articulate those outcomes by way of ecological sensemaking. To continue to manage as if captains are rational-acting supermen, capable of plucking only certain species out of the ocean—if they just try hard enough, or care deeply enough, is to allow thousands and thousands of tons of natural resources to go to waste in adherence to fantastical notions of what should-be, rather than realistic analyses of what is. It is the misregulation, mismanagement, and misuse of natural resources.

This misregulation, mismanagement, and misuse is somewhat tempered in the GOA (as well as in the Bering Sea) by a prohibited species bycatch donation program. Prior to 2011, the year in which infrastructure for donating prohibited species catch in the GOA was first constructed, donating prohibited species catch in the GOA was largely not an option. In 2011, after the regulatory and political fallout of the extreme Chinook salmon bycatch event, the GOA trawl fleet took the initiative to establish procedures to regularly deliver Chinook salmon bycatch to the food bank SeaShare. SeaShare is the organization that manages all food bank donations from federal trawl fisheries in Alaska. Limited available data suggest that under 10% of the Pacific halibut caught each year in the GOA trawl fisheries is tallied at the dock as donated to food banks. Due to the mismatch of the way Chinook salmon bycatch is managed (by numbers) and the way they are recorded by food banks (by dressed weight), it is exceedingly difficult to derive an accurate percentage of the amount of Chinook that is donated. Nonetheless, based on personal communication with SeaShare, in 2013, 19,373 pounds of the 29,367 individual salmon caught in GOA trawl fisheries (which tends to be 90% Chinook and 10% chum) made its way into the food bank system. Using the conservative calculations explained earlier in the chapter, 29,367 fish Chinook weigh in at around 220,000 pounds, while 19,373 pounds is about 2,600 fish, or about 11% of the fish that were bycaught. Donations are relatively low because the process of getting fish from vessel decks at sea to a food bank in Anchorage or Seattle requires expenditures of resources for both vessels and processing plants. The upshot is that every year thousands of tons of prohibited species are discarded and wasted.

Yet, the amount of wasted resources is not critical to my recommendations. What is important is that fisheries are regulated, and in turn managed, by a system that requires *any* natural resource to be wasted. Throughout history, fisheries developed where certain desired species aggregated to an extent that catching them was a profitable endeavor. But just as 'history is written by the victors,' fisheries' boundaries and properites have been written into regulatory structures in terms of the species sold at market, not the species that were discarded along the way. In Alaskan fisheries, the agencies that seized management control of marketable fisheries determined who gets to deliver which fish to market, as well as when, where, and how those selected actors could catch them. Those agencies have largely maintained their control over certain species and fisheries in the face of changes to political boundaries that, had the fisheries formed after those changes, those species and fisheries would have been managed by different authorities. Thus, the International Pacific Halibut Commission continues to manage Pacific halibut, even though since its formation in 1930 new political boundaries have been established, such as Alaska being granted statehood in 1959 and the US enacting its Exclusive Economic Zone (EEZ) in 1976; these political boundaries situate a large amount of halibut fishing effort within Alaskan state and US federal waters, though management of that fishing effort still remains with the International Pacific Halibut Commission. Similarly, the State of Alaska seized control of the king crab and salmon fisheries upon its statehood in 1959, and continues to have primary manage authority over those fisheries today, regardless of the fact that king crab is regularly fished in what is now, after the creation of the EEZ in 1976, federal waters. On the whole, fisheries that were established prior to the passage of the Magnuson-Stevens Act (MSA) in 1976 (which created the EEZ) are managed today based on who managed them when they were first established, yet fisheries that were established after the passage of the MSA, such as all cod, pollock, flatfish, and rockfish fisheries (including all trawl fisheries), are managed based on the location of fishing effort relative to state, federal, and international boundaries. Species that were established and managed by non-federal (i.e., state and international) agencies prior to the passage of the MSA are in turn declared 'prohibited species' in federal fisheries that were established *after* the MSA.

Trawl captains have to discard certain species based on when directed fisheries for those species were developed in relation to when political boundaries were established. Thus, prohibited species regulations in the federal groundfish fisheries require captains to differentiate (i.e., cut boundaries into) their catch in terms of the boundaries of agency authorities, and to then discard and waste fish that belong to the species whose primary regulatory authority (e.g., the State of Alaska, the International Halibut Commission) is not the same as the agency under which the captains are fishing (e.g., the federal government). For instance, GOA trawl vessels must disaggregate Chinook salmon from their catch, and then discard and waste that fish, because its species falls under the management authority of the State of Alaska while GOA trawl fisheries fall under the authority of the federal government.

The regulatory differentiations of catch into target and bycatch species, and into bycatch that can be retained and prohibited bycatch that must be discarded, are historical political boundaries that are continually cut into the current articulation of fishing practices. The takeaway is that the prohibited species discard requirement is a political differentiation, a boundary agentially enacted from both on land and long ago into at-sea trawl fishing practice today. As we have learned, with the enactment of boundaries come constitutive inclusions and exclusions; constitutive exclusions in this context involve the discarding and wasting of natural resources. The requirement for prohibited species discard is an ongoing materialization of political management, and its continual re-enactment today is an abdication of responsibility to make the best use of national natural resources.

The question of who has responsibility for the materialization of bycatch boils down to Bohr's 'central lesson of quantum mechanics.' This is the lesson that 'we are part of the nature that we seek to understand.' In other words, "knowledge making practices are material enactments that contribute to, and are part of, the phenomena we describe" (Barad, 2007, p. 247). Thus, apparatuses of knowledge-making, organizing, and enactment, such as ecological sensemaking, are created through, contain, and perform the activities, which is to say, the 'intra-actions,' through which the boundaries and properties that are essential for determinate meanings materialize. Bohr's central lesson of quantum mechanics means that concepts, theories, and the like, are *physical* arrangements. The conceptual world does not exist above the physical world in some separate abstract realm; instead, concepts are articulated by the world, and their unambiguous character is insepar-able from their physical materialization. Particular physical apparatuses in turn give rise to particular concepts. As Barad explains,

> For Bohr, apparatuses are particular physical arrangements that give meaning to certain concepts to the exclusion of others; they are the local physical conditions that constrain and enable knowledge practices such as con-ceptualizing and measuring ... concepts are not ideational but rather actual physical arrangements.
>
> *(Barad, 2007, p. 147)*

What this means for bycatch is that the concept of individual bycaught species is meaningful, or unambiguous, only when it is physically articulated. But as the data show, and as the axiom 'You never know until you tow' testifies, the unambig-uous manifestation of individual bycatch species, such that they are differentiated from target species, is only possible after captains tow and perform the agential cut of 'measuring' the catch for its species composition. It is only after they tow and have catch on their deck, already extracted (and for the most part already dead), that captains can differentiate their catch into mutually exclusive, and com-plementary, 'target catch' and 'bycatch' categories. The same holds for the more nuanced concept of 'prohibited species catch'—it also requires catch to be on deck, already extracted, and for the most part already dead, before it can be rendered (unambiguously) meaningful. The apparatus of ecological sensemaking does not create determinate meaning in terms of the concept of what one will catch until after it enacts the agential cut of extracting catch from the depths and categorizing it by species. Until then, the concepts of bycatch, as well as prohibited species bycatch, are ambiguous. And as I argued in previous chapters, this ambiguity, and the resulting indeterminacy, holds for every tow. The determinacy captains gain after they tow is retrospective; the next tow is always laden with indeterminacy.

Captains can increase the plausibility of their propositions as to what's next, but they cannot create determinacy before they tow. They can work to increase the conformity of their propositions, but they will never know if those propositions are conformal at least until after they tow, and, as we saw in the 2010 extreme bycatch event, in some instances they do not know until after they deliver their catch to a processing plant, and in even more extreme instances they do not know until after they complete their next fishing trip. Absent technology for prospectively differentiating target species from non-target species,[5] the only hope of captains being able to avoid bycatch is perfect information regarding how their nets will carve their pathway through a particular aggregation of fish. Until captains are afforded relatively perfect information regarding the natural phenomena they are entangled with, and how that entanglement will play out, which would allow captains to construct rational decision-making processes at sea, there will be bycatch.

The mass discarding of certain species is a regulatorily constructed 'solution' to the regulatorily constructed 'problem' of species being naturally entangled at sea but, due to historical contingencies, managed by separate agencies on land. Yet, the regulatory construction of both the prohibited species problem and the discard solution appears to be little recognized in the literature, which instead falls back on the easy and fantastical notion of the rational decision-making superhero. For example, Bellido et al. (2011, p. 318), in an article on discarding on a global scale, state that "Discarding involves a conscious decision made by fishers to reject some part of the catch." Similarly, Kelleher (2005, p. 56) states that discards "indicate undesirable fishing practices." The reality is that federal Alaskan prohibited species regulations, as they agentially cut boundaries into ecological sensemaking apparatuses at sea, take discarding decisions, as they relate to prohibited species, out of the hands of captains and their fishing practices, and instead predetermine the practice. As Chapter 4 argued, savvy captains can learn to 'make their gear work in any different situation to its utmost potential,' but they will always have bycatch. Captains of course should be encouraged, or incentivized, to be savvy fishermen. But even those fishermen catch bycatch on an ongoing basis, and intermittently incur lightning strikes. There will always be bycatch; that is what the captains' axiom communicates. The question is, how to manage it? One of the more perverse answers one can give is, 'waste it.'

Discarding is a retrospective means of matching the inherently indeterminate nature of at-sea fishing practices to the inherently rational nature of on-land management systems. The practice may solve the problem in which captains catch fish whose management is 'owned' by other agencies, but it does so through the wastage of thousands of tons of salable, edible fish every year in Alaska alone. The ecological and economic issues that discarding creates, in the interest of solving a chiefly socio-political problem, makes it a perverse management tool.

Discarding salable fish is antithetical to commercial fishing. During my field research, GOA trawl captains lamented on multiple occasions having to discard dead fish. Bratton found similar sentiment in her study of commercial fisheries:

> This author and her students, in a series of interviews of both commercial fishers and charter fishers, on the Pacific coast of the US and in Ireland, found that fishers dislike waste of any commercial species, and protest regulations which force them to toss edible catch overboard.
>
> *(Bratton, 2000, p. 2)*

Several captains in my research argued that "full retention" is the solution to the bycatch discard problem. Likewise, Kelleher (2005, p. 60) states, "Discard bans have wide support among fishers if they are applied in a fair and pragmatic manner." Both in my research and my experience working as a fisheries observer, I do not recall encountering a captain who expressed pleasure in dumping salable or edible fish overboard, yet I do recall multiple captains expressing displeasure with the practice. Full retention, which means that captains must keep all catch, save certain exceptions related to safety (e.g., a codend is dangerously overfilled) and ecology (e.g., species that survive being caught in a trawl net are discarded), coupled with catch share systems, and the requirement that fish processors must buy retained catch, is the only real, complete solution to the problem in which captains 'do not know until they tow.' It is the only solution that accounts for the entangled, mutually constitutive nature of fishing practices and natural phenomena, in which the only concepts that are physically articulated prior to performing the species-based measurement of catch on deck (when most of the catch is dead) are multi-species behavioral patterns and morphological characteristics. The ambiguity of regulations needs to complement the ambiguity of the entangled materiality of fishing practice; put differently, the determinacy of how fisheries are regulated should match the determinacy of how entangled human-natural practices unfold. Regulations need to be constructed so that they complement how fishing actually works, including its varying levels of determinacy/ambiguity, rather than fantastical notions of how rational superheroes actors can work.

Thus, regulators need to incorporate mutual constitution into their rule-making (i.e., boundary-making) processes. This starts with transitioning all fisheries to catch share/cooperative structures. Under catch share regimes, captains will be better equipped with the potentiality needed to update their actualities in response to bycatch. Yet, because operations at sea are indeterminate, and because multiple species will always be constitutively embedded in the same phenomena, bycatch cannot be adequately resolved just through the facilitation of ecological sensemaking. Thus, even if the NPFMC enacts catch share structures, captains will still never know until they tow. Regulations can incentivize captains to make more adaptive sense of how to reduce bycatch (e.g., both seeing what they have caught and moving when it contains bycatch), but trawl captains will always catch multiple species when organizing with ecological phenomena that are constitutively embedded with multiple species, and when the ecological sensemaking at the heart of those organizing practices cannot disambiguate that phenomena at the species level prior to towing.

My recommendation is that rather than imposing historical actualities into present resource extraction practices, which function to limit potentialities and create wasteful actualities, regulations need to give nature its due in the management and regulation of the ecological sensemaking apparatus. Catching fish ancillary to the species one is targeting is unavoidable, but requiring the wastage of those species is not. If we constructed fisheries management divisions anew today, it is difficult to imagine that we would divide the management of species that are regularly caught together into different agencies, and further require that those species that 'belong' to one agency be discarded when caught under the authority of another agency. Fisheries should be managed based on current entangled realities, not solely on historical management authorities. Such an approach means that whatever is caught and is actually, and in some cases merely potentially, usable, salable, or edible, is kept. Regulations should of course limit what can be extracted from the sea (perhaps through the continued use of gear-based requirements and limitations), as well as how much, when, and where it can be extracted, but never which natural resources, already extracted and dead, can be used. Regulations can incentivize captains to make more adaptive sense of how to reduce bycatch, and at the same time *not* require the wastage of natural resources.

The PES framework, in which fishing practices and ecological phenomena are entangled, can play a key role in fisheries management. From this framework, my recommendation for beginning to resolve the discard problem is to interject rules which allow fisheries to be structured from both the ground up and the top-down. This construction starts at the natural end of the human-natural spectrum, with typical fisheries science-based assessments of fish populations, from which species-level fishing quotas are derived. Thus, we maintain a quota-based management approach for both target and bycatch species. From there the approach to management and regulation moves to mutually constituted, human-natural ecological sensemaking, within and through which ecological phenomena and fishing operations are entangled. Fishing activity should be regulated according to how it is actually assembled, which is to say, according to its entangled nature, rather than the fantasy that it is assembled apart from ecological phenomena, and in which frontline managers *interact* with ecological phenomena, and engage in rational decision-making to do so. When captains encounter other species that are constitutively embedded in the same ecological phenomena as their target species, captains must keep those species and deliver them for sale or, only when sale is not possible, donation. Nothing potentially or actually usable (but dead) should be discarded at sea or wasted by a processing plant. Further, bycaught fish should fundamentally be used at their highest value; they should not, as is the case today, be turned into low-value fishmeal simply because a plant is processing primarily one species at the time another species is delivered, or because a market has not yet been developed for the fish. We should always adhere to the principle of making the best use of the natural resources we extract, which means extracting as much value from them as is ethically and sustainably possible. This principle is in keeping with current developments in economic systems, particular the circular economy, and should be entrenched into the foundation of commercial fisheries management and regulation (as well as all other natural resource extraction industries). This means that regulators and industry must take responsibility for capturing and maintaining as much value in the system as is ethically and sustainably possible, which requires them to develop markets, support structures, and institutions for using bycaught fish at their highest value.

In turn, as long as captains do not exceed quotas they are fishing under, be it target or bycatch limit, they must sell all that they catch (unless infrastructure is created such that certain traditional user groups can be delivered certain species, or certain species can be delivered to food banks). This means that processing plants must buy all fish that are delivered to them (except under extreme exceptions). Outside of at-sea operations, this regime would force the fishing and processing industry to adapt to receiving multiple species at a time, and would incentivize them, and the seafood industry, to be more entrepreneurial in terms of developing markets for fish that are currently considered 'trash' fish, and which are currently processed into low-value fishmeal (or simply wasted). Urgency is, as they say, the mother of invention. There have been multiple instances in which new markets have been developed for species that were 'trash fish,' such as spiny dogfish on the US east coast and skate wings in Alaska. The 'Chefs Collaborative' serves 'Trash Fish Dinners,' which are dinners, held in different locations nationwide, where leading chefs introduce the public to fish for which markets have not yet been locally developed, helping to develop demand. Much more effort needs to be put into developing such business opportunities.

Of course this raises the potential issue of captains targeting species that they are not licensed to target, but would be required to retain and potentially sell. To avoid such practices, quota amounts could be crafted in ways that incentivize captains to avoid certain species in favor of targeting another (such as avoiding Chinook salmon as they target pollock). This approach is simply a matter of setting the limit for one species, say Chinook salmon, low relative to the amount of Chinook salmon captains are likely to encounter when fishing for pollock. When captains reach their Chinook limit, but have not reached their pollock limit, they must stop fishing. Such an approach is already taken in multiple Alaskan fisheries, as was exemplified above in terms of the NPFMC creating a 'hard cap' in the pollock fishery. An accompanying catch share structure would give captains the potential to engage in the ecological sensemaking necessary to keep their Chinook salmon numbers low. Further, the issue of captains potentially targeting Chinook salmon can be reduced through the regular monitoring of captains' fishing practices, including data submitted from fisheries observers and satellite tracking.

Nature should not be wasted in the interest of maintaining ownership that has been determined by bygone socio-political events. Instead, what a captain can keep and sell should emerge from the ground-up based on ecological sensemaking at-sea, while also being structured from the top-down through incentives created on-land. This catch share no-discard regime is a mere sketch, or merely a collection of ideas and principles, meant to be explored as a way to shift current metaphysical individualism-based regimes into entangled-based human-natural systems, ones that do not perversely use the wastage of natural resources as a management crutch. Such a shift, however, has to also be flexible, allowing discarding when it is necessary. Norway is an exemplar of this approach, in which, as Kelleher describes,

> It is incumbent on a particular fishery to justify discards or show why they are unavoidable. Then, legislation may make allowance for such unavoidable discards, and agencies can examine means of reducing the discard, developing alternative fishing opportunities, or financing the phasing out of the wasteful fishing technologies.
>
> (Kelleher, 2005, p. 61)

Alaskan federal fisheries regulators, now that they understand the ecological sensemaking processes through which captains catch fish, should use the PES framework to help them construct regulatory regimes to accommodate and encourage the ecological sensemaking of catching target species and avoiding non-target species, while also recognizing the posthumanistic limitations of such processes. Rather than taking the simplistic approach of regulating according to how rational decision-making theory assumes captains *should* catch fish, regulators should help construct a system that accounts for how captains, constitutively embedded in entanglements of human-natural phenomena, *can* catch fish.

Notes

1   A few Pacific halibut survive being caught in a trawl net due to these fish being muscularly dense and morphologically flat, while also having the good fortune of evolving without scales or the aid of an air bladder, which are attributes that lead to most roundfish dying in the process of being caught. Further, some crab, due to their tough exoskeletons, and also not having air bladders and scales, survive being caught by a trawl net. All other fish, from pollock to P. cod, and sharks, from spiny dogfish to salmon sharks, are dead upon arrival on the back of a trawl vessel. If any of these species are caught but not retained, for whatever reason, they are wasted.
2   See NOAA Fisheries, Fisheries Catch and Landings Reports, available at www.fisheries. noaa.gov/alaska/commercial-fishing/fisheries-catch-and-landings-reports#goa-prohibited-species.
3   See data available at www.uaa.alaska.edu/academics/college-of-health/departments/justice-center/alaska-justice-forum/26/2summer2009/b_homelessness.cshtml.
4   This knowledge comes from personal experience working as a fisheries observer on board trawl vessels delivering to processing plants in Alaska.
5   Prohibited species excluder technology (e.g., salmon excluders, halibut excluders) is a method of prospectively differentiating target species and prohibited species based on behavioral and biological characteristics. Thus, this technology, which selects and deselects fish during the process of towing, based on their biophysical characteristics, is a way in which captains can 'know before they tow.' Salmon excluders have been shown to reduce Chinook salmon catch by 25–40% on Bering Sea trawl vessels, which tend to be larger and more powerful than Gulf trawl vessels (Gauvin, 2012), and halibut excluders have been shown to reduce halibut in the Gulf trawl vessels by 86% (NPFMC, 2014). Thus, while excluders allow some fish that are trapped in the net to escape before they are towed up from the depths, bycatch numbers are based on what is actually caught. This means that while excluders reduce overall amounts of prohibited species catch, perhaps their biggest benefit is allowing captains to catch more of their target species before they catch all of their prohibited species bycatch limit (as soon as captains reach these latter limits, they have to stop fishing for their target species). Thus, for the same amount of prohibited bycatch caught, captains can catch more of their target species. In terms of the theory elaborated in this book, excluders, embedded with potentiality based on the actuality of fish biophysiology, perform agential cuts during the process of towing. Thus, they are physical boundary-making tools, which help articulate meaning in terms of catching certain species and not catching other species. Yet, excluders are still at their early stages of development. Due to their potential for having significant impacts on bycatch, funding for their development and testing should be increased.

REFERENCES

Abbott, J. K., & Wilen, J. E. (2009). Regulation of fisheries bycatch with common-pool output quotas. *Journal of Environmental Economics and Management, 57*(2), 195–204.

Abolafia, M. Y. (2010). Narrative construction as sensemaking: How a central bank thinks. *Organization Studies,* 31(3), 349–367.

Acheson, J. M. (2006). Lobster and groundfish management in the Gulf of Maine: A rational choice perspective. *Human Organization,* 65(3), 240–252.

Alaska Newspaper Staff. (2011). Coastal Alaskans ask federal council to cap gulf bycatch. *The Cordova Times,* June 3.

Allen, S., Cunliffe, A. L., & Easterby-Smith, M. (2019). Understanding sustainability through the lens of ecocentric radical-reflexivity: Implications for management education. *Journal of Business Ethics, 154*(3), 781–795.

Allison, G. T., & Zelikow, P. (1999). *Essence of decision: Explaining the Cuban missile crisis.* New York: Longman.

Alverson, D., Freeberg, M., Murawski, S., & Pope, J. (1994). *A global assessment of fisheries bycatch and discards.* FAO Fisheries Technical Paper 339. Rome: Food and Agriculture Organization of the United Nations.

Alvesson, M. (1996). *Communication, Power and Organization.* Berlin: Walter de Gruyter.

A'mar, T., & Palsson, W. (2014). Assessment of the northern and southern rock sole (*Lepidopsetta polyxystra* and *bilineata*) stocks in the Gulf of Alaska for 2016. Chapter 4.1 of the Stock Assessment and Fishery Evaluation Reports for 2014. Retrieved from www.afsc.noaa.gov/REFM/Docs/2015/GOAnsrocksole.pdf.

A'mar, T., Thompson, G., Martin, M., & Palsson, W. (2013). Assessment of the Pacific cod (*Gadus macrocephalus*) stock in the Gulf of Alaska for 2013. Chapter 2 of the Stock Assessment and Fishery Evaluation Reports for 2013. *North Pacific Fishery Management Council, Gulf of Alaska Stock Assessment and Fishery Evaluation Report.* Retrieved from www.afsc.noaa.gov/REFM/Docs/2012/GOApcod.pdf.

Bansal, P., & Knox-Hayes, J. (2013). The time and space of materiality in organizations and the natural environment. *Organization & Environment,* 26(1), 61–82.

Barad, K. (1998). Getting real: Technoscientific practices and the materialization of reality. *Differences*, 10(2), 87–126.

Barad, K. (2003). Posthumanist performativity: Toward an understanding of how matter comes to matter. *Signs*, 28(3), 801–831.

Barad, K. (2007). *Meeting the universe halfway: Quantum physics and the entanglement of matter and meaning*. Durham, NC: Duke University Press.

Barad, K. (2011). Nature's queer performativity. *Qui Parle*, 19(2), 121–158.

Barad, K. (2014). Diffracting diffraction: Cutting together-apart. *Parallax*, 20(3), 168–187.

Bartumeus, F., Giuggioli, L., Louzao, M., Bretagnolle, V., Oro, D., & Levin, S. A. (2010). Fishery discards impact on seabird movement patterns at regional scales. *Current Biology*, 20(3), 215–222.

Bateson, G. (1972). *Steps to an ecology of mind*. Chicago, IL: University of Chicago Press.

Bauman, M. (2011). Federal council moves to stem Chinook bycatch in Gulf. *The Seward Pheonix*, April 3.

Bazigos, G. P. (1981). *A manual on acoustic surveys: Sampling methods for acoustic surveys*. Rome: Food and Agriculture Organization of the United Nations.

Bean, C. J. and E. M. Eisenberg (2006), Employee sensemaking in the transition to nomadic work. *Journal of Organizational Change Management*, 19(2), 210–222.

Bellido, J. M., Santos, M. B., Pennino, M. G., Valeiras, X., & Pierce, G. J. (2011). Fishery discards and bycatch: Solutions for an ecosystem approach to fisheries management? *Hydrobiologia*, 670(1), 317–333.

Bergson, H. L. (2007). *An introduction to metaphysics*. Basingstoke: Palgrave Macmillan.

Berthod, O., & Müller-Seitz, G. (2018). Making sense in pitch darkness: An exploration of the sociomateriality of sensemaking in crises. *Journal of Management Inquiry*, 27(1), 52–68.

Birkenbach, A. M., Kaczan, D. J., & Smith, M. D. (2017). Catch shares slow the race to fish. *Nature*, 544(7649), 223–226.

Birnholtz, J. P., Cohen, M. D., & Hoch, S. V. (2007). Organizational character: On the regeneration of camp poplar grove. *Organization Science*, 18, 315–332.

Bohr, N. (1958). *Atomic physics and human knowledge*. New York: Wiley.

Bohr, N. (1963). *Essays, 1958–1962, on atomic physics and human knowledge*. New York: Interscience Publishers.

Boiral, O., Heras-Saizarbitoria, I., & Brotherton, M. (2019). Nature connectedness and environmental management in natural resources companies: An exploratory study. *Journal of Cleaner Production, 206*, 227–237.

Bond, J. (2015) Making Sense of Human–Elephant Conflict in Laikipia County, Kenya, *Society & Natural Resources, 28*(3), 312-327.

Boons, F. (2013). Organizing within dynamic ecosystems: Conceptualizing socio-ecological mechanisms. *Organization & Environment*, 26, 281–297.

BP. (2018). *Responding to the dual challenge: BP sustainability report*. Retrieved from www.bp.com/content/dam/bp-country/fr_ch/PDF/bp-sustainability-report-2018.pdf.

Branch, T. A., Hilborn, R., Haynie, A. C., Fay, G., Flynn, L., Griffiths, J., … Young, M. (2006). Fleet dynamics and fishermen behavior: Lessons for fisheries managers. *Canadian Journal of Fisheries and Aquatic Sciences*, 63(7), 1647–1668.

Branch, T. A., Rutherford, K., & Hilborn, R. (2006). Replacing trip limits with individual transferable quotas: Implications for discarding. *Marine Policy*, 30(3), 281–292.

Bratton, S.P. (2000). Is "waste not, want not" an adequate ethic for by-catch? Five biblical ethical models for addressing incidental fisheries catch and ecosystem disturbance. Retrieved from https://ir.library.oregonstate.edu/xmlui/bitstream/1957/35472/1/075.pdf

Brown, A. D. (2000). Making sense of inquiry sensemaking. *Journal of Management Studies, 37*(1), 45–76.

Butler, J. (1990). *Gender trouble: Feminism and the subversion of identity*. New York: Routledge.

Callon, M. (1986). Éléments pour une sociologie de la traduction: La domestication des coquilles saint-jacques et des marins-pêcheurs dans la Baie de Saint-Brieuc. *L'Année Sociologique (1940/1948–)*, 36, 169–208.

Campbell, M. (2010). Bycatch kings irk sport fishermen—CONTROVERSY: 59,000 were caught unintentionally by pollock trawlers. *Alaska Daily News*, November 9.

Chapman, C. J. (1981). Discarding and tailing Nephrops at sea. *Scottish Fisheries Bulletin*, 46, 10–13.

Cheilari, A., Guillen, J., Damalas, D., & Barbas, T. (2013). Effects of the fuel price crisis on the energy efficiency and the economic performance of the European Union fishing fleets. *Marine Policy*, 40, 18–24.

Chia, R. (2003). Ontology: Organization as "world-making." In R. Westwood & S. Clegg (Eds.), *Debating organization: Point-counterpoint in organization studies* (pp. 98–113). Malden, MA: Blackwell.

Christianson, M. K., Farkas, M. T., Sutcliffe, K. M., & Weick, K. E. (2009). Learning through rare events: Significant interruptions at the Baltimore & Ohio Railroad Museum. *Organization Science*, 20(5), 846–860.

Condie, H. M., Grant, A., & Catchpole, T. L. (2014). Incentivising selective fishing under a policy to ban discards; lessons from European and global fisheries. *Marine Policy*, 45, 287–292.

Cooper, R., & Law, J. (1995). Organization: Distal and proximal views. In S. B. Bachrach, P. Gagliardi, & B. Mundell (Eds.), *Research in the sociology of organizations: Studies of organizations in the European tradition*, vol. 13, 237–274. London: JAI Press.

Cornelissen, J. P. (2012). Sensemaking under pressure: The influence of professional roles and social accountability on the creation of sense. *Organization Science*, 23(1), 118–137.

Cornelissen, J. P., Mantere, S., & Vaara, E. (2014). The contraction of meaning: The combined effect of communication, emotions, and materiality on sensemaking in the Stockwell shooting. *Journal of Management Studies, 51*(5), 699–736.

Crutzen, P. J. (2006) The "Anthropocene." In E. Ehlers & T. Krafft (Eds.), *Earth system science in the Anthropocene*. Berlin: Springer.

Csabai, D., Good, J., & Parham, S. (2020). Duality or dualism? how firms formulate their relations with nature. Unpublished manuscript.

Cunliffe, A., & Coupland, C. (2012). From hero to villain to hero: Making experience sensible through embodied narrative sensemaking. *Human Relations*, 65(1), 63–88.

Cyert, R. M., & March, J. G. (1963), *A behavioral theory of the firm*. Upper Saddle River, NJ, Prentice Hall.

Czarniawska, B. (2004). On time, space, and action nets. *Organization*, 11(6).

Daft, R. L., & Macintosh, N. B. (1981). A tentative exploration into the amount and equivocality of information processing in organizational work units. *Administrative Science Quarterly*, 26(2), 207–224.

Daft, R. L., & Weick, K. E. (1984). Toward a model of organizations as interpretation systems. *The Academy of Management Review, 9*(2), 284–295.

Davies, R. W. D., Cripps, S. J., Nickson, A., & Porter, G. (2009). Defining and estimating global marine fisheries bycatch. *Marine Policy, 33*(4), 661–672.

Davis, M. W. (2002). Key principles for understanding fish bycatch discard mortality. *Canadian Journal of Fisheries and Aquatic Sciences*, 59(11), 1834–1843.

Davis, N. D., Armstrong, J. L., & Myers, K. W. (2003). *Bering Sea salmon food habits: Diet overlap in fall and potential for interactions among salmon*. Seattle, WA: High Seas Salmon Research Program, Fisheries Research Institute, School of Aquatic and Fishery Sciences, University of Washington.

de Haan, M., Johnson, M. H., & Halit, H. (2003). Development of face-sensitive event-related potentials during infancy: A review. *International Journal of Psychophysiology: Official Journal of the International Organization of Psychophysiology, 51*(1), 45–58.

de Vaujany, F., & Vaast, E. (2014). If these walls could talk: The mutual construction of organizational space and legitimacy. *Organization Science, 25*(3), 713–731.

del Giudice, M., Manera, V., & Keysers, C. (2009). Programmed to learn? The ontogeny of mirror neurons. *Developmental Science, 12*(2), 350–363.

Diamond, B., & Beukers-Stewart, B. D. (2011). Fisheries discards in the north sea: Waste of resources or a necessary evil? *Reviews in Fisheries Science*, 19(3), 231–245.

DiMaggio, P. J., & Powell, W. W. (1983). The iron cage revisited: Institutional isomorphism and collective rationality in organizational fields. *American Sociological Review*, 48, 147–160.

Dirzo, R., Young, H. S., Galetti, M., Ceballos, G., Isaac, N. J. B., & Collen, B. (2014). Defaunation in the anthropocene. *Science, 345*(6195), 401–406.

Dorn, M., Aydin, K., Barbeaux, S., Jones, D., Spalinger, K., & Palsson, W. (2012). Assessment of the walleye pollock stock in the Gulf of Alaska. Retrieved from www.afsc.noaa.gov/REFM/Docs/2012/GOApollock.pdf.

Eisenhardt, K. M. (1989). Building theories from case-study research. *Academy of Management Review*, 14(4), 532–550.

Eliasen, S. Q., Papadopoulou, K., Vassilopoulou, V., & Catchpole, T. L. (2014). Socio-economic and institutional incentives influencing fishers' behaviour in relation to fishing practices and discard. *ICES Journal of Marine Science*, 71(5), 1298–1307.

Elster, J. (1989). *Nuts and bolts for the social sciences*. New York: Cambridge University Press.

Emery, F. E. & Trist, E. L. (1969). The causal texture of organizational environments. In F. E. Emery (Ed.), *Systems thinking*, 241–257. Harmondsworth: Penguin.

Enberg, K., Jørgensen, C., Dunlop, E. S., Varpe, Ø., Boukal, D. S., Baulier, L., … Heino, M. (2012). Fishing-induced evolution of growth: Concepts, mechanisms and the empirical evidence. *Marine Ecology*, 33(1), 1–25.

Fabrizio F., Pfeffer, J., & and Sutton, R. I. (2005). Economics Language and Assumptions: How Theories can Become Self-Fulfilling, Academy of Management Review, Vol. 30, 8–24.

FAO. (2010). *Report of the technical consultation to develop international guidelines on bycatch management and reduction of discards*. FAO Fisheries and Aquaculture Report no. 957. Rome: Food and Agriculture Organization of the United Nations.

FAO. (2018). *The State of World Fisheries and Aquaculture 2018: Meeting the sustainable development goals*. Rome: Food and Agriculture Organization of the United Nations. Retrieved from www.fao.org/3/i9540en/i9540en.pdf.

Farjoun, M. (2010). Beyond dualism: Stability and change as a duality. *Academy of Management Review*, 35(2), 202–225.

Fazey, I., Proust, K., Newell, B., Johnson, B., & Fazey, J. A. (2006). Eliciting the implicit knowledge and perceptions of on-ground conservation managers of the Macquarie Marshes. *Ecology and Society*, 11, 25.

Fein, Y. Y., Geyer, P., Zwick, P., Kiałka, F., Pedalino, S., Mayor, M., … Arndt, M. (2019). Quantum superposition of molecules beyond 25 kDa. *Nature Physics*, 15, 1242–1245.

Ferraro, F., Pfeffer, J., & Sutton, R. I. (2005). Economics language and assumptions: How theories can become self-fulfilling. *The Academy of Management Review, 30*(1), 8–24.

Feynman, R., Leighton, R.B., & Sands, M. (1964). *Lectures on physics, vol. I*. London: Addison-Wesley.

Fitzgerald, D., & Callard, F. (2015). Social science and neuroscience beyond inter-disciplinarity: Experimental entanglements. *Theory, Culture & Society*, 32(1), 3–32.

Follett, M. P. (1924) *Creative experience*. New York: Peter Smith.

Foucault, M. (1978). *The history of sexuality, Vol. 1: An introduction* (trans. R. Hurley). London: Penguin Press.

Gatewood, J. B. (1984). Cooperation, competition, and synergy: Information-Sharing groups among southeast Alaskan salmon seiners. *American Ethnologist*, 11(2), 350–370.

Gauvin, J. (2012). Request for an exempted fishing permit (EFP) to conduct research on Chinook salmon bycatch reduction device for the Central Gulf of Alaska pollock fishery. Retrieved from https://alaskafisheries.noaa.gov/sustainablefisheries/efp/applicationsalm onexdevice12.pdf.

Gephart, R. P. (1984). Making sense of organizationally based environmental disasters. *Journal of Management*, 10(2), 205–225.

Gephart, R. P. (1993). The textual approach—risk and blame in disaster sensemaking. *Academy of Management Journal*, 36(6), 1465–1514.

Gerlich, S., Eibenberger, S., Tomandl, M., Nimmrichter, S., Hornberger, K., Fagan, P. J., ... Arndt, M. (2011). Quantum interference of large organic molecules. *Nature Communications*, 2(1), 263.

Gezelius, S. (2007). The social aspects of fishing effort. *Human Ecology*, 35(5), 587–599.

Ghoshal, S., & Moran, P. (1996). Bad for practice: A critique of the transaction cost theory. *The Academy of Management Review*, 21(1), 13–47.

Gillis, D. M., Peterman, R. M., & Pikitch, E. K. (1995). Implications of trip regulations for high-grading; a model of the behavior of fishermen. *Canadian Journal of Fisheries and Aquatic Sciences*, 52(2), 402–415.

Gioia, D. A., & Chittipeddi, K. (1991). Sensemaking and sensegiving in strategic change initiation. *Strategic Management Journal*, 12(6), 433–448.

Gioia, D. A., Corley, K. G., & Hamilton, A. L. (2013). Seeking qualitative rigor in inductive research: Notes on the Gioia methodology. *Organizational Research Methods*, 16(1), 15–31.

Glaser, B. G., & Strauss, A. L. (1965). *The discovery of grounded theory: Strategies for qualitative research*. New Brunswick, NJ: Transaction Publishers.

Golden-Biddle, K., & Locke, K. D. (1997). *Composing qualitative research*. Thousand Oaks, CA: Sage Publications.

Good, J., & Thorpe, A. (2019). The nature of organizing: A relational approach to understanding business sustainability. *Organization & Environment*, online first.

Grafton, R. Q., Arnason, R., Bjorndal, T., Campbell, D., Campbell, H. F., Clark, C. W., ... Weninger, Q. (2006). Incentive-based approaches to sustainable fisheries. *Canadian Journal of Fisheries and Aquatic Sciences*, 63(3), 699–710.

Grafton, R. Q., Kompas, T., & Hilborn, R. W. (2007). Economics of overexploitation revisited. *Science, 318*(5856), 1601.

Grémillet, D., Pichegru, L., Kuntz, G., Woakes, A. G., Wilkinson, S., Crawford, R. J. M., & Ryan, P. G. (2008) A junk-food hypothesis for gannets feeding on fishery waste. *Proceedings of the Royal Society B*, 275(639).

Gustavsson, J., Cederberg, C., Sonesson, U., van Otterdijk, R. & Meybeck, A. 2011. Global food losses and food waste—extent, causes and prevention. Study conducted for the Save Food! International Congress, Düsseldorf, Germany, 16–17 May.

Hacking, I. (1983). *Representing and intervening: Introductory topics in the philosophy of natural science*. Cambridge: Cambridge University Press.

Hahn, T., & Knight, E. (in press). The ontology of organizational paradox: A quantum approach. *Academy of Management Review*.

Haraway, D. J. (1991). *Simians, cyborgs, and women: The re-invention of nature*. London: Free Association.

Haraway, D. (1992). The promises of monsters: A regenerative politics for inappropriate/d others. In L. Grossberg, C. Nelson, & P. Treichler (Eds.), *Cultural studies*, 295–337. New York: Routledge.

Harrington, J. M., Myers, R. A., & Rosenberg, A. A. (2005). Wasted fishery resources: discarded by-catch in the USA. *Fish*, 6, 350–361.

Harrowitz, N. (1983). The body of the detective model: Charles S. Peirce and Edgar Allan Poe. In U. Eco & T. A. Sebeok (Eds.), *The sign of three: Dupin, Holmes, Peirce*, 179–197. Bloomington, IN: Indiana University Press.

Heery, E., & Cope, J. M. (2014). Co-occurrence of bycatch and target species in the groundfish demersal trawl fishery of the US West coast; with special consideration of rebuilding stocks. *Fishery Bulletin*, 112(1), 36–48.

Hernes, T. (2008). *Understanding organization as process: Theory for a tangled world*. New York: Routledge.

Hilborn, R. (2007). Managing fisheries is managing people: What has been learned? *Fish and Fisheries*, 8(4), 285–296.

Hilborn, R., Orensanz, J. M., & Parma, A. M. (2005). Institutions, incentives and the future of fisheries. *Philosophical Transactions of the Royal Society of Biological Sciences*, 360(1453), 47–57.

Hindorff, L. A., Sethupathy, P., Junkins, H. A., Ramos, E. M., Mehta, J. P., Collins, F. S., & Manolio, T. A. (2009). Potential etiologic and functional implications of genome-wide association loci for human diseases and traits. *Proceedings of the National Academy of Sciences of the United States of America*, 106(23), 9362–9367.

Hoffman, A. J. (1999). Institutional evolution and change: Environmentalism and the US chemical industry. *Academy of Management Journal*, 42, 351–371.

Hoffman, A. J., & Jennings, P. D. (2015). Institutional theory and the natural environment: Research in (and on) the Anthropocene. *Organization & Environment, 28*(1), 8–31.

Holland, D. S. (2008). Are fishermen rational? A fishing expedition. *Marine Resource Economics*, 23(3), 325–344.

Hollin, G., Forsyth, I., Giraud, E., & Potts, T. (2017). (Dis)entangling barad: Materialisms and ethics. *Soc Stud Sci, 47*(6), 918–941.

Hulson, P.-J. F., Hanselman, D. H., Shotwel, S. K., Lunsford, C. R., & Ianelli, J. N. (2013). Assessment of the Pacific Ocean perch stock in the Gulf of Alaska. Retrieved from www.afsc.noaa.gov/REFM/Docs/2013/GOApop.pdf.

Hultin, L., & Mähring, M. (2017). How practice makes sense in healthcare operations: Studying sensemaking as performative, material-discursive practice. *Human Relations*, 70 (5), 566–593.

Islam, G. (2013). Finding a space for story: Sensemaking, stories and epistemic impasse. *Journal of Organizational Change Management*, 26(1), 29–48.

Jensen, A. (2011). Fishery council to take bite out of bycatch in Nome. *Alaska Journal of Commerce*, June 3.

Jentoft, S. (2006). Beyond fisheries management: The phronetic dimension. *Marine Policy*, 30 (6), 671–680.

Jentoft, S., McCay, B. J., & Wilson, D. C. (1998). Social theory and fisheries co-management. *Marine Policy*, 22(4–5), 423–436.

Jeong, H. S., & Brower, R. S. (2008). Extending the present understanding of organizational sensemaking—three stages and three contexts. *Administration & Society*, 40(3), 223–252.

Jett, Q. R., & J. George (2003). Work interrupted: A closer look at the role of interruptions in organizational life. *Academy of Management Review*, 28(3), 494–507.

Kayes, D. (2004). The 1996 Mount Everest climbing disaster: The breakdown of learning in teams. *Human Relations*, 57(10), 1263–1284.

Kelleher, K. (2005). *Discards in the world's marine fisheries. An update*. FAO Fisheries Technical Paper no. 470. Rome: Food and Agriculture Organization of the United Nations. Retrieved from https://bibliotheekuniversiteitvanamsterdam.on.worldcat.org/oclc/109641194.

King, A. (1995). Avoiding ecological surprise: Lessons from long-standing communities. *Academy of Management Review*, 20, 961–985.

Kodiak Chamber of Commerce. (2013). *Kodiak community profile and economic indicators: 4th quarter*. Retrieved from www.kodiakchamber.org/uploads/pdfs/4th_qt_community_profile_econ_indicators_2013.pdf

Kramer, F. J. (2007). *Organizing doubt: Self-organization and army units in crisis operations*. Eindhoven: Technische Universiteit Eindhoven.

Lagadec, P. (1993). *Preventing chaos in a crisis: strategies for prevention, control, and damage limitation*. Maidenhead: McGraw Hill Europe.

Langley, A. (1999). Strategies for theorizing from process data. *The Academy of Management Review*, 24(4), 691–710.

Latour, B. (2005). *Reassembling the social: An introduction to actor–network theory*. Oxford: Oxford University Press.

Law, J. (1994). *Organizing modernity*. Cambridge, MA: Blackwell.

Lawrence, P., and Lorsch, J. (1967). Differentiation and integration in complex organizations. *Administrative Science Quarterly*, 12, 1–30.

Leonardi, P. M. (2011). When flexible routines meet flexible technologies: Affordance, constraint, and the imbrication of human and material agencies. *Mis Quarterly*, 35(1), 147–167.

Levins, R., & Lewontin, R. C. (1985). *The dialectical biologist*. Cambridge, MA: Harvard University Press.

Lewis, S. L., & Maslin, M. A. (2015). Defining the Anthropocene. *Nature, 519*(7542), 171–180.

Lewison, R. L., Soykan, C. U., Cox, T., Peckham, H., Pilcher, N., LeBoeuf, N., … Crowder, L. B. (2011). Ingredients for addressing the challenges of fisheries bycatch. *Bulletin of Marine Science*, 87(2), 235–250.

Lewontin, R. C. (2000). *The triple helix: Gene, organism, and environment*. Cambridge, MA: Harvard University Press.

Linnenluecke, M. K., Griffiths, A., & Winn, M. (2012). Extreme weather events and the critical importance of anticipatory adaptation and organizational resilience in responding to impacts. *Business Strategy and the Environment, 21*(1), 17-32.

Lofland, J., Snow, D., Anderson, L., & Lofland, L. H. (2006). *Analyzing social settings: A guide to qualitative observation and analysis* (4th ed.). Australia: Wadsworth Pub Co.

Lord, R. G., Dinh, J. E., & Hoffman, E. L. (2015). A quantum approach to time and organizational change. *Academy of Management Review*, 40, 263–290.

Lunsford, C. R., Hulson, P-J. F., Shotwell, S. K., & Hanselman, D. H. (2015). Assessment of the Dusky Rockfish stock in the Gulf of Alaska. Retrieved from www.afsc.noaa.gov/REFM/Docs/2015/GOAdusky.pdf.

Ma, X., Herbst, T., Scheidl, T., Wang, D., Kropatschek, S., Naylor, W., … Zeilinger, A. (2012). Quantum teleportation over 143 kilometres using active feed-forward. *Nature*, 489(7415), 269–273.

Maclean, N. (1992). *Young men and fire*. Chicago, IL: University of Chicago Press.

Maitlis, S. (2005). The social processes of organizational sensemaking. *Academy of Management Journal, 48*(1), 21–49.

Maitlis, S., & Christianson, M. K. (2014). Sensemaking in organizations: Taking stock and moving forward. *Academy of Management Annals, 8*(1), 57–125.

Maitlis, S., & Lawrence, T. B. (2007). Triggers and enablers of sensegiving in organizations, *Academy of Management Journal*, 50(1), 57–84.

Maitlis, S., & Sonenshein, S. (2010). Sensemaking in crisis and change: Inspiration and insights from Weick (1988). *Journal of Management Studies, 47*(3), 551–580.

March, J. G., & Simon, H. A. (1958) *Organizations.* New York: Wiley.

McCay, B. J., Micheli, F., Ponce-Diaz, G., Murray, G., Shester, G., Ramirez-Sanchez, S., & Weisman, W. (2014). Cooperatives, concessions, and co-management on the pacific coast of Mexico. *Marine Policy, 44,* 49–59.

McGilliard, C. R., Palsson, W., Stockhausen, W., & Ianelli, J. (2013). *Assessment of the flathead sole stock in the Gulf of Alaska.* Gulf of Alaska Stock Assessment and Fishery Evaluation Report. Anchorage, AK: North Pacific Fishery Management Council.

Meacham, J. A. (1983). Wisdom and the context of knowledge: Knowing that one doesn't know. In D. Kuhn & J. A. Meacham (Eds.), *On the development of developmental psychology,* 111–134. New York: Karger.

Mermin, D. (1998). What Is Quantum Mechanics Trying to Tell Us? *American Journal of Physics, 66*(9), 753–767.

Meyer, J. W., & Rowan, B. (1977). Institutionalized organizations: Formal structure as myth and ceremony. *American Journal of Sociology, 83*(2), 340–363. Retrieved from www.jstor.org/stable/2778293.

Mills, J. H. (2003). *Making sense of organizational change.* London: Routledge.

Mumby, D. K., & Putnam, L. L. (1992). The politics of emotion: A feminist reading of bounded rationality. *The Academy of Management Review, 17*(3), 465–486.

Murawski, S. A. (1996). Factors influencing by-catch and discard rates: Analyses from multispecies/multifishery sea sampling. *Journal of Northwest Atlantic Fishery Science,* 19, 31–40.

Neubauer, P., Jensen, O. P., Hutchings, J. A., & Baum, J. K. (2013). Resilience and recovery of overexploited marine populations. *Science,* 340(6130), 347–349.

Neukirch, G. M., Rouleau, L., Mellet, C., Sitri, F., & de Vogue, S. (2018). From boat to bags: The role of material chronotopes in adaptive sensemaking. *Management,* 21(2), 705–737.

Nicolini, D. (2011). Practice as the site of knowing: Insights from the field of telemedicine. *Organization Science,* 22(3), 602–620.

Nicolini, D., Mengis, J., & Swan, J. (2012). Understanding the role of objects in cross-disciplinary collaboration. *Organization Science,* 23(3), 612–629.

NMFS. (2010). *Endangered Species Act—Section 7. Consultation Biological Opinion for Steller Sea Lion.* Silver Spring, MD: National Marine Fisheries Service.

NMFS. (2013). *2013 Observer Sampling Manual.* Fisheries Monitoring and Analysis Division. North Pacific Groundfish Observer Program, Alaska Fisheries Science Center, Seattle, WA. Silver Spring, MD: National Marine Fisheries Service.

NOAA. (2006). *Fish glossary.* Technical Memorandum NMFS-F/SPO-69. Silver Spring, MD: National Oceanic & Atmospheric Administration.

NPFMC. (2007). BSAI crab bycatch. In Plan Team for the King and Tanner Crab Fisheries of the Bering Sea and Aleutian Islands Region (Ed.), *Stock assessment and fishery evaluation report for the king and tanner crab fisheries of the Bering Sea and Aleutian Islands region.* Anchorage, AK: North Pacific Fishery Management Council.

NPFMC. (2011). *Public review draft: Environmental assessment/regulatory impact review/initial regulatory flexibility analysis for Amendment 90 to the Fishery Management Plan for the Gulf of Alaska.* Presented at North Pacific Fishery Management Council meeting, June. Anchorage, AK: North Pacific Fishery Management Council.

NPFMC. (2014). Halibut mortality rates. Retrieved from https://alaskafisheries.noaa.gov/sustainablefisheries/specs14_15/goatable21.pdf.

NPFMC. (2019). Fishery management plan for groundfish of the Gulf of Alaska. Retrieved from www.npfmc.org/wp-content/PDFdocuments/fmp/GOA/GOAfmp.pdf.

Orlikowski, W. J. (2007). Sociomaterial practices: Exploring technology at work. *Organization Studies, 28*(9), 1435–1448.

Orlikowski, W. J., & Scott, S. V. (2008). Sociomateriality: Challenging the separation of technology, work and organization. *Academy of Management Annals, 2*(1), 433–474.

Orlikowski, W. J., & Scott, S. V. (2014). Exploring material-discursive practices. *Journal of Management Studies, 52*(5), 697–705.

Orth, G. C. (1987). Fishing in Alaska, and the sharing of information. *American Ethnologist, 14*(2), 377–379.

Ostrom, E. (1998). *The comparative study of public economies.* Memphis, TN: S. K. Seidman Foundation.

Palumbi, S. R. (2001). Humans as the world's greatest evolutionary force. *Science, 293* (5536), 1786–1790.

Pascoe, S., (1997). *Bycatch management and the economics of discarding.* FAO Fisheries Technical Paper 370. Rome: Food and Agriculture Organization of the United Nations.

Patrick, W. S., & Benaka, L. R. (2013). Estimating the economic impacts of bycatch in us commercial fisheries. *Marine Policy,* 38, 470–475.

Patriotta, G. (2003). Sensemaking on the shop floor: Narratives of knowledge in organizations. *Journal of Management Studies, 40*(2), 349–375.

Patriotta, G., & Gruber, D. A. (2015). Newsmaking and sensemaking: Navigating temporal transitions between planned and unexpected events. *Organization Science,* 26, 1574–1591.

Patriotta, G. & S. Spedale (2009). Making sense through face: Identity and social interaction in a consultancy task force. *Organization Studies, 30*(11), 1227–1248.

Pauly, D., Palomares, M. L., Froese, R., Sa-a, P., Vakily, M., Preikshot, D., & Wallace, S. (2001). Fishing down Canadian aquatic food webs. *Canadian Journal of Fisheries and Aquatic Sciences, 58*(1), 51–62.

Pearson, C. M., & Clair, J. A. (1998). Reframing crisis management. *The Academy of Management Review, 23*(1), 59–76.

Peirce, C. S. (1931–1958). *Collected papers of Charles Sanders Peirce* (Eds. C. Hartshorne, P. Weiss, & A. Brooks), 8 vols. Cambridge, MA: Harvard University Press.

Peirce, C. S. (1955). Abduction and induction. In J. Buchler (Ed.), *Philosophical writings of Peirce.* New York: Dover.

Perey, R., & Benn, S. (2015). Organising for ecological repair: Reconstructing land management practice. *Organization & Environment,* 28, 458–477.

Phillips, R. A., Gales, R., Baker, G. B., Double, M. C., Favero, M., Quintana, F., ... Wolfaardt, A. (2016). The conservation status and priorities for albatrosses and large petrels. *Biological Conservation,* 201, 169–183.

Pickering, A. (1995). *The mangle of practice: Time, agency, and science.* Chicago, IL: University of Chicago Press.

Plummer, R., & Fitzgibbon, J. (2004). Co-management of natural resources: A proposed framework. *Environmental Management, 33*(6), 876–885.

Pohl, R., Antognini, A., Nez, F., Amaro, F. D., Biraben, F., Cardoso, J. M. R., ... Kottmann, F. (2010). The size of the proton. *Nature, 466*(7303), 213–216.

Polkinghorne, D. E. (1988). *Narrative knowing and the human sciences.* Albany, NY: State University of New York Press.

Pratt, M. G. (2000). The good, the bad, and the ambivalent: Managing identification among Amway distributors. *Administrative Science Quarterly, 45*(3), 456–493.

Priour, D. (2009). Numerical optimisation of trawls design to improve their energy efficiency. *Fisheries Research, 98*(1–3), 40–50.

Pruitt, J. N., & Goodnight, C. J. (2014). Site-specific group selection drives locally adapted group compositions. *Nature, 514*(7522), 359–362.

Pulver, J. R., Liu, H., & Scott-Denton, E. (2016). Modelling community structure and species co-occurrence using fishery observer data. *ICES Journal of Marine Science, 73*(7), 1750–1763.

Pulver, J. R., & Stephen, J. A. (2019). Factors that influence discarding in the Gulf of Mexico commercial grouper-tilefish IFQ reef fish fishery. *Fisheries Research, 218*, 218–228.

Raby, G. D., Packer, J. R., Danylchuk, A. J., & Cooke, S. J. (2014). The understudied and underappreciated role of predation in the mortality of fish released from fishing gears. *Fish and Fisheries, 15*(3), 489–505.

Rao, H., Monin, P., & Durand, R. (2003). Institutional change in Tocqueville: Nouvelle cuisine as an identity movement in French gastronomy. *American Journal of Sociology, 108* (4), 795–843.

Raworth, K. (2017). *Doughnut economics: Seven ways to think like a 21st century economist.* White River Junction, VT: Chelsea Green Publishing.

Rerup, C. (2009). Attentional triangulation: Learning from unexpected rare crises. *Organization Science, 20*(5), 876–893.

Rescher, N. (1978). *Peirce's philosophy of science: Critical studies in his theory of induction and scientific method.* Notre Dame, IN: University of Notre Dame Press.

Rinke, C., Schwientek, P., Sczyrba, A., Ivanova, N. N., Anderson, I. J., Cheng, J., … Woyke, T. (2013). Insights into the phylogeny and coding potential of microbial dark matter. *Nature, 499*(7459), 431–437.

Roff, D. A. (1992). *Evolution of life histories: Theory and analysis.* New York: Chapman & Hall Press.

Rose, C., Munk, E., Hammond, C., & Stoner, A. (2010). *Cooperative research to reduce the effects of Bering Sea flatfish trawling on seafloor habitat and crabs.* Seattle, WA: NOAA Fisheries, Alaska Fisheries Science Center.

Rosenberg, A. A. (2017). The race to fish slows down. *Nature, 544*(7649), 165–166.

Rouse, J. (2002). *How scientific practices matter: Reclaiming philosophical naturalism.* Chicago, IL: University of Chicago Press.

Rudolph, J. W., Morrison, J. B., & Carroll, J. S. (2009). The dynamics of action-oriented problem solving: Linking interpretation and choice. *The Academy of Management Review, 34*(4), 733–756. Retrieved from www.jstor.org/stable/27760034.

Schön, D. A. (1983). *The reflective practitioner: How professionals think in action.* New York: Basic Books.

Schrödinger, E. 1935/1983. "The Present Situation in Quantum Mechanics." In J. Wheeler & W. H. Zurek (Eds.), *Quantum Theory and Measurement.* Princeton, N.J.: Princeton University Press.

Schruz, G. (2008). Patterns of abduction. *Synthese, 164*(2), 201–234.

Scott, W. R., & Davis, G. F. (2006). *Organizations and organizing: Rational, natural and open systems perspectives.* Upper Saddle River, NJ: Pearson Prentice Hall.

Scott, S. V., & Orlikowski, W. J. (2012). Reconfiguring relations of accountability: Materialization of social media in the travel sector. *Accounting Organizations and Society, 37*(1), 26–40.

Shotter, J. (2014). Agential realism, social constructionism, and our living relations to our surroundings: Sensing similarities rather than seeing patterns. *Theory & Psychology, 24*(3), 305–325.

Simon, H. A. (1979). *Models of thought.* New Haven, CT: Yale University Press.

Simon, H. A. (1983). *Reason in human affairs.* Stanford, CA: Stanford University Press.

Shrivastava, P. (1987). *Bhopal: Anatomy of a crisis.* Cambridge, MA: Ballinger.

Shrivastava, P. (1994). Castrated environment: Greening organizational studies. *Organization Studies, 15*, 705–726.

Slife, B. D. (2004). Taking practice seriously: Toward a relational ontology. *Journal of Theoretical and Philosophical Psychology, 24*(2), 157–178.

Sonenshein, S. (2010). We're changing—or are we? Untangling the role of progressive, regressive, and stability narratives during strategic change implementation. *Academy of Management Journal*, 53(3), 477–512.

Starik, M. (1995). Should trees have managerial standing? Toward stakeholder status for non-human nature. *Journal of Business Ethics, 14*, 207–218.

Stearns, S. C. (1992). *The evolution of life histories.* Oxford: Oxford University Press.

Steffen, W., Persson, A., Deutsch, L., Zalasiewicz, J., Williams, M., Richardson, K., … Svedin, U. (2011). The Anthropocene: from global change to planetary stewardship. *Ambio*, 40(7), 739–761.

Stengers, I. (2005). Whitehead's account of the sixth day. *Configurations*, 13(1), 35–55.

Stengers, I. (2008). A constructivist reading of process and reality. *Theory, Culture & Society, 25*(4), 91–110.

Stigliani, I., & Ravasi, D. (2012). Organizing thoughts and connecting brains: material practices and the transition from individual to group-level prospective sensemaking. *The Academy of Management Journal*, 55(5), 1232–1259.

Stokesbury, K. D. E., Bethoney, N. D., Georgianna, D., Inglis, S., & Keiley, E. (2019). Convergence of a disease and litigation leading to increased scallop discard mortality and economic loss in the georges bank fishery. *North American Journal of Fisheries Management*, 39(2), 299–306.

Teller, P. 1989. Relativity, relational holism, and the Bell inequalities. In J. T. Cushing & E. McMullin (Eds.), *Philosophical consequences of quantum theory*, 208–223. Notre Dame, IN: University of Notre Dame Press.

Thornton, P. H., & Ocasio, W. (1999). Institutional logics and the historical contingency of power in organizations: Executive succession in the higher education publishing industry, 1958–1990. *American Journal of Sociology*, 105(3), 801–843.

Tisch, D. & Galbreath, J. (2018). Building organizational resilience through sensemaking: The case of climate change and extreme weather events. *Business Strategy and the Environment, 27*, 1197– 1208.

Wallas, G. (1926). *The art of thought.* London: Jonathan Cape.

Weick, K. E. (1969). *Topics in social psychology: The social psychology of organizing.* Reading, MA: Addison-Wesley.

Weick, K. E. (1979). *The social psychology of organizing.* New York: McGraw-Hill.

Weick, K. E. (1988). Enacted sensemaking in crisis situations. *The Journal of Management Studies*, 25(4), 305–317.

Weick, K. E. (1990). The vulnerable system: An analysis of the Tenerife air disaster. *Journal of Management, 16*(3), 571.

Weick, K. E. (1993). The collapse of sensemaking in organizations: The Mann Gulch disaster. *Administrative Science Quarterly*, 38(4), 628–652.

Weick, K. E. (1995). *Sensemaking in organizations.* Thousand Oaks, CA: Sage Publications.

Weick, K. E. (2001). *Making sense of the organization.* Malden, MA: Blackwell Publishers.

Weick, K. E. (2003). Enacting an environment: The infrastructure of organizing. In R. Westwood & S. Clegg (Eds.), *Point/counterpoint: Central debates in organization theory.* (pp. 184–194). London: Blackwell.

Weick, K. E. (2006). Faith, evidence, and action: Better guesses in an unknowable world. *Organization Studies*, 27(11), 1723–1736.

Weick, K. E. (2009). *Making sense of the organization: The impermanent organization* (Vol. 2). Chichester: Wiley.

Weick, K. E. (2010). Reflections on enacted sensemaking in the Bhopal disaster. *Journal of Management Studies, 47*, 537–550.

Weick, K. E. (2012). Organized sensemaking: A commentary on processes of interpretive work. *Human Relations*, 65, 141–153.

Weick, K. E., & Sutcliffe, K. M. (2007). *Managing the unexpected: Resilient performance in an age of uncertainty*. San Francisco, CA: Jossey-Bass.

Weick, K. E., Sutcliffe, K. M., & Obstfeld, D. (2005). Organizing and the process of sensemaking. *Organization Science*, 16(4), 409–421.

Wendt, A. (2015). *Quantum mind and social science: Unifying physical and social ontology*. Cambridge: Cambridge University Press.

Whitehead, A. N. (1919). *The concept of nature: Tarner lectures delivered in trinity college, November, 1919*. Cambridge: Cambridge University Press.

Whitehead, A. N. (1929). *The function of reason*. Princeton, NJ: Princeton University Press.

Whitehead, A. N. (1967a). *Adventures of ideas*. New York: The Free Press.

Whitehead, A. N. (1967b). *Science and the modern world: Lowell lectures, 1925*. New York: The Free Press.

Whitehead, A. N. (1968). *Modes of thought*. New York: Free Press.

Whitehead, A. N. (1978). *Process and reality: An essay in cosmology*. New York: Free Press.

Whiteman, G., & Cooper, W. H. (2011). Ecological sensemaking. *Academy of Management Journal*, 54(5), 889–911.

Wilson, C. M., Johansson, G., Pourkabirian, A., Simoen, M., Johansson, J. R., Duty, T., … Delsing, P. (2011). Observation of the dynamical casimir effect in a superconducting circuit. *Nature, 479*(7373), 376–379.

Winn, M. I., & Pogutz, S. (2013). Business ecosystems, and biodiversity: New horizons for management research. *Organization & Environment*, 26, 1–27.

Witherell, D., Ackley, D., & Coon, C. (2002). An overview of salmon bycatch in Alaska groundfish fisheries. *Alaska Fishery Research Bulletin*, 9(1), 53–64.

Yin, R. K. (2009). *Case study research: Design and methods*. Thousand Oaks, CA: Sage.

Zalasiewicz, J., Williams, M., Haywood, A., & Ellis, M. (2011). The Anthropocene: A new epoch of geological time? *Philosophical Transactions Series A, Mathematical, Physical, and Engineering Sciences*, 369(1938), 835–841.

INDEX

and incentives 59–60, 62–65, 164;
lightning strikes *see* lightning strikes; and
MSA 38, 40, 160; and NPFMC 40–41,
47–49; and prohibited species *see*
prohibited species; and propositions 113,
114; *see also* Chinook salmon extreme
bycatch event (2010)
bycatch discard 27–28, 33, 40, 49, 77n3, 86,
101, 155–158, 184, 191–200; ban on,
detrimental effects of 28; extent of 27,
157–158; and prohibited species *see*
prohibited species; regulations on 63–64,
96, 151, 156–157, 160; three reasons for
156; and trash fish 200, *see also* Chinook
salmon extreme bycatch event (2010)

Callon, Michel 11, 20
Campbell, Mike 161–163
Cartesian dualism *see* dualism, Cartesian
catch data, delivery, accounting 49–52
catch limits 48–49, 59
catch rates 48, 50; monitoring 99, 103n4
catch share cooperative system/privatized
fisheries 35, 46, 52, 163, 185–190,
198, 200
causality 184–185, 191
Central Gulf (GOA) 39, 44, 45, 47,
157, 162
Chinook salmon 47–48, 63–64, 66–67, 144,
187–190, 193–195, 200, 201n5;
migratory patterns of 161, 172; spawning
of 172
Chinook salmon extreme bycatch event
(2010) 35, 47, 157–182; and altering
potentiality to change actuality by
moving 181–182; and ambiguity/
under-specification of catch and bycatch
168–175; and captains' ecological
sensemaking 164–171, 173–182; and
captains' testimonies 167, 168, 173, 178,
179–181, 187, 188–189; and
communication between captains 177,
180–182, 185–186; and entanglement
164–166, 169, 183, 191–192, 197; extent
of bycatch 157–160, *159*; and food banks
158, 171, 194; and full retention 190–201;
and importance of Chinook salmon 156,
157; and lightning strikes of Chinook
salmon 170–172, 173, 175–176, 177, 180,
187; and limitations of trawl nets 177–178;
media reporting of 161–163; and mutual
constitution of catch actuality 175–176;
and mutual constitution of feed band
actuality 167–170, *169*; and mutual
constitution of potentiality for a place to

fish 164–167, 170–175; and NMFS
observers 179–180; and NPFMC/ESA
160–164, 165, 166, 168, 172, 173, 177,
179–184, 187–190, 192, 198, 200; and
perverse management 182–201; and PES
framework 155, 157, 164, 167, 169, 175,
176; and race fisheries 185–190; and
regulatory boundary-making at sea
164–167, 200; and salmon runs 161; and
steaming potentiality 159–162, *162*; and
systemic lags 178–179; and unchecked
potentiality 176–177
Christianson, M. K. 34, 79, 85, 87, 117, 157
climate change xii, 8–10, 25, 110
co-articulation 68, 71, 91–92, 102, 113,
118, 122, 134–138, 142–143, 152, 155,
157, 166, 174; *see also* apparatus;
materiality, materialization
co-occurrence 170
codends 40–41, 177–178, 198
Cohen, M. D. 107
communication between captains 145–148,
170, 180–181; and race structure
180–182, 185–190
competition 46, 64, 186, 190
constitutive embeddedness 84, 88, 134
constitutive exclusions 17, 68, 71, 75, 89,
99, 123–124, 184–185, 195
Cooper, R. 18, 56
Cooper, W. H. 18–21, 24–25, *25*, 33, 29,
81–82, 85, 87, 135
Cope, J. M. 170
costs of trawl fishing 115–116, 189
Cree tallymen 19
crisis events 81, 85, 89
Crutzen, P. J. 8

Daft, R. L. viii–xi, 26, 83
data collection 52–55
Davis, G.F. 26, 33, 43, 61, 187
Davis, M.W. 27
Davis, N.D. 172
decision-making, 91, 190; fetishizing the
right decision 79; hyper focus on 80
derby fisheries *see* race fisheries
determinism xii, 61–62
Diamond, B. 27–28
Differentiation: and agential realism x–xiii,
6, 15, 17, 32, 68–69, 70–71, 76, 86–87,
97–98, 100, 127, 131, 139, 155–156,
174, 176, 178, 184, 195–196; ambiguity/
under-specification 127, 144, 155,
168–170, 174, 176; and fisheries
management 143, 144, 154–156,
169–171, 173, 176–177, 184, 192,